D1603776

1/22/18

Six Turkish Filmmakers

WISCONSIN FILM STUDIES

Patrick McGilligan
Series Editor

Six Turkish Filmmakers

LAURENCE RAW

The University of Wisconsin Press

The University of Wisconsin Press
1930 Monroe Street, 3rd Floor
Madison, Wisconsin 53711-2059
uwpress.wisc.edu

3 Henrietta Street, Covent Garden
London WC2E 8LU, United Kingdom
eurospanbookstore.com

Printed in the United States of America

This book may be available in a digital edition.

Library of Congress Cataloging-in-Publication Data
Names: Raw, Laurence, author.
Title: Six Turkish filmmakers / Laurence Raw.
Other titles: Wisconsin film studies.
Description: Madison, Wisconsin: The University of Wisconsin Press, [2017]
| Series: Wisconsin film studies
| Includes bibliographical references and index.
Identifiers: LCCN 2017010437 | ISBN 9780299315405 (cloth: alk. paper)
Subjects: LCSH: Motion pictures—Turkey—History—21st century.
| Motion pictures—Turkey—History—20th century.
| Zaim, Derviş, 1964- —Criticism and interpretation.
| Demirkubuz, Zeki, 1964- —Criticism and interpretation.
| Kaplanoğlu, Semih, 1963- —Criticism and interpretation.
| Irmak, Çağan, 1970- —Criticism and interpretation.
| Örnek, Tolga—Criticism and interpretation.
| Ceylan, Nuri Bilge, 1959- —Criticism and interpretation.
Classification: LCC PN1993.5.T8 R39 2017 | DDC 791.4309561—dc23
LC record available at https://lccn.loc.gov/2017010437

Contents

Acknowledgments

I first became interested in Turkish films past and present when they were regularly broadcast on TRT (Turkish State Radio and Television) in the days before the explosion of television channels in the mid-1990s. Sadly the *Yeşilçam* films do not appear as regularly as they did in the past—unless you have a specific cable channel—but I would like to thank the anonymous schedulers whose efforts first attracted my attention to a very specific type of film.

I first engaged with Turkish filmmakers in my book *Exploring Turkish Cultures* (2011). I had the privilege of talking personally to Derviş Zaim, Tolga Örnek, Genco Erkal, Pelin Esmer, Orhan Eskiköy, Özgür Doğan, and Ben Hopkins. I also received considerable help and advice from Ahmet Gürata, Gönül Pultar, Yıldız Kenter, and Zeynep Tül Akbal Sualp. Tony Gurr has always been an inspirational force in discovering new insights about myself and my relationship to the world I live in.

Early drafts of the chapters on Derviş Zaim first appeared as "Cyprus Past and Present: The Derviş Zaim Trilogy" in *Cypriot Cinemas: Memory, Conflict, and Identity in the Margins of Europe* (Bloomsbury Academic, 2015). My thanks to Costas Constandinides and Yiannis Papadakis for commissioning it as well as providing constructive feedback. I'd also like to thank Patrick McGilligan and Matthew Cosby of the University of Wisconsin Press for keeping faith with the project through difficult times.

I'd like to thanks the staffs of Başkent University Library, Bilkent University Library, the British Library, the Library of Congress, and the library of the British Film Institute for their assistance. I also pay tribute to the numerous secondhand booksellers in the Republic of Turkey, whose catalogs proved so useful on the website nadirkitap.com and who were so prompt in sending me vital resources.

My dear learners, both graduate and undergraduate, in the Department of Education at Başkent University, have been more of an inspiration to me than they would ever realize. May they continue to be so.

I'd like to thank Jackie Bierman Spicer, whose wise counsel and continual support, both moral and emotional, has enabled me to make this journey in the wake of my cancer surgery. I know it is a cliché, but I really could not have made it without her.

Lastly I'd like to thank my wife, Meltem Kıran Raw, who not only shares my love of Turkish films past and present but continually provides me with inspiration and the will to continue writing, even through the most difficult of times. I dedicate this volume to her.

Six Turkish Filmmakers

Introduction

In 2011 I published *Exploring Turkish Cultures*, an extended collection of writings dating back to my first years as an academic based in the Republic of Turkey in the late eighties and early nineties. I conceived it as a retrospective not only covering the range of projects in which I had been involved — cinematic, literary, educational — but representing an attempt to make sense of my complicated sense of identity as a Briton spending most of his time outside his country of origins. I found the experience of watching and discussing recent Turkish films particularly fruitful; from director Derviş Zaim I learned what it was to be an alluvionic filmmaker, in which levels of narrative and symbol are layered in a fashion similar "to the sediments of alluvium that coagulate to form an alluvion" (Raw, *Exploring Turkish Cultures*, 295). A film such as *Filler ve Çimen* (*Elephants and Grass*) (2001) operates as a piece of social criticism of government corruption yet includes overt references to the Ottoman craft of marbling, emphasizing the intimate relationship between past and present and the ways in which people exploit that relationship to move beyond the mundane realities of day-to-day living and communicate with their ancestors. Although stylistically very different from Zaim, Tolga Örnek has been equally preoccupied with the past and its effect on the present. In *Devrim Arabaları* (*Cars of the Revolution*) (2008), set in the early sixties, he underlines the idealism of a group of engineers dedicated to producing the first Turkish-made car. They succeed in their task, but no one possesses sufficient wherewithal to put the model into mass production. The project is quietly abandoned in the wake of a disastrous maiden journey, when the car runs out of gas with President Cemal Gürsel (Saït Genay) inside. Örnek reads the entire project as symptomatic of a general lack of adventure in Turkish cultures that prevents the country from advancing as rapidly as it should. Both filmmakers taught me a lot about the importance of local ways of thinking; to appreciate the Republic of Turkey's past as well as its present, I had to cast aside well-entrenched binary oppositions between "Eastern" and "Western" cultures and approach films on their own terms as responses to a fast-changing world in the late twentieth century and beyond, in which rapid economic growth was accompanied by an advance in government corruption.

As I reread what I published five years ago, I realize that my work to date on Turkish directors constitutes only a partial attempt to understand their preoccupations and (more significantly) ascertain my relationship to them. This book looks at six filmmakers — Zaim, Örnek, Semih Kaplanoğlu, Zeki Demirkubuz, Çağan Irmak, and Nuri Bilge Ceylan — the majority of whom are exponents of what Asuman Suner terms the "New Turkish Cinema," which preoccupies itself "with the question of belonging and interrogates it from different social, political and aesthetic perspectives. . . . [They] revolve round the figure of a 'spectral home,' which takes different forms and meanings" (16). Bearing the notion of "belonging" in mind, I explore how the filmmakers' work has helped me explore my identity in a culture undergoing rapid social, political, and economic change. Örnek's *Kaybedenler Külübü* (*The Losers' Club*) (2011) considers the issue of loneliness in a capitalist environment: mostly shot in the İstanbul suburb of Kadıköy, its two central characters (Nejat İşler, Yiğit Özsener) learn how to rethink their conceptions of masculinity as well as their relationships with their predominantly female fans. Örnek's next work *Labirent* (*Labyrinth*) (2011) centers on the operations of the Turkish intelligence community in the wake of the 9/11 tragedy; can they combine their high-pressure professional lives with personal relationships? Çağan Irmak's best-known film, *Babam ve Oğlum* (*Fathers and Sons*) (2005), set during the turmoil of the late seventies and early eighties leading up to the coup of 12 September 1980, involves Sadık (Fikret Kuşkan) and his father Hüseyin (Çetin Tekindor). The film gains much of its power from a conflict of values: rural stability versus political and (mostly) urban aspects of forward thinking. *Issiz Adam* (*Alone*) (2008) develops the theme through the life of prosperous chef Alper (Cemal Hünal) who is incapable of finding love until he meets costume designer Ada (Melis Birkan). They fall in love, albeit tentatively; in a status-conscious İstanbul dominated by money, no one dares to reveal their emotions. Through a soundtrack comprised of old Turkish pop standards, Irmak emphasizes the protagonists' nostalgia for an imaginary world wherein true love always runs smoothly. It would seem that industrial development has ruined the quality of people's lives. Currently I live in the suburbs of Ankara, about two kilometers from the center; when I moved to my current house in 1999, this area was on the city's outskirts. Now urban expansion has advanced with bewildering celerity: tower blocks dominate the landscape in a radius of nearly fifty kilometers from the center. This process represents a triumph of capitalism, but whether it benefits communities as a whole is questionable. Murat Germen's recent photo exhibit "Ankara: From Pioneering Modernism to Revivalist Mimicry and Fake Futurism" charts the city's progress, in which people have been transformed "into hostages of a depleting economic order where authority is not questioned" (3).

This process of acclimatizing to this environment has not been easy. I began at Bilkent University in Ankara, the country's first private university (established in 1984) that attracted the offspring of the *nouveaux riches*. Many parents who paid for their offspring's education expected a degree to be awarded in return: the capitalist mentality seldom considers issues of academic excellence. Zaim's two latest releases *Devir* (*The Cycle*) (2013) and *Balık* (*Fish*) (2014) examine the ways in which capitalism destroys long-established rural traditions—for example, through unauthorized building. Ceylan's *Bir Zamanlar Anadolu'da* (*Once Upon a Time in Anatolia*) (2011) takes up the same issue in an area replete with history, while *Kış Uykusu* (*Winter Sleep*) (2014) wonders how capitalism affects individuals' worldviews: should money assume more significance than personal relationships? Previously established notions of social stability are now being questioned—in Demirkubuz's *İtiraf* (*The Confession*) (2002), for instance, the director considers the pressures of capitalism on domestic life—although families still function as the core of society (as promulgated by successive governments), that does not guarantee happiness for individual people. With more than a passing reference to Dostoyevsky, *Yeraltı* (*Underground*) (2012) looks at the ways in which gender conceptions have shifted away from the familiar constructions of the dominant man and submissive woman.

None of these issues are especially culture specific, but what renders them especially interesting for me is how they have helped me challenge the kind of institutional compartmentalization that conventionally defines me as an English native speaker improving learners' levels of spoken and written English while trying to come to terms with the complexities of Turkish cultures. The experience of watching Nuri Bilge Ceylan or Derviş Zaim's work has helped me to construct what Robert J. Nash terms SPNs (scholarly personal narratives), through which I can learn something about myself and my shifting personal identities over the last twenty-five years: "It's [in this case, the cinematic experience] all about loving ideas so much that we are willing to play with them, to take chances with them, to express our passions about them, to deliver them in some fresh, new ways, to nurture and care for them; and to continually test and challenge them in the company of others" (48). By constructing my own SPNs out of the filmmakers' narratives I have come to understand the cultural and spiritual *connections* between myself and others around me—learners, friends, and others—rather than the *differences*. This book comprises a series of six

SPNs, each designed to prove that inter- or cross-cultural interactions are a lot more complex than many Western scholars would have us believe. The American Sam Kaplan considers the Turkish education system in light of "collectivist" local cultures, rendering methods of learning fundamentally different from their equivalents in Western Europe or the United States: "The curriculum has consciously worked at inculcating authoritative interpretations of society and policy. . . . The entire school system links didactic methods with monologic themes to demonstrate clear-cut definitions of citizenship and classificatory boundaries between state and society with which each child will identify" (219). While "individualism . . . has become both a desirable means and an end for those young men and women trying to exert some degree of autonomy" (220), it does not flourish in cultures whose schools are instrumental "in fashioning an individual's identification with nation and state" (227).

Kaplan's arguments remind me of my early days in the Republic of Turkey when I was encouraged by my (European) colleagues both inside and outside the country to cultivate "intercultural competence" based on an awareness of differences and how to negotiate them. These differences were not only situational but psychological as well. Being accustomed to a system based on memorization and loyalty to the state, learners might find it difficult to indulge in the active process of synthesizing different kinds of information into argumentative essays. From the evidence of the directors' work in this book, the reality is precisely the opposite: difference assumes less significance than individuality as people strive to formulate new identities in a fast-changing world. Yet this does not mean that difference isn't important; we just have to conceive it in an alternative way. Both Zaim and Kaplanoğlu spend a lot of time focusing on landscapes, both urban and rural: Kaplanoğlu's *Yumurta* (*Egg*) (2007) begins with a shot of an elderly lady walking in a sylvan setting; on the soundtrack we hear dogs barking and birds singing. The woman walks toward the camera, pauses, and looks left to right before moving toward some cypress trees. Yusuf (Nejat İşler) enters, carrying a quail's egg; as it cracks in his hand, crystals form and birds flutter in the sky. Comprising a series of lengthy takes, these sequences underline humanity's relationship to nature: the cypress trees are associated with death, and the woman's walking toward them adumbrates her fate. The fact that the birds fly away after the egg breaks further underlines the connection between humans and animals; if you destroy one life, you put everyone else's at risk. Zaim's *Tabutta Rövaşata* (*Somersault in a Coffin*) (1996) is set in a rundown area close to the Bosphorus, where Mahsun (Mustafa Uğurlu) spends much of his time watching the waves ebbing and flowing on cold winter's days. Like Kaplanoğlu, Zaim examines humanity's connection to the natural world: water not only represents life but purifies the body from impurities such as the dirt that dominates Mahsun's life. For the thirteenth-century poet Jalāl ad-Dīn Muhammad Rūmī, water (as with all natural elements) possesses powerful associations:

> A naked man jumps in the river, hornets swarming
> above him. The water is the *zikr*;
> remembering. *There is no reality but God.*
> *There is only God* . . .
>
> A person blended unto God does not disappear.
> He or she is just completely soaked
> in God's qualities . . .
>
> *All shall be brought into our presence.* . . .
>
> This is the story of the animal soul,
> not the divine soul. The sun shines on every house.
> When it goes down, all houses get dark.
>
> (Barks 94–95)

We are all part of the music of the spheres, presided over by a God who suffuses all things. Rūmī's "The Music We Are" explains:

> Did you hear that winter's over?
> The basil and the carnations
>
> cannot control their laughter
> The nightingale, back from his wandering,
>
> has been made singing master over
> All the birds. The trees reach out
>
> their congratulations. The soul
> goes dancing through the king's doorway.
>
> (Barks 26)

Listening to that music requires us to stand outside the rhythms of our daily lives and become more mindful. Rūmī's "Special Plates" advises:

Notice how each particle moves.
Notice how everyone has just arrived here
from a journey. Notice how each wants
a different food. Notice how
the stars vanish as the sun comes up,
and how all streams stream toward the ocean.

(Barks 13)

Kaplanoğlu and Zaim communicate this meditative mood through consciously slow movement, the use of the static camera focusing lengthily on the characters' profiles with a minimal soundtrack of sound effects (the endless throb of İstanbul traffic in *Tabutta Rövaşata*). Their films might be slight in terms of plot and character development, but the directors are more preoccupied with an individual's place in a world where life and death are less important than understanding God's presence in all things. The old woman in *Yumurta* is not frightened of death as she moves toward the cypress trees; Mahsun in *Tabutta Rövaşata* is at his happiest while traveling by boat down the Bosphorus.

For many Western readers, Rūmī's poems have proved exceptionally popular as they help them "articulate what it feels like to be alive. . . . They help us understand our own search for love and the ecstatic in the coil of everyday life" (Clabbatari). On this view it might seem that by invoking his ideas, Kaplanoğlu and Zaim are trying to universalize him, to show their protagonists engaging in similar existential quests. This might be true thematically, but both directors are more preoccupied with showing how (and whether) their characters "notice how each particle moves . . . and how all streams stream toward the ocean," while encouraging viewers to participate in similar mindful processes. Throughout his lengthy career as an academic, poet, and translator, Talât Saït Halman celebrated Rūmī as one of the principal representatives of the Anatolian Renaissance that took place a full century before the European equivalent, wherein he introduced "a powerful new ideal of love and humanitarian solidarity" transcending "conventional religious tenets and institutions," in pursuit of ecstasy and "a glimpse of God the beloved [as embodied in Mother Anatolia]" (Halman, *Love Is All*, 6). Contemporary filmmakers like Kaplanoğlu embrace similar objectives: to underline the impact of the Anatolian Renaissance on contemporary Turkish cultures, whether urban or rural. Non-Turkish viewers should try to come to terms with this different way of thinking; it is my aim to relate it to Anatolian history as well as more modern histories in the Republic of Turkey.

This framework has important political dimensions. Henry Kissinger's recent *World Order* (2014) identifies İslam as "at once a religion, a multiethnic superstate, and a new world order" (117), rendering its people unable to empathize with the American way of thinking, committed to the democratization of the Middle East through negotiation. His formulation reinforces the popular belief that difference inhibits rather than promotes understanding. As a long-term resident of an İslamic country, I wonder whether my position is any different from that embraced by my ancestors such as the writer Marmaduke Pickthall who, despite long residence in the country, remained perpetually separated from local cultures until he took the decision to "turn Turk" by converting to İslam. Owing in no small part to the propaganda disseminated by former Prime Minister William Ewart Gladstone, who considered the Turk "the one great inhuman specimen of inhumanity," Pickthall found himself torn in two, especially during World War I and afterward (Rogerson 32). Things don't seem to have changed much today: Kemal Aydın's *Images of the Turk in Western Literature* (1999) traces a long history of conscious othering by Western writers either visiting or residing in the Republic of Turkey over the last century and a half. Charles Cumming's spy thriller *A Colder War* (2014) offers a case in point, with its negative representation of Turkey as "a light touch police state" (117), with "disgusting" food (129), "hot and crowded and traffic-stalled" cities (231), and tea on offer "which, even by Turkish standards, was so stewed as to be undrinkable" (252). Even those writers of Turkish ancestry adopting a more liberal perspective such as Elif Şafak claim that politics and culture in the republic has been blighted by "cultural dogma" (Şafak). Understanding the place of Rūmī and his relationship to Anatolian thought, and the way it has influenced modern Turkish filmmakers, can help us to transcend dogma and thereby permit more pluralistic constructions of identity through the SPN.

It might be argued with justification that this approach is a variation on methods pioneered by the "New Cinephilia" movement, which collapses the distinctions between critics, filmmakers, theorists, and cinephiles, thereby permitting "creative encounters with words and images disengaged from their association with recognized authorities" (Baumbach 52). This movement can be divided into two strands: the first has been described as "a discourse braided around love, in all the richly contradictory, narcissistic, altruistic, communicative and artistic forms." Reacting against the theory-driven film studies of the seventies, this strand turns to cinephilia based on memory, "a recaptured attempt at self-presence: possessing the experience in order to possess the memory, in order to possess the self" (Elsaesser 40). The second strand adopts a more active position, expressing cinephilia through the fan flick or other forms of creative fandom that transforms "the unlimited archive of our media memory . . . into desirable and much valued clips, . . . which proves that cinephilia is not only an anxious love, but can always turn itself into a happy perversion" (Elsaesser 41). The Fan Studies Network was formed in 2012 to provide a forum for different people in this field, with a special interest in the way the Internet and social media offer new opportunities for creative fandom, presenting new challenges to the way we respond to films (Bennett and Phillips 53). Paul Willemen's observations about cinephilia appear to have been vindicated: everyone can now employ "multiple sets of discourses" to prove that "readers, like texts . . . are always sites where pluralities intersect." Out of such pluralities new self-narratives (or SPNs) are continually formed and reformed—not only texts such as fan flicks but also responses to the external world existing beyond the cinematic text (78).

Yet this form of interpretation is overtly Western in its prioritization of self-interest as a powerful determinant of behavior. This norm influences the cinephile's actions and opinions as well as the account they provide of their research. It is the "text" and the social, political, or cinematic contexts shaping it that redefine the reader's or writer's personality. In a piece of quantitative research focusing on the ways in which films promote "comforting behavior" both mentally as well as physically, twenty-one undergraduates (eleven male, ten female) were interviewed. Those who watched horror films tended to react in a less comforting manner, resulting in their being less willing to help those in difficulties. On the other hand, those who watched comedies were more favorably disposed. Such findings might have been expected; but nonetheless, the researchers managed to conclude that those witnessing horror suffered from a "dysphoric affective state" that could only be negotiated through "coping behaviors" unrelated to the experience of watching the film (Tamborini, Salomonson, and Bahk 736). I don't want to pursue this argument too far (fans of horror films react in different ways, depending on the situation), but I would, nonetheless, suggest that self-interest assumes less significance in the Republic of Turkey. An awareness of one's place in the universal order of things creates a feeling of humility; a realization that human beings are part of nature and hence do not regard themselves exclusively as social animals. Nazım Hikmet's poem "Eğer Alan Vardır" ("You Are the Field") exemplifies this point of view:

> You are a village
>   high in an Anatolian mountain
> You are my city
>   most lovely and most suffering

> You are a cry for help; that is,
>   you are my country
> The steps running to you—
>   are mine.
>
>   (qtd. in Silay 328–29)[1]

The filmmakers covered in this book are equally preoccupied with this relationship. Ceylan's *Kış Uykusu* uses the snow-covered fairy chimneys in Cappadochia to suggest Aydın's (Haluk Bilginer's) disturbed state of mind: unable to sustain his family life or his livelihood as a hotel owner, he sees his aspirations collapse in front of him. The world becomes bleak, full of strange shapes and unearthly apparitions. Örnek's documentaries *Hititler* (*The Hittites*) (2003) and *Gelibolu* (*Gallipoli*) (2005) use specific historical sites to suggest the importance of layering: underneath the apparently peaceful terrain of the Gallipoli peninsula lie the bones of those with stories to tell of the past and its fundamental contribution to the present. Kaplanoğlu's *Bal* (*Honey*) (2010) explores the childhood of central character Yusuf (Bora Altaş) growing up in rural Anatolia, whose father (Erdal Beşikçioğlu) makes a living collecting honey. When the father does not return, Yusuf experiences a life-changing moment that redefines his relationship to the landscape. In Karen Lury's apt formulation, Yusuf's presence "situates the child as betwixt and between the animate and inanimate, or the earth and sky, and this means they are not separate from the land" (287). Lury identifies this relationship as political in outlook, revealing "the confining qualities of rural life." Even though the child might think of his world as open, it is "repetitive, boring and dangerous"; his only hope in life is to cultivate resilience, persistence, and hope (287, 289, 292). I would counter by saying that Kaplanoğlu places less emphasis on Yusuf's state of mind and more on his place in the order of things. He has no need to be intimidated by the landscape as he is part of it and thus learns how to be rather than assume any particular course of direct action. When the action is set in an urban context, characters often refer to this loss of being. In Zaim's *Filler ve Çimen*, Adem (Sanem Çelik), living in a squalid apartment in one of the less salubrious districts of İstanbul, tries to recover it by practicing the ancient Ottoman craft of marbling—making shapes in water. She tries to realign herself with the elements, a state of mind that transcends the capitalist's get-rich-quick obsessions.

     In suggesting that Turkish directors might embrace a view of the world different from that of their Western counterparts, I am not trying to substitute one framework for another.[2] Cinephilia and its relationship to human psychology is as strong in the republic as anywhere else. An exhibition held at İstanbul

Modern art gallery celebrating the centenary of cinema in late 2014 explored the history of cinephilia through various forms of ephemera (posters, fanzines, etc.) as well as recorded interviews with the actors Türkan Şoray and Filiz Akın, who recalled how their ways of life had been continually reshaped by their fans' demands. Selim İleri's 2004 novel *Yarım Yapayalnız* (translated a decade later as *Boundless Solitude*) has one of its narrators reminiscing about visiting the now-demolished Emek Cinema in Beyoğlu during his childhood. He saw a film about Chopin and decided there and then to become a composer (he eventually embraced the writing profession) (140).[3] The female protagonist Handan recounts her autobiography, especially her love of female star Belgin Doruk, who provided an invaluable guide to what "style" meant during the sixties and seventies (377). Using Clark Gable as a model, Ayhan Işık was another popular figure at that time; with his rugged good looks and pencil mustache, he offered an ideal of masculinity for male and female filmgoers alike (Raw, "Ayhan"). What differentiates cinephilia in the Republic of Turkey is its fundamentally *organic* nature: adopting the fashions and mannerisms of a star might increase one's self-esteem, but it should never be considered as an end in itself. İleri relates his female protagonist's love of Doruk to her youth, when she believed in her God-given looks as a basis for experiment. Her cinephilia was not viewed through a capitalist prism—for example, by wanting to buy fashionable clothes similar to those worn by her idol. According to Janet Staiger, the freedom associated with Western cinephilia "exceeds the typical . . . [through] a production of new materials, an extension into the rest of living, and an alternative social grouping" (14). For İleri's protagonist the need to forge new social groupings has no intrinsic value. Now she has grown older, she has learned to accept that her looks have gone, although her place in the universe remains as secure as ever.

It should be noted that this belief teaches us that humankind should love God because He is the creator; this should be taught at schools as well as a belief in family-related issues including the relationship between husbands and wives and the raising of children. Only then can we appreciate the "Divine Decree" and thereby acquire freedom and eternal life.

In common with most filmmakers covered in this book, Halman offers a more secular interpretation based on an alternative to the logical connection between words and objects characteristic of Western Enlightenment rationalism. Rūmī concentrates on the involuntary musical order of the world discovered by listening to ourselves; an awareness of the inner reality of being. Orhan Veli Kanık's poem "İstanbul'u Dinliyorum" ("I Am Listening to İstanbul") offers a prime example:

I am listening to İstanbul, intent, my eyes closed;
Still giddy from the revelries of the past,
A seaside mansion with dingy boathouses is fast asleep.
Amid the din and drone of southern winds, reposed,
I am listening to İstanbul, intent, my eyes closed.

. . . .

I am listening to İstanbul, intent, my eyes closed.
A bird flutters round your skirt;
On your brow, is there sweat? Or not? I know.
Are your lips wet? Or not? I know.
A silver moon rises beyond the pine trees:
I can sense it all in my heart's throbbing.
I am listening to İstanbul, intent, my eyes closed.

(Kanık 25–26)

How do such notions affect my constructing an SPN out of the experience of watching modern Turkish films? This book will show how; it offers a unique opportunity for self-evaluation in the wake of a serious operation in 2014 that affected my vocal capabilities. Beforehand I had been an extrovert personality, possessed of a loud voice that could silence crowds of learners at the secondary and tertiary levels. Colleagues could always hear me down the corridor; when I began my career some of them admitted to "running for cover" when they sensed my impending presence. I liked to perform on stage as well as at the front of the class, wrapping my voice round Shakespearean vowels as I tried to unravel the mysteries of the iambic pentameter. Following my illness I had to learn how to reconstruct my personality by learning how to love myself as well as others: "Think to yourself 'I am completely good' and 'I am completely lovable.' . . . Imagine yourself shining with golden light. The more open you feel, the more light you shine. Prevent any negative thoughts from settling in your mind" (Sweet 77). I began to redefine my life narrative through SPNs concentrating on openness with an emphasis on the here and now rather than past encounters, inspired by my learners as well as regular viewings of contemporary Turkish films. I felt intrinsically different to someone like Pickthall, whose conversion to İslam transformed him into a supporter of its values: "once more what it ought to be, the standard of İslam, a faithful witness to the greater Khalifat—the viceroyalty of Man to God—showing mankind only the way of human progress" (qtd. in Clark 58). By contrast, the Christian church upholds "an ideal remote from life. . . . The down-trodden, envious of the privileges which the rich enjoy, aim at themselves attaining such wealth and privilege rather than adjusting the balance. Thus there is no equilibrium" (Pickthall 176). The SPNs I create shy away from such essentialist leanings in favor of embracing a variety of value systems; I listen to others as well as to myself and thereby imagine possibilities in their fullness—historical, personal, and political (Calloway-Thomas 2). Through this approach I try to rediscover the real purpose of cinema, which in common with other artistic forms (whether viewed on one's own or discussed in class) can inspire ontological reflection both on oneself and on other people's relationship to the world. Julian Barnes's recent collection of essays *Keeping an Eye Open* (2015) sums up this point admirably: art inspires "great truth-speaking combined with a fundamental reexamination of the forms [of existence]" ("Introduction"). We need "to bring things into focus, to make everyone take stock of themselves, of their methods, . . . of life and success" (chap. 6). This might not be a rational process; sometimes "the only thing that matters in art is what cannot be explained. . . . To define a thing is to substitute the definition for the thing" (chap. 12). An SPN should be able to set dogma aside and understand the connections between people and environment: "What matters is the surviving object and our living response to it" (Barnes, chap. 15). On this view we can approach the filmmaker's work not just as a comment on contemporary Turkish society but rather as an attempt to "bring things into focus, to make everyone take stock . . . of life and success." We can use their visions as a basis for similar forms of evaluation.

What follows in the next six chapters represents a personal quest, where films form the basis for self-reflection while taking the significance of the environment into account, in a fashion similar to that set forth in Orhan Veli Kanık's "İstanbul'u Dinliyorum." In doing so, I adopt the kind of interdisciplinary framework described by Robert J. Nash and Jennifer J. J. Jang in their recent book *Preparing Students for Life Beyond College*, encompassing "multiperspectival" methods to stimulate creativity and reflection: "For us, interdisciplinarity is a word that applies to the fullest understanding of the real world that we . . . live, work, learn, and love in" (117). Only through this strategy can we learn how to construct and reconstruct meanings through our encounters with texts of various kinds. Hence I make no apology for quoting from Turkish literary texts in translation past and present (as well as texts from other cultures) that I have found beneficial in understanding the six directors' oeuvres. The metaphor I draw upon here is that of a suitcase; by packing in as much material as possible, I try to show how my evaluations of each film depend on a series of complex, often contradictory, responses, transcending the kind of binary oppositions that inhibit rather than broaden our understanding of the world around us. Such strategies have helped me acquire a more mindful outlook on life as well as made me aware of how perfectly possible it is to forge a trans-cultural connection to material produced in entirely different contexts, drawing on entirely different belief systems. It is simply a matter of remaining both resilient and open to experience.

This book makes no claim to academic comprehensiveness. Although a wealth of material has appeared on all six directors in Turkish, I have restricted myself largely to secondary material published in English rather than Turkish, in the belief that the book will be mostly read by English-speaking readers. To this end I quote extensively from previously published translations, especially poetry and fiction. Readers seeking more extensive bibliographies of work available in Turkish—especially on the six directors—are invited to consult their respective websites or to look at the YÖK (or Ministry of Higher Education) site (www.yok.gov.tr).

All quotations from the films will be from the English subtitles available on the DVD versions. In the written text, the titles of all works—whether literary or otherwise—will be cited in Turkish with the English translation in parentheses. Any subsequent references to the same texts will be written in Turkish only. In the Works Cited the titles will be given in Turkish, together with the published translation title.

1

Derviş Zaim

"A Universe of Sky and Snow"

I first encountered Derviş Zaim when he enrolled as a graduate learner on the British Council/University of Warwick program in British Cultural Studies in 1993. At that time he came across as taciturn, eager to participate, but perhaps not as vociferous as his classmates. He produced the twenty-minute film *Camii Çevresinde Rock* (*Rock around the Mosque*) as part of his final assignment, combining archival footage, interviews, and live performances shot around the bars and clubs of Taksim Square, İstanbul. The film showed how Great Britain and the Republic of Turkey experienced the development of youth cultures differently: the advent of Teddy Boys, Mods, and Rockers in fifties Britain was paralleled four decades later by the growth of Turkish Rockers. The difference between the two constructions of Rockers was that, whereas the movement originated among the British working class, its Turkish counterpart was confined to the educated middle class who possessed sufficient linguistic competence to understand the lyrics of English and American songs as a basis for creating Turkish versions. The film ended with a shot of a young British musician essaying the work of the Anatolian rock pioneer Erkin Koray.[1] I enjoyed the video for its treatment of cross-cultural issues: avoiding essentialist tendencies, Zaim argues that cultures develop through continual and harmonious interaction and thereby come to understand one another.

It was not until I reencountered the director seventeen years later that I realized how important cross-cultural issues were to his worldview. Born in Famagusta, Cyprus, he attended the local high school but left the country of his birth and moved to İstanbul to pursue his education. As an exile his existence has been shaped by conflict — political as well as cultural — and it is thus hardly surprising that his films look for some kind of resolution. To understand ourselves we should appreciate how the past continues to impact the present and determines our future course of action as well. This is highly significant to anyone associated in any way with Cyprus, where the two communities—Greek and Turkish—have made efforts toward reconciliation despite the civil war dating back to the mid-fifties. For Zaim the success of such initiatives depends on adopting a long view of history, moving beyond immediate concerns toward understanding the island's ancient past. He also shows this process at work in his interpretations of Turkish as well as Cypriot history. More generally his films emphasize how ancient Turkish arts such as calligraphy, miniature painting, and marbling offer an important means of making sense of our lives, even if they seem at first glance to be difficult to understand. We should be prepared to look beneath the surface of the object and use it as a means to reflect on our relationship to the environment, focusing on what is *felt* rather than what is seen. This is where the tradition of Turkish arts becomes so significant; it can help us rediscover our essential selves and our intimate connection to those around us. As an exile like Zaim, I have found that watching his oeuvre has helped me engage with transcultural issues as well as develop a way of thinking based on humanity's intimate relationship to the elements as the basis for establishing a more just world.

The Urban Jungle:
Tabutta Rövaşata (1996) and *Filler ve Çimen* (2000)

Shot on low budgets, Zaim's first two features both take place in nineties İstanbul and deal with the consequences of poverty. They offer a bleak representation of an indifferent society riddled with corruption, where money talks and everyone seeks to profit at others' expense. Even at the lowest social levels individuals exploit one another ruthlessly. This view of the city is the antithesis of "cool İstanbul" that Derya Özkan suggests is characteristic of the contemporary metropolis—a post-Fordist space of increased cultural as well as commercial initiatives (18-19). Yet Zaim identifies more positive alternatives lurking beneath the workaday world, so long as we are prepared to acknowledge the presence of a higher, spiritual truth governing our lives. Sometimes we discover this through direct experience; on other occasions art can encourage us toward illumination. While humanity might not be able to extricate itself from corruption, at least one can achieve a more fulfilling life.

Tabutta Rövaşata (*Somersault in a Coffin*) has a straightforward plot centering on Mahsun (Mustafa Uğurlu), a down-and-out sheltering by the Bosphorus. He encounters a female drug addict (Ayşen Aydemir) and dreams of escaping with her on a boat: nothing comes of the idea. Desperate for food, he ends up killing a peacock in the Rümeli Hisarı (Rumeli Fortress) and roasting it over an open fire, a criminal act for which he receives inevitable retribution from the police.

The film uses sequences to create mood; we watch the fishermen gathering in their daily catch by the seafront, the fish moving feebly in their nets, unable to move. Like Mahsun, their fate is predetermined. Mahsun whiles much of his time away in a café; as he looks out of the window, the other patrons are shown sitting in silence, listening to the television news. The drug addict tries to write a letter but cannot emerge from her heroin-induced haze. No one, it seems, can exchange even minor pleasantries. With no money for tea, Mahsun is summarily ejected from the café and forced to sit round a fire with his fellow down-and-outs, munching a crust of stale bread. A stray dog crosses the frame, reminding us of how little there is to separate human beings from animals.[2] The camera tracks upward to show a stream of vehicles crossing the Second Bosphorus Bridge connecting the European and Asian sides of İstanbul—a telling reminder of the prosperity accessible to those who can afford it.[3] Since the Third Bosphorus Bridge (the Yavuz Sultan Selim Bridge) opened on 25 August 2016, the gap between prosperous and deprived areas of the city has become more pronounced.

The television's presence in the café introduces one of Zaim's principal thematic concerns—the gulf between the worlds represented in the media and the viewers' daily realities. In one sequence Mahsun hovers close to Rümeli Hisarı as a heavily made-up television presenter rehearses a piece in front of the camera. During filming he moves uncomfortably close to the lens and is summarily pushed away; no one wants to look at down-and-outs in an historical documentary. The desperation of his plight is underlined through cross-cutting between close-ups of his haggard face and medium shots of a party of Japanese tourists excitedly preparing to enter the fortress, cameras in hand. With disposable income at the ready, they are the kind of people who are enthusiastically welcomed in the new Turkish Republic and its media products. This contrast is emphasized once more through Mahsun's relationship to the peacocks. Brought in to Rümeli Hisarı to celebrate a similar act of generosity by Sultan Mehmet the Conqueror in 1451-52, they symbolize immortality, wisdom, and universal unity, depending on one's religious persuasion (Raw, "Derviş Zaim," 283). For Mahsun they represent something far more fundamental—a potential source of food—as he picks one of them up and conceals it beneath his overcoat. This is an act of liberation, as shown when he walks past a cash machine, oblivious to anyone around him; he has no need for material wealth.

The peacocks' presence in *Tabutta Rövaşata* also demonstrates that there are more ways of looking at objects, if we are prepared to make the imaginative effort. Peacocks are not just there to decorate a tourist site but evoke more lasting religious values transcending time, space, and cultures. Mahsun appreciates this; he is a much more mindful person than anyone gives him credit for. Zaim reinforces the point through a series of shots of the Bosphorus with Mahsun at the edge of the frame, suggesting some kind of close relationship between human beings and the elements. This is a common theme in Turkish literature: Reşat Nuri Güntekin's famous novel *Çalıkuşu* (*The Autobiography of a Turkish Girl*) (1922) shows the narrator and protagonist Feride standing by the seashore in the evening, a time when "the waters seemed so vast and lonely, that they really brought a pang to the heart. Fortunately, I was alive to this danger, and I would make the beach echo with my cheerful laughter" (56). This is a transient reaction: when Feride later throws some stones into the sea, she delights in observing how they "lit up the water with a flash of phosphorus" (59) as if a chemical reaction had taken place. Nazım Hikmet's poem "Eğer Alan Vardır" ("You Are the Field") likens the beloved to "the drinker," while the male speaker is "the water," suggesting some of kind of indissoluble link between the two (328–29). In *Tabutta Rövaşata* Mahsun aspires to a similar state of being as he takes the drug addict out in a boat, far away from the clutches of the river police. He tries to kiss her and stroke her hair; but the idyll is abruptly interrupted when the boat capsizes, throwing him into the sea. The next sequence shows him in hospital shivering in a blanket, being interrogated by a police officer (played by Zaim himself). His dreams have not entirely evaporated: Zaim cuts to a shot of the slate gray Bosphorus on a winter's morning, followed by a medium close-up of Mahsun sleeping in one of Rümeli's towers, the sound of water plashing in the background. Although unable to escape his miserable fate, he dreams of the sea transporting him into an alternative world, in a fashion similar to that described in Oktay Rıfat's poem "Sandalda" ("In the Rowing Boat"):

> I understood it again on that sea
> Stretched out in the rowing boat I closed my eyes
> To be alive is so good
> It's worth fighting for this life and one can die
>   by good luck or fate.
> I understood that love of freedom and love of peace
>   Are the same as the joy of living.

                                                              (269-70)

Buket Uzuner's novel *Uyumsuz Defne Kaman'ın Maceraları* (*The Adventures of Misfit Defne Kaman*) (2012) (inspired by Kaman [shaman] traditions) has this to say about the power of water:

> *There was WATER. In the beginning there was only WATER.*
> *At first there was no sky, no moon, no air, fire, earth, nor tree: There was only WATER.*
> *WATER was the beginning before time and before it no life was possible.*
> *WATER is aqua vitae . . .*
> *WATER is time. Before WATER there was no time.*
> *And after WATER there will be no such thing as time.*
> *Running WATER is the metaphor for the passage of time.*
> *"WATER has seen the face of God," said Dede Korkut.*
>
> (98–99)

On this view, Mahsun's dream has unmistakable religious connotations; by associating himself with the Bosphorus he hopes to be able to see God once more as well as return to a pure state of being that defies time, space, and the other elements. For anyone conversant with Jung, the shot of Mahsun denotes an acknowledgment of the unconscious, that "valley spirit" permitting the mind to wander where it will, unfettered by worldly concerns. Having discovered the potential of mindfulness to deal with my own trauma, I find this shot especially meaningful, drawing attention to our capacity to overcome even the most straitened of circumstances.

Needless to say Mahsun dies an ignominious death, the victim of hunger and neglect. The news is broadcast over the airwaves; this is the first time any of his so-called acquaintances have heard about it. The image of them listening carefully—perhaps for the first time—to the broadcast sums up life in a capitalist world where the poorest classes are ignored in life but become newsworthy in death. On the other hand, the ending can be considered optimistic as we understand that Mahsun has at last escaped from "an artificially enclosed world" and been reunited with the elements (Raw, "Derviş Zaim," 291).

In *Filler ve Çimen* (*Elephants and Grass*) Zaim shows how the main character Havva (Sanem Çeilk) achieves a similar inner peace through the practice of marbling (*ebru*). Confronted with the seemingly endless responsibility of caring for her crippled brother (Rıza Sönmez), compelling her to visit a luxury hotel for food prepared by a chef, she attends a class to learn about the ancient art. The camera fixes our attention on the colored liquids slowly placed into the water, creating new and suggestive shapes that help her to forget her troubles, if only temporarily. In the film's final sequence she tries to recreate similar patterns in a snow-covered graveyard; as she does so, the camera tracks upward to show her handiwork with a train clattering past at the edge of the shot.

Ebru enjoyed a peak of popularity during the sixteenth and seventeenth centuries when the Ottomans regularly traded with neighboring territories. The earliest written example in Western museums is a "Turkish Paper" (1586–89), described by traveler Reinhold Lubernau as an example of goods on sale in "all kinds of special markets." A century later *ebru* developed into a full-scale export industry, with the recipes being transcribed for foreign as well as domestic markets, rather than being handed down orally from generation to generation (Sönmez 35). The art flourished; it was regarded as something precious not only for its delicacy but also because it possessed mystical traits through which the artist could communicate with the deity. Several branches of *ebru* were established in religious lodges, designed to create "a perfect pattern" of an ordered universe ("The Turkish Art"). The art depends for its success on accurate balances: purity and application guidelines need to be respected, while the relationship between the water and the colored dye, the dye and the agent (gall), and the quality of gall need to be ascertained. This trial-and-error aspect renders it ideal for therapeutic purposes ("Ebru: The Art of Paper Marbling"). In the contemporary era *ebru* has been identified with "the search for a new language to make cultural diversity in Turkey visible and intelligible. . . . It is a metaphor that offers a promising alternative to others, such as 'mosaic' or 'quilt' when thinking through the new and old dilemmas of cultural politics at the turn of the century" (Altınay 19). The blending of dyes in water emphasizes the capacity of humanity to achieve similar blending, both among themselves and with the Mother Goddess, so long as they set aside differences that often act as obstacles rather than facilitators for communication.

In *Filler ve Çimen* Havva comes to appreciate this function, although not without considerable mental anguish in the process. On one of her daily hotel visits, she witnesses the assassination of a mobster and, as a result, becomes involved in a complicated intrigue revolving around cocaine smuggling. Taken into custody, accused of being a terrorist threatening the future of the state, she subsequently returns home to find her apartment ransacked and her brother missing. In this kind of situation, where chance rules her life (often for the worse), it's hardly surprising that she should try to reunite herself with the Mother Goddess and the elements through *ebru*. Zaim emphasizes the wisdom of her decision by photographing her walking alongside the Bosphorus, looking out to sea in a pose strongly reminiscent of Mahsun in *Tabutta Rövaşata*.

The links between the two films also surface in their use of fish imagery. As in *Tabutta Rövaşata* some of the action of *Filler ve Çimen* takes place among fishermen: the police make an arrest in the market surrounded by boxes and boxes of fish of all kinds. İstanbul's daily rhythms have been disrupted, preventing its citizens from carrying out their legitimate business. The sight of the dead fish heads also serves a thematic purpose, reminding us that the luxury hotel manager Şeref (Uğur Polat) used to be a fish farmer. Now he has sacrificed an honest profession to become involved in the cocaine-smuggling plot and, by doing so, resembles a fish out of water.

The Minister (Bülent Kayabaş) has sacrificed his integrity in pursuit of ill-gotten gains. He carefully cultivates a public image of someone striving for the public good, as he associates himself with a campaign to increase state-sponsored circumcisions for young boys. By doing so he associates himself with what might be termed a traditional view of society, where value is not dependent on use or performance but on who people are. The state respects the people; in turn the people respect the state for everything they do, both in terms of providing services and preserving the status quo (Ülgener 122). In private he has embraced capitalist individuality, being obsessively concerned with feathering his own financial nest by working with a series of gangsters including Sabit (Haluk Bilginer) and Camoka (Ali Sürmeli). This is a high-risk strategy culminating in the Minister's brutal murder aboard a boat. Up to that point, however, Zaim has shown how he exploits the media for his own ends. He strides through the circumcision hall smiling for the benefit of the cameras and holding a bewildered toddler in his arms; in the background the sound of tranquil music can be heard. In the waiting room a clown plays with the boys nervously awaiting their turn. Meanwhile in an anteroom the gangsters continue to plot against one another. The peace of the sequence is rudely interrupted as a youngster screams in agony following the operation; no one, least of all the Minister, takes much notice, as it represents part of every boy's transition into manhood. For him it represents a public relations triumph similar to that in 2011 when the real-life mayor of İstanbul İbrahim Kavuncu attended a similar event at the historic Eyüp Sultan Mosque. He was quoted as saying: "Circumcision is an important tradition in Islam. . . . We place great importance in the festival, not only because it's a tradition but it offers a chance for healthy and hygienic expectations for children" ("Free Circumcision"). The boys' piercing screams in *Filler ve Çimen* suggest that they have been somehow crippled and thereby reduced to a vegetative state similar to that of Havva's brother, who lost his legs fighting against the PKK (Kurdistan Workers' Party) in the east of Turkey. Corruption destroys ordinary people; it reduces public gatherings to a sham, a photomedia opportunity for rapacious politicians to consolidate their reputation, secure in the knowledge that there will be no resistance to their will.

As explained in a card at the beginning, the film's title comes from a quotation ("when elephants hump, it's the grass that gets beat"). Honest families like Havva and her brother resemble blades of grass trampled under the feet of capitalism. Likewise two luckless down-and-outs are forced by the mobsters to carry out Salih's murder and experience extreme torture as a result, with the police tying them up and beating the soles of their feet in the hope of extracting a confession. Nazım Hikmet's poem "Üzücü Özgürlük" ("Sad Freedom") vividly expresses their plight:

> You say man must live not as a tool or number or cog,
>> but as a human being.
> All that great freedom is yours, for them to handcuff you
>> yours to be jostled, jailed or even hanged:
>>> You are free.
>
> (216)

Zaim has suggested that the film's content was inspired by the corruption debates of the mid-nineties, especially the Susurluk scandal, when the then-prime minister Tansu Çiller asked the police, led by Mehmet Ağar, to cripple the PKK and its leader Abdullah Öcalan. This caused panic in the National Intelligence Service (MİT), which had irreconcilable differences with Ağar. Ağar and Çiller resigned as a result, and no one was sentenced (Raw, "Derviş Zaim," 292).

When *Filler ve Çimen* opened in 2001, some critics found the plot too political, others not political enough; the violence was applauded and derided. I saw the film at a neighborhood theater in Ankara and considered it a complex piece whose implications extended far beyond the social and political spheres. I now understood what I felt; by following Havva's example and turning one's back on the corruption inherent in daily life, it is possible to identify a rhythm uniting past, present, and future. Through appreciating this rhythm (through meditation or through the practice of *ebru*) it is possible to learn how to *be* rather than worrying about the consequences of our actions or what the future might bring.

Rethinking Histories:
Cenneti Beklerken (2006) and *Nokta* (2008)

I have to admit that on first viewing, *Cenneti Beklerken* (*Waiting for Heaven*) seemed virtually incomprehensible with its combination of lush period drama and animation. It was not until I had seen similar examples of the historical genre such as the blockbuster *Fetih 1453* (*Fatih 1453*) (2012) and the television series *Muhteşem Yüzyıl* (*The Magnificent Century*) (2011-14) that I began to uncover the nuances of Zaim's film. *Fatih 1453* is a highly profitable neo-Ottoman work where the past is deliberately used to celebrate the present; it celebrates the achievement of Sultan Mehmed II and his conquest of Constantinople and thereby demonstrates the Republic of Turkey's greatness and ambition. Such messages serve a cheerleading purpose for a country trying to reestablish itself as a regional as well as a commercial power (Daloğlu). *Cenneti Beklerken* uses similar material to offer a quite different (re-)interpretation of the past. The combination of live action and animation reminds us that all histories are narratives constructed for ideological purposes in which the distinctions between past, present, and future are arbitrarily drawn. Rather than concerning ourselves with issues of truth versus fiction, we should focus more on how and why such histories are formulated. Zaim invites us to ponder these issues through the central character Eflâtun (Serhat Tutumler), a master miniaturist at the sultan's court.

These issues are especially pertinent in a sequence where Eflâtun is asked by Prince Danyal (Nihat İleri) to create an image capturing the prince's hopes and dreams that will serve propagandist purposes for his people. Danyal wants it in the European rather than the Ottoman style and thereby to legitimate what has hitherto been branded "an infidel practice." The image Eflâtun has to work from is a copy of Velázquez's "Las Meninas" ("The Maids of Europe") (1656), a complex image inviting us to reconsider the relationship between ourselves as viewers and the figures depicted. The young infanta Margaret Theresa is surrounded by her courtiers, with Velázquez working on a canvas in the background. In the mirror the king and queen's upper torsos are reflected; they exist outside the picture space in a position similar to that of the viewer, although their image might be a reflection of the painting Velázquez is working on. In *Cenneti Beklerken* the copy shows the sultan rather than King Philip; Danyal wants a new version with an image of himself and his dead son Yakup (Mehmet Ali Nuroğlu) replacing the sultan, thereby investing them with the power to transcend "different realities, times and spaces." Eflâtun proves artistically incapable of fulfilling the commission—although conversant with prevailing conventions of European art (although protesting otherwise), he cannot entertain the idea of painting over the sultan's image, as the sultan is God's representative on earth. To do so would be tantamount to denying the deity's existence. In a complicated sequence making repeated use of light and mirrors, Eflâtun's female companion Leyla (Melisa Sözen) cuts out an image from one of Eflâtun's drawings of Danyal and pastes it over the sultan's head. The fact that the colors of the painting and the image are totally different doesn't matter as the task has been fulfilled. This sequence invites us to contrast our prior knowledge of the Velázquez portrait with the image depicted in the film; both contain a representation of the artist at work, thereby reminding us of his or her status as a free spirit possessed of the capacity to understand the rhythms of existence. The image fashioned by Leyla is a palimpsest comprising Western and Eastern motifs; differences no longer matter. What the sequence reminds us is that the manifold histories of the painting (both the Velázquez version as well as the versions depicted in the film) have been constructed for particular purposes—propagandist, artistic, or both. This notion runs throughout the film through the repeated transitions between live action and animation, which make us understand the futility of trying to create any objective realities.

Visually speaking, *Cenneti Beklerken* includes a series of panning shots with distinct echoes of the classic Hollywood western. Osman and his band of soldiers cross mountainous landscapes, their bulky figures reduced to specks on the vast horizon. This allusion I believe is entirely deliberate, designed to emphasize once more the constructedness of reality. Zaim explains his purpose thus:

> I reflect on them [images] a lot, especially in the ways in which they problema-tize fundamental issues of space and time. For example, I am talking to you now in a café: a miniature painter of this scene might include elements that took place twenty years ago in the picture of us, or images of what might take place thirty years later. He can play with issues of time and space to create a more comprehensive representation of what he identifies as "reality." (Raw, "Derviş Zaim," 296)

The recurrence of water images—for example, in the representation of Eflâtun's dead son—reinforces Zaim's intention to create a "more comprehensive" version of reality.

For Eflâtun, the film represents a process of self-discovery, as he under-stands the power wielded by any artist able to achieve this representation of reality. Despite his name (the Turkish translation of Plato), he begins the film by being treated as a minion by the sultan, a common practice during the Otto-man period (And 105). Forced to embark on a mission led by Osman (Mesut Akusta) to eliminate Danyal in the interests of justice, he is ordered to draw Danyal's head once it has been severed from the body. Eflâtun deliberately maims himself to escape responsibility but eventually fulfills his task; chance dictates that he draws the head of Yakup instead. Faced by such struggles, the best course of action is for Eflâtun to follow Havva's example and trust in his art by "painting what's in [his] head" and disregarding what others think of him. Trusting in his imagination alone, he realizes that he can do no more than create images of his subjects that assume their own reality, depending on the context for which they have been created.

Even when he has created his images, he no longer knows who owns them—as witnessed at the film's end, when he discovers to his cost that the sultan has seen the palimpsestic image of "Las Meninas" with Danyal's head pasted on top. In the public world of the court the miniaturist has no real control over what he produces and who sees it. The only way he can "recover" himself, in his own words, is to trust in his imagination, that power he possesses to conjure up reassuring images of his dead wife and son in his mind. Zaim reinforces the point at the end in a sequence that begins with a shot of the son standing by a lake on a glorious summer day, a mirror on the left of the frame. The action switches to a shot of Eflâtun walking away from his house toward his son's grave; this is followed by a dissolve to a miniature of Eflâtun kneeling and a repeated shot of the "Las Meninas" image with Danyal's head superimposed on it. We understand the power given to all of us to transcend past and present and thereby establish a communion with the dead. We can establish a similar circuit of communication while viewing a miniature or a painting and, hence, savor the "out-of-timelessness" that according to novelist and essayist Ahmet Hamdi Tanpınar is comprised of "accumulated separations, huddled deaths, memories, and forgetfulnesses. Even the living contemplated . . . the death of their own childhood and prime of life. The heap of things . . . [give] the impression of a ship run aground" (*Saatleri*, 92). Understanding how this accumulation works helps to answer the existential questions Tanpınar asks later on: "What could I conjure up, with whom could I communicate? What man can in fact communicate? How can man communicate to man any of his ills? Stars can communicate with each other, but not men!" (113). In fact all human beings can communicate, provided they are prepared to look into themselves and meditate upon their relationship to the past, present, and future. Miniaturists achieve this task on a daily basis; as viewers, we are encouraged to do the same.

Ahmet (Mehmet Ali Nuroğlu), one of the protagonists of *Nokta* (*Dot*) (2008) aspires to achieve similar aims through practicing calligraphy. Newly released from prison, he travels to the Tuz Gölü (Salt Lake) in Central Anatolia to study with a *hoca* (teacher). Like *ebru*, calligraphy possesses culturally specific significance: the medieval scholar Muhammad Ibn Ishaq Ibn al-Nadim described the pen as "a messenger and ambassador of the mind, its fluent tongue and celebrated interpreter. The intellect of men flows from the tips of their pens."[4] The pen's special position during writing, its bowed head, ink dripping from its tip, and its obedience to the calligrapher's will evoked epithets such as chaste, kneeling, prostrating oneself before the deity, or the weeping one. The left tip of the pen was called *insi* (human), the right tip *wahshi* (raptorial) (qtd. in Gasimova 9). In *Nokta* the *hoca* Hamdullah (Şener Kökkaya) believes that calligraphy can help uncover the mysteries of life as well as help understand the power of the deity.[5] He declines to work with Ahmet, in the belief that the younger man will never become a true artist. The film's title emphasizes this notion; hitherto Ahmet has created calligraphy lacking the dot that would render it whole. In its present state, his art is worthless. Ahmet comes to realize this; later on he is shown sitting at a desk trying out more calligraphy, but as he does so the camera swings violently to the left and abruptly swings back to him getting up, his work left unfinished.

Like the other two films dealing with ancient arts, *Nokta* shows how palimpsests work as different civilizations leave their imprint on the same area over time. Ahmet is inveigled by close friend Selim (Serhat Kılıç) into a plot to steal a fifteenth century Qu'ran, which will be sold on to a gang of mobsters. The two men claim that the book has been concealed under the salt in the Tuz Gölü; later Selim takes a spade and begins to dig. Whether the Qu'ran is there or not doesn't really matter; as an ancient site peopled by different civilizations, the Tuz Gölü conceals secrets from the past beneath its surface. At the beginning of the film a group of medieval nomads, led by another *hoca* (Hikmet Karagöz) are shown burying books for posterity. Selim's act of digging represents an attempt to bring these historical actions to the surface once more and thereby deepen (or should it be complicate?) the relationship between present and past.

Yet this is not Selim's reason for digging; in his efforts to palm the Qu'ran off as speedily as possible, he has become involved with a particularly ruthless outfit led by Cengiz (Mustafa Uzunyılmaz). With their black suits and sleek automobiles, they represent capitalism at its worst: anything, even ancient artifacts, can be sacrificed in pursuit of financial gain. Hence it comes as no surprise to find Selim being gunned down in cold blood. Cengiz's presence in the film reminds us that the spiritual state achieved through calligraphy is perpetually under threat from worldly concerns, which explains why Ahmet can never achieve his aim. He has been too easily deflected from the path of righteousness by the prospect of instant riches. The film ends with him walking slowly into the distance and collapsing in an otherwise deserted lake. He resembles nothing more than another dot on the horizon, an insignificant footnote to history, perhaps. Beşir Ayvazoğlu's poem ("Grief Strikes Suddenly") sums up the effect of this sequence:

The road suddenly grows thin
And stretches without me
I don't know what's behind the mountains . . .

Death smiles suddenly
A voice thoroughly
Divides history in half
The majestic dead rise from their graves.

(116)

Confronted by the vastness of the lake, which quite literally swallows Ahmet up, we have to find our own way through, both psychologically as well as physically. Zaim proposes a solution through the image of the footprint, which appears at least twice — once at the beginning, when the nomads traverse the lake, and once when the conspirators try to dispose of the Qu'ran. The footprint suggests that while humanity can always make an impression on the landscape, it disappears over the passage of time, to be discovered by future generations. Nothing taking place in the past can ever be erased, whether material or imaginative. Hence we should learn to reflect on how history impacts our lives; the more we know about our ancestors, the better we can understand the futility of materialism and come to respect more lasting values, as represented through Turkish arts. This is a transhistorical as well as a transcultural process of significance to us all, even if we are not well versed in Turkish history.

The Cyprus Trilogy:
Çamur (2003), Paralel Yolculuklar (2004), Gölgeler ve Suretler (2010)

An interesting question pertaining to Zaim's oeuvre is the extent to which his ideological position changes in his treatment of Cypriot as opposed to Ottoman history. I have previously analyzed his Cypriot trilogy and its representation of recent history (Raw, "Cyprus Past," 96–117); what interests me here is to discover how the films make use of some of the themes and visual imagery already discussed in this chapter.

The bulk of the action of *Çamur* (*Mud*) takes place on a salt plain (reminiscent of *Nokta*) that surrounds a compound belonging to the Turkish army, which has occupied the northern territory of Cyprus since 1974. Nothing much happens there, save for the regular visits of local people armed with small bags coming to collect mud in the belief that it possesses curative powers. Most of these people are crippled in some way—victims of the civil war who cannot afford hospital treatment and who trust in the elements instead. The film's protagonist Ali (Mustafa Uğurlu), another war veteran now completing his national service in the Turkish army, shares this belief as he smears his throat with mud in the hope of recovering the power of speech. Symbolically speaking, this gesture represents an attempt to return to the elemental embrace, the Goddess Anatolia who bore him and will swallow him up when he passes away. Although taking regular injections provided by the local hospital, his process of recovery only begins when he discovers a well inside the barracks and climbs down it to search for more mud. Hitherto a passive personality, he rediscovers the power to come to terms with past traumas, both personal and political.

If mud and water possess life-giving powers, they can also conceal guilty secrets. Temel (Taner Birsel) travels out to sea in a skiff to bury a statue of Ali, a perpetual reminder of the civil war. If it is out of sight, then it might be out of mind too. This decision to bury something proves futile, as Temel discovers to his cost when he tells a gang of mobsters that another valuable statue (discovered by Ali) has been buried for safekeeping in the mud. When this turns out to be false, Temel (like Selim in *Nokta*) is gunned down in cold blood. Nothing can be concealed: the mud contains the remains of Greek Cypriot soldiers ruthlessly murdered by Turkish Cypriots during the invasion, which haunt Temel and Ali alike. The only way to come to terms with the past is suggested by the film's concluding shot, when Ayşe (Yelda Reynaud) sits by the seashore nursing a newly born child, the product of Ali's sperm (previously stored in a sperm bank). Next to her stands Ali's statue, previously dragged from the sea bed by Temel before his sudden demise. The scene suggests several things: the baby represents Ali's future, the statue, his past. Behind them the ebb and flow of the sea reminds us of life's timelessness. Ayşe looks serenely out to sea, her back to the camera; it seems that she has accepted circumstances as they are, rather than trying to run away from them, and has thereby acquired an inner serenity.

This process of personal self-discovery is contrasted with the superficial ways in which the media likes to represent current events. As in *Filler ve Çimen*, Zaim incorporates a sequence where a television reporter describes a truce between the Greek and Turkish Cypriots. Politically speaking, this news is perfectly true, but the initiative produces no change to the existing situation: the Turkish army remains in the barracks, preventing the locals from gathering mud. For the most part the media tends to oversimplify rather than explain, as suggested by a complex shot in which an ancient statue of a man sitting down has a television placed on it. The statue formerly belonged to the Greek Cypriot owner of a house now inhabited by Ayşe and her boyfriend Halil (Bülent

Yarar); it has been returned to the house as part of a project to reconcile the two communities: even though Greek Cypriot dwellings are now occupied by Turkish Cypriots, Greek Cypriots can now come and relive the past. The television's presence trivializes the initiative, reducing the statue to a piece of furniture. Our impressions of this sequence affect the way in which we view Temel's attempts to create oral history on his videocamera. The initiative might be praiseworthy but will inevitably oversimplify complex and often traumatic experiences. Hence it is hardly surprising that his questions are deemed over-intrusive by one Turkish Cypriot war veteran.

At heart *Çamur* is an intensely political piece of work, examining how politics continues to blight ordinary people's lives, both Turkish and Greek Cypriots alike. The Turkish Cypriot poet Taner Baybars's poem "Memlekete Mektup" ("Letter to Homeland") captures the feelings of many residents:

> Homesick?
> I am not because I've never had a home
> but you are not responsible for that.
> Yet I still remember the sea and the mountain
> together, at night infinitely apart,
> and the space between them my cradle.
> I must not digress in a letter
> so I stop living in that alien past.
> In the present, I mean right just now,
> the summer rain is beating on the sash
> and a conceited sun is falling on the mirror.
> Very, very strange.
>
> (32)

Although living in physical spaces, few Cypriots—especially those experiencing the pain of enforced migration—have ever felt they have had a stable home. Ali feels much the same, even though he lives an apparently stable life with Ayşe and Halil. Past traumas—especially his experiences as a soldier in 1974—render him tongue-tied; like Baybars's speaker, he tries to suppress "that alien past" through silence. By doing so Ali resembles his statue, which the United Nations peacekeepers have transported from the Greek to the Turkish sector of the island in another futile peace initiative. Zaim's camera tracks the statue, lying open to the elements in a truck driving along an isolated country lane, drawing our attention to the fact that no one really wants to work toward reconciliation. They would far rather deal in commodities, just like the gang of mobsters who murder Temel later on. Ali is likewise treated as a commodity—a soldier forcibly called on to serve in Cyprus with no power to challenge the decision.

Zaim suggests that perhaps a solution to the deadlock could be established if politicians bothered to listen to ordinary people rather than making grand yet futile gestures. One of Ali's fellow conscripts remarks at one point that "everything [in Cyprus] is just fate" as he patrols the military compound: individuals have no power of self-determination. The sight of Ali smearing his face with mud suggests quite the opposite; if people can discover their own solutions, unfettered by petty restrictions, then they can come to terms with the past and use the self-knowledge gained thereby to determine their future. Temel learns that lesson, but too late; Ayşe discovers it right at the film's end. As a British-born viewer and writer, the experience of watching *Çamur* is an uncomfortable one, especially since it was the so-called "compromise" agreement initiated by the British in 1960 that transformed Cyprus into an independent republic and exacerbated the conflict between the two communities. While Zaim refrains from making any postcolonial criticism of the former occupying power, he implies that the presence of a multinational peacekeeping force fulfills little or no useful function. Greek and Turkish Cypriots should not be forcibly kept apart; the only way forward is through direct contact as a basis for healing the wounds of the past.

More generally the film forces me to consider my role as a native speaker in the Republic of Turkey, working in a context where learners try to improve their second language abilities as well as develop cross-cultural awareness. If I want to avoid repeating the mistakes made by the British in the past, I should negotiate so as to understand that my opinions are as much subject to revision as those of my learners. Compromise is the only way forward as a means of understanding people as well as increasing self-knowledge. Watching *Çamur* helps me to understand what Zaim was doing in *Rock around the Mosque*; the earlier documentary called for cross-cultural negotiation through music. Out of such processes emerge new identity constructions, for example the Turkish Rocker. *Çamur* calls for a solution based on a "bottom-up" strategy, in which ordinary people's views assume infinitely more significance than those expressed by politicians or military leaders.

Paralel Yolculuklar (*Parallel Tracks*) comprises a series of interviews with members of several Greek and Turkish Cypriot families recalling their experiences of recent history while offering tentative solutions to the country's political difficulties. Codirected with the Greek Cypriot Panicos Chrysanthou, the documentary breaks new ground in Greek-Turkish relations, with the two communities cooperating both in front of and behind the camera. Several of the ideas raised in *Çamur* are addressed once more; at first we hear the testimony of Turkish Cypriots from the village of Murtağa recalling how during the colonial period the two communities coexisted peacefully. They might never have been close, but they did not resent one another. The defining moment came with the onset of EOKA (the Greek nationalist movement), an organization dedicated to securing Greek majority rule. Throughout the late fifties and sixties the Turkish Cypriot community's plight grew gradually worse, culminating in the 1974 invasion, when the Greek Cypriot army rounded up all the men in the village and incarcerated them. The same fate befell the Greek Cypriot villagers at the Turkish army's hands. Zaim sets these reminiscences against shots of the now-derelict land where the Turkish Cypriots once lived. Some men were callously murdered; their remains still lie among the detritus of deserted caves. The trauma of enforced migration is rendered even more poignant through close-ups of black-and-white family photographs pre-1974, when everyone smiled at the camera. In the post-invasion era these same families had been decimated — 37 members died in one, 60 in another. It's hardly surprising that many of the remaining members felt in deep darkness.

At the end of this segment family members from both the Greek and Turkish sectors meet on one of the few occasions when the border has been opened — albeit briefly — thereby permitting freedom of movement. They revisit their former homes (from which they were forcibly removed in 1974) and contemplate the graves of their fellow villagers who were massacred in cold blood when the respective armies forced them to leave. The occasion is a painful one, bringing memories to the surface that everyone would rather conceal; but reconciliation can only be achieved through acknowledgment rather than repression of the past. To achieve such harmony, however temporary, is no easy task, as the documentary's second segment suggests. Comprising a series of one-on-one interviews with Turkish and Greek Cypriots from different generations, it shows how the experience of 1974 has damaged individual lives. Born in 1968, Şirin teaches poetry in a Turkish Cypriot high school as a means of helping her young learners understand the importance of reconciliation between the two communities. On the other hand, the only way she could deal with her past was by writing about it. Although the film makes no direct reference, we feel that Şirin's experiences parallel those of the director. In another interview Saīm recalls his experience of conflict that left him permanently disabled; it was only after considerable struggle, both mental as well as physical, that he could come to terms with it. He opened a small market (*bakkal*) and subsequently embraced a second career as a fisherman. Zaim shows him at work steering the boat and gathering in the nets in a sequence reminiscent of *Tabutta Rövaşata*. The decision to go to sea puts him in touch with the elements, helping him to discover the presence of a distant past transcending the immediate realities of Cypriot history. This awareness helps him to realize that revenge is no solution; the only way to achieve peace is for people to listen to each other.

The narrative of *Paralel Yolculuklar* subsequently takes an unexpected turn that challenges our assumptions concerning Cyprus's future. Initially it seems as if Saīm is a mild-mannered person dedicated to others' welfare through his work for the Handicapped Persons' Association. He vows he could live side by side with a Greek Cypriot family; but his hesitation in answering the question suggests otherwise. Baybars's poem "Gerçek" ("Reality") emphasizes the inherent difficulties of trying to forge harmony between the two communities in this situation:

> I have been to countries
> to cities over land and sea.
> Have seen . . .
> . . . .
> the grey corn shed its seed
> above the door of a municipal hall
> in a very remote town.
> But only tonight
> seeing the cracks in the ceiling
> I begin my journey into the attic
> after all these long years.
>
> Lost?

(65)

Saīm seems "lost," despite his protestations to the contrary.

Perhaps the best way forward is to trust in the power of art. This might seem a naïve, even improbable suggestion, but *Paralel Yolculuklar* shows how it might work through an interview with Salih. Having suffered the childhood horror of seeing his father blown up by a Greek Cypriot bomb in 1957, he has at last come to terms with the experience. Living in a dwelling once belonging to a Greek Cypriot, he has discovered a cache of photographs belonging to the former owner that he wishes to return. Zaim cuts to the Bi-Communal Choir (of which Salih is a proud member) in rehearsal; comprised of Greek and Turkish Cypriots singing in both their native languages, it gives concerts in various venues all over the island as well as İstanbul. In a context where the politicians' attempts to negotiate proceed extremely slowly, the choir offers a prime example of how ordinary people from both communities can achieve reconciliation, free from bureaucratic interference.

This climax to what has been an absorbing documentary offers a good example of Zaim's principal aim as a filmmaker. When I interviewed him in 2010 for *Exploring Turkish Cultures*, he called himself "alluvionic," sharing many of the concerns of his fellow directors but choosing on occasions to branch out on his own (Raw, "Derviş Zaim," 281–82). I have to admit that I did not quite understand what he meant by that term; after five years, I venture to suggest that "alluvionic"—literally, the action of a sea or river forming a new land by deposition—has less to do with overt politics and more about the need to investigate the future through the past. The Bi-Communal Choir acknowledges what happened in Cyprus's past, but uses its repertoire to raise the possibility of future harmony. Both the politicians and the media are preoccupied with superficialities; for real change to occur, ordinary people have to assume responsibility for themselves as well as the communities they inhabit. They should be mindful of what happens around them as well as of the histories shaping their existence. Music, film, and literature, with their capacity to transcend temporal divisions, can prove extremely helpful in this respect.[6] I referred in the introduction to the ways in which Jalāl ad-Dīn Muhammad Rūmī's thought shapes the thinking of several Turkish filmmakers. His ideas shape the ending of *Paralel Yolculuklar*: the communal experience of art helps us understand the importance of "oneness," a belief in the power of the Goddess Anatolia (or other deities) and the elements. Although not necessarily a religious experience, it can prompt us to meditate existentially on our futures (Harmless 186).

The point is reemphasized in *Gölgeler ve Suretler* (*Shadows and Faces*). Set in the early sixties at a time when Green Cypriot forces evicted Turkish Cypriot villagers from their long-inhabited homes. The action rehearses many of the points expressed in *Paralel Yolculuklar*: the two communities once cohabited in relative harmony, with the Turkish Cypriots buying their bread in a Greek Cypriot bakery. The Greek Cypriot Anna (Popi Avraam) and the Turkish Cypriot Veli (Osman Alkaş) have been close for a long time, to such an extent that they willingly exchange confidences. With the escalation of the civil war, the status quo rapidly dissolves: Anna's son Hristo (Constantinos Gavriel) collaborates with the Greek Cypriots in expelling the Turks and shoots in earnest at his erstwhile neighbors. He tries to prevent his mother from fraternizing with Veli; when she visits the deserted Turkish Cypriot village, she is stopped and roughed up by the Greek police. Even members of the same community cannot coexist harmoniously. We hear a television report drawing our attention to the

Turkish Cypriots' poverty as prisoners within their own country, but no one, not least the politicians, can intervene on their behalf. They are rendered helpless, victims of circumstances beyond their control.

The action acquires an added dimension of meaning through the introduction of shadow puppeteer Salih (Settar Tanrıoğen) and his daughter Ruhsar (Hazar Ergüçlü). Like the other arts explored in Zaim's oeuvre, shadow puppetry (Karagöz) has a distinguished history as a means to communicate social, moral, and religious lessons passed down from generation to generation. Ayşe Didem Uslu suggests that Karagöz differs from Western versions of puppetry in the way it refrains from equating death and chaos with evil but, rather, sees such themes as "indispensable aspects of life and the universe." God embraces all opposites—good/evil, self/other. Karagöz offers "an ambivalence that has to do with the mythical (shamanism) and the mundane (patrilinear) cohabiting a single space. Rather than confining, such a space activates liberation" (233–34). Zaim invokes Karagöz associations throughout *Gölgeler ve Suretler* through the use of a large white sheet suspended from a clothesline with a light shining behind it. We witness the characters' actions in shadow resembling living marionettes, prompting reflection as to whether they are "real" or not. Perhaps it doesn't really matter—as Uslu suggests, in the world of Karagöz binary oppositions possess little or no significance, as we are invited to listen to our inner selves.

Sadly, few people seem either willing or able to make that imaginative leap. Forced to leave the village post-haste, Salih leaves his puppets behind. While this is exceptionally traumatic for him, Veli shows little interest in wanting to recover them, despite Ruhsar's entreaties. In a situation where the community's survival is in doubt, the puppets are unimportant pieces of cardboard, representatives of a long-extinct tradition.

As the film unfolds, we come to understand their significance. The shepherd Cevdet (Cihan Tanman) buries them in the ground, next to a field; Hristo watches him from afar and calls in the troops, convinced that Cevdet has concealed something dangerous. The shepherd is shot dead at point-blank range; the puppets are disinterred, and one of them placed beside the corpse in a gesture of contempt. Symbolically speaking this consequence reminds us of the impossibility of burying the past. The puppets are restored to Ruhsar as she makes the hazardous trip from the war-torn village to the relative safety of the city of Famagusta. Zaim underlines the destruction wrought by the civil war as his camera tracks along a queue of refugees seeking food and shelter. Ruhsar is about to bury the puppets for good when she overhears another Karagöz show being performed nearby. She discovers her long-lost father behind a white sheet in the middle of a diatribe against lust and greed; they embrace and continue the performance. While this ending is perhaps a little sentimental in view of what we have previously seen, Zaim underlines the Karagöz's power to evoke a prelapsarian world stretching far beyond the Cyprus conflict in which human beings from all cultures live together harmoniously. In war-torn Famagusta this spirit of community might only be temporary—once the performance finishes all the Turkish Cypriot refugees have to confront a violent and uncertain future. Yet we are left in no doubt of the power of art to offer the prospect of a better world transcending past, present, and future.

In a 2012 interview Zaim claimed that the film's inspiration came from Plato, although the director was particularly skeptical about the notion of harmony. In the film he tries to show the two sides of human nature—good and evil—and the importance of coming to terms with our dark sides, so as to avoid being overpowered by shadows or transformed into slaves (Menken). I am not sure that such ideas emerge in the finished product: the fact that the characters are frequently photographed in shadow makes us aware of how flimsy the distinctions are between good and evil. Maybe they only exist in our collective imagination. A shadow does not necessarily denote evil; it might remind us of our connection to the elements. While politics is intrinsic to all three films discussed in this section, Zaim seems more preoccupied with enduring truths discovered through reflection. Sometimes we need certain stimuli to expedite this process of self-discovery, which explains the enduring importance of artistic endeavor and our reaction to it.

Back to Anatolia:
Devir (2013) and Balık (2014)

In Çamur we saw how Ali picked up handfuls of mud and smeared them over his face in a bid to return symbolically to Mother Anatolia's embrace. Devir (The Cycle) and Balık (Fish) return to this issue from an insider's rather than an outsider's perspective: is it possible for human beings to sustain such a close identification with their roots during a time of apparently unrestricted capitalist expansion? To understand Zaim's concern, we need to realize that "Anatolia" represents a state of mind as well as a physical area in the Turkish psyche. Güngör Dilmen's one-woman play Ben Anatolia (I, Anatolia) (1984) explores this idea through the stories of sixteen different characters from a variety of sociocultural backgrounds; cumulatively they tell the story of the rise and fall of Anatolian civilizations from the Phrygian to the modern era. The play uses an historical framework to emphasize the importance of common humanity. Ceyhun Atuf

Kansu's poem "Anadolu Ristoranlar" ("Anatolian Restaurants") sums up this transcultural spirit:

> I leave the restaurant, oh, the gardens smell sweet.
> The stars shine from their silent balconies.
> Our youth seems, yes, to beckon to all of us.
> I go to my room where a Van Gogh chair greets me,
> On the seat there are apples, and dark grapes.
>
> (315)

Devir asks whether that form of identification can survive in contemporary Anatolia. The action focuses on the intergenerational relationships between three generations of shepherds—Ramazan (Ramazan Bayar), Mustafa (Mustafa Salman), and Ali (Ali Özel). Ali leaves his home village of Hasanpaşa in southeast Turkey to seek his fortune in İstanbul, providing a means for Zaim to contrast the bare windswept steppes of his hometown with the anonymous-looking concrete blocks that dominate the contemporary city, transforming it into an even grayer and less attractive environment than *Filler ve Çimen*. Thirteen years of relentless building has significantly affected the quality of the residents' lives. Ali travels by metro to the city center; once there, he finds it impossible to obtain employment except in a slaughterhouse. Imprisoned in a dingy room by night, his future looks bleak, especially when his boss deducts significant amounts from his wages for "surcharges." Zaim includes a point-of-view shot as Ali contrasts the snow-covered mountains in the background with the anonymous-looking concrete blocks immediately before him. His future course of action seems assured; to return home.

Yet the alternative back in Hasanpaşa seems equally fraught with difficulty. As the shepherds pursue their time-honored rituals, we observe bulldozers in the background preparing to dig up the land and build yet more luxury apartments in the village. Superficially they might offer a superior life for their prospective residents, with electric appliances taking on the backbreaking chores normally undertaken by women, but they also threaten the rhythms of the Anatolian world celebrated in Kansu's poem. Ali expedites this process of destruction by establishing a new business attracting city dwellers from İstanbul and İzmir—reindeer hunting. We see a fleet of expensive cars traveling along snow-covered roads, the mountains once again in the background; followed by a shot of Ali welcoming his guests to the village. The action shifts to a virgin landscape with a reindeer corpse in the background without its horns. Ali comes up to it and places a pair of imitation horns on its head as the sun sets. The entire operation might prove financially profitable, but it destroys the balance of nature. All we are left with is an imitation of life, as symbolized by Ali's horns. What renders this process so painful is that it has not been initiated by city dwellers but by the villagers themselves, in the hope of attracting quick riches.

If Ali—the last in a line of shepherds—chooses this way of life, what prospects are there for the survival of ancient life cycles? Zaim offers no comforting solutions, other than suggesting that we should appreciate the experience of the moment as we witness the villagers running their flocks of sheep through the village, firing shotguns in celebration. This forms the prelude to a communal feast where the men dance to traditional music. In the background a television broadcasts the latest news from home and abroad, but no one bothers to listen, suggesting that in spite of evidence to the contrary (as represented in Zaim's earlier films), it is possible to ignore the media. Timeless rituals occupy far greater prominence in the villagers' lives.

The action moves forward in time to midwinter, when a sheep is killed and eaten in celebration of Kurban Bayram (the Feast of the Sacrifice).[7] As the men enjoy their food, Mustafa hugs his sheep. Once the meal has concluded, the bones of the roasted animal are scattered across the landscape, reminding us once more that every living thing springs from and returns to the elemental world. Yet even within this tranquil scene the winds of change are blowing, as the villagers watch a program about shepherds on television. We are faced with a choice: either appreciate the lasting significance of the Bayram celebration or accept that it has been reduced into cannon fodder for the apparently insatiable broadcast media. Zaim leaves us in no doubt as to where our preferences should lie.

In common with his earlier films, *Devir* incorporates shots of the protagonists set against the vast landscape. Ramazan picks up some sheep bones from the ground and surveys the snow-covered view in front of him. The shot suggests that if the villagers understand the elements, they can enjoy a symbiotic relationship with them and thereby become more in tune with the rhythms of life. This is what Anatolianness truly represents—a state of mind achievable by anyone, regardless of their socioeconomic background, so long as they are prepared to make the effort. This belief helps to inspire Filiz (Sanem Çelik), one of the main protagonists in *Balık*. Living in a small village near Bursa, central Anatolia, she identifies so much with the local lake that she believes that she might be the granddaughter of a local shaman. She shares the same emotional feelings experienced by Hamit Bey, the protagonist of Reşat Nuri Güntekin's short story "Bir Yudum Su" ("One Drink of Water"):

"Let me drink . . . so our deaths won't be left without water!" he said.

When Hamit Bey drank the water from those hands that in a few months would be earth, he felt a new life. Crying silently, the young girl wrapped her arms round her father's neck and kissed him again and again with wet, trembling lips. (99)

Zaim emphasizes the strength of Filiz's feelings by photographing her beside the lake, looking at the birds flying past in a shot reminiscent of the dead son in *Cenneti Beklerken*.

Her daughter Deniz (Myraslava Kostyeva Akay) suffers from a mysterious illness, one that (like Ali in *Çamur*) reduces her to silence. Medical science cannot cure her, which inspires Filiz to tell her husband Kaya (Bülent İnal) that if he catches the right kind of fish and takes care of it, her daughter will be cured. We witness several sequences where Kaya creates a specially constructed tank and spends considerable time and energy trying to keep the water at the right temperature and thereby ensure the fish's continued existence. Although the scheme has been conceived with the best of intentions, Zaim emphasizes its unnaturalness: a fish has been plucked from its natural habit and imprisoned in an artificial tank. Interfering with the balance of nature will never produce positive results.

Yet it seems that people remain oblivious to this basic tenet. Unable to look after his family financially, Kaya embroils himself in a get-rich-quick scheme to increase his daily catch by deliberately polluting the lake. Inevitably the outcome proves disastrous, as witnessed by repeated close-ups of the polluted water, followed by a dead seagull floating lifelessly in the current. Filiz experiences a similar fate as she eats polluted fish and dies. Yet Zaim does not condemn Kaya for his actions; by means of repeated close-ups of soiled banknotes in his friends' hands, he draws attention once more to the dominance of capitalist values. The fishmarket exists solely to perpetuate such values, with the traders continuing their business in blissful ignorance of Kaya's plight.

Kaya deserves our admiration as he makes every effort to atone for his deeds. Released from jail, he returns to the house where Deniz now lives; the frozen lake in the background sets the mood for the occasion. As she peeps out from behind a curtain watching her father approach, Zaim cuts back to a medium shot of Kaya shrouded in shadow; this evil presence is what Deniz sees as she looks out of the window. Unable to see his daughter, Kaya wanders forlornly toward Filiz's grave. As he kneels, Deniz comes up behind him and starts to speak once more. She understands his willingness to observe the laws of nature and hence recovers her "natural" abilities. Now the two of them can learn how to bond together once more as a means of negotiating the future. Kaya resumes his former occupation as a fisherman; sitting alone in a small boat, he crosses the lake as Zaim's camera tracks upward to the sky. At last he has come to share his late wife's point of view: that human beings should value their relationship to the elements to ensure their future. The importance of this viewpoint to Anatolians is emphasized in Dilmen's *Ben Anatolia*, as the speaker celebrates the "thousands of years . . . [of] the human spirit, with its treasons and loves" (242–43).

Unlike some of Zaim's earlier work, both *Devir* and *Balık* adopt a low-key tone, with the emphasis placed less on plot and character and more on the characters' relationship to their environment. This is not necessarily a criticism; what we have seen is that the director is as much, if not more, preoccupied with metaphysical as with political issues.

Politics versus Metaphysics

Throughout the nineties I coedited a series of proceedings emanating from an annual (now biennial) conference on cultural studies held at Ege University in İzmir. Contributors regularly alluded to what they identified as a fundamental sea change in Turkish society, with successive governments foregrounding free-market values as well as encouraging greater foreign investment. Chris Rumford wrote in 1999 that the decade had witnessed the "development of a much needed civil society, a multiplicity of autonomous cultures with their own, popular voice" that challenged the unifying tendencies of Kemalism: "This [process] has liberated the 'dynamics of modernization rather than extinguished the promise of modernity,' offering the best solution to the crisis of identity that Turkey now faces" (146). Fourteen years later another researcher claimed that Turkish women welcomed the rapid process of modernization: "There is more variety of products to reflect self or create the ideal salon environment" (Dazkır and Read). Zaim takes a more skeptical stance toward consumerism by showing how it creates acquisitive societies based on greed. Traditional notions of community based on family and friendship count for little: some people can commit murder if it suits their interests. Zaim invites us to turn away from day-to-day politics and take a more distanced view; if a "crisis of identity" exists, as Rumford claims, it can be healed through understanding the importance of tradition as the foundation of any society, while realizing simultaneously that such traditions need to be reexamined over time. What invests his films with such emotional and intellectual depth is his willingness to go beyond critical generalizations (as expressed by Rumford and Dazkır) and focus instead on the ways in which individuals negotiate the worlds they inhabit. In a capitalist environment, perhaps it's more advantageous to emphasize the relationship between human beings and the elements, which depends as much on *unconscious* as on *conscious* identification. We should trust in our imagination, as well as have faith in Mother Anatolia, to guide us through life's obstacles. This does not require us to turn away from everyday affairs but demands a shift in perception as we reflect on circumstances and how they affect us rather than let ourselves be ruled by those circumstances. Once we have acquired such insight, we can understand why *Tabutta Rövaşata*'s ending might be considered optimistic, or why the final shot of Ayşe looking out to sea in *Çamur* might seem so life enhancing. Even Kaya in *Balık* acquires a modicum of self-knowledge as he fishes in the deserted lake. Notions of happiness or sadness seem insignificant: what matters more is that the characters—as well as viewers like ourselves—acknowledge the inspiration of the moment. It might not be a permanent state of mind, but it can prove extremely pleasurable, as witnessed, for instance, through Salih's and Ruhsar's embrace at the end of *Gölger ve Suretler*.

2

Zeki Demirkubuz

Fitting In

I became aware of the work of Zeki Demirkubuz during the late nineties as I tried to make sense of my experience of walking round the cramped pedestrian streets of Kızılay in the center of Ankara. Thronged with people at the best of times, it is filled with *dershanes* (crammers), bookstores, cafés, and bars. Two decades ago several bars were shoehorned into an aging six-story block; on the ground floor was a butcher's shop, a supermarket, and an offal shop (*sakatat*), while the upper floors were filled with extremely popular haunts for learners, artists, and regular drinkers alike. During daytime the sound of muffled conversation could be heard both inside and outside; by night they were transformed into throbbing hubs blasting out music, both Turkish as well as Western. Superficially the scene did not appear very different from the center of London on a Friday or Saturday night—except for the presence of middle-aged men standing outside the bars, smoking and staring into the middle distance. They certainly weren't seeking female company; rather they watched the world go by without engaging with anyone, either friend or foe. There were so many of them that they eventually spilled over into the pedestrianized area of Kızılay, while posing no threat to anyone.

My perception of these people was greatly enhanced after a chat with a Turkish colleague who had been imprisoned in the aftermath of the military takeover in 1980. Once a civilian government had been restored, there existed a degree of optimism about the country's democratic future. Writing in 1991, Samuel Huntington cited the republic as a good example of the so-called "Third Wave" of democracy designed "to reinforce modernizing and democratic tendencies . . . and so contain and isolate the forces in Turkey supporting Islamic fundamentalism" (14). By the end of that decade many hopes had soured; although financial liberalization created a market-oriented economy offering money-making opportunities, the gap between rich and poor had widened. A succession of weak coalition governments offered various blueprints for reform, but their policies were scuppered by internal disagreements among the governing parties. Ümit Cizre-Sakallıoğlu and Erinç Yeldan commented in 2000: "The most visible signs of political stress . . . have been the disappearance of alternative coherent political philosophies. . . . The economically weaker segments of society have been further sub-divided into distinct rural identities . . . reflecting economic resentment against the nation-state" (506). Resentment was soon transformed into disillusion as the prospects for major social reform evaporated. It would be unfair to generalize, but many of those loitering outside Kızılay bars certainly felt that way.

The films of Zeki Demirkubuz examine this feeling through a succession of (male) protagonists of differing socioeconomic backgrounds who find it impossible to make sense of their lives. For the most part Demirkubuz treats the problem existentially: do people in the contemporary Republic of Turkey possess freedom of choice or are they forced into social roles for which they are palpably ill equipped? He cites one occasion when as a child he sat on a wall and watched two boys who "played for a little while and soon were tired. They left the ball there and sat by the side of the wall. The ball continues rolling and stopped very slowly at the side of the building. It is impossible for me to describe how silent that moment was. I just sat there staring at the ball and the kids. Then I looked at the school building and felt a very strong and weird kind of pain. It grew stronger and stronger inside. I met with pain there, that day, for the first time in my life." The pain outlined here is an awareness of the futility of life (Dadak and Köstepen 19). Unlike Derviş Zaim, Demirkubuz does not acknowledge the existence of an alternative universe symbolized by the elements; hence his oeuvre tends toward the pessimistic. Occasionally the protagonists stare out on expanses of water such as the Bosphorus but discover no salvation. Perhaps this state of mind is a consequence of the director having been imprisoned without trial for alleged communist activities as a seventeen-year-old. Aslı Kotaman comments: "The darkness of the underground is a fate to be borne by human beings in life" (233).[1]

The Urban Jungle:
C Blok (1994) and Üçüncü Sayfa (1999)

Demirkubuz's first feature *C Blok* covers similar thematic territory to Zaim's early films. Set in an anonymous-looking housing estate close to the Bosphorus, the action centers on two protagonists—Tülay (Serap Aksoy), a rich home-maker coping with a sterile marriage, and Halit (Fikret Kuşkan), a janitor's son with a penchant for observation at a distance. Materially speaking the residents want for nothing: satellite dishes protrude from the roof of each block while the parking lots are packed with expensive cars. Yet daily life is sterile; the characters are frequently photographed behind panes of opaque glass or fea-tured in shots with bars at the front or the back of the frame to denote imprison-ment, whether physical or emotional. Frequently they look out across the Bos-phorus for inspiration, but pollution has destroyed all living creatures therein, as shown in a shot of a fisherman emerging from a boat with two dead sea bass streaked in grime. A ferry boat chugs across from the European to the Asian side of İstanbul as Halit reflects on a better life dominated by "merciful slow running water." But this water is not merciful: gray waves crash onto the sea-shore as if they were repelling rather than admitting human interaction.

As the film opens we witness Halit making passionless love to Tülay's cleaner Aslı (Zuhal Gencer). Once they have finished, they resume their daily chores. Later on Tülay drives her car to a nearby jetty and looks out to sea, without noticing that a group of young men have sidled threateningly up to her. We might expect her to be scared, or at least tell them to go away; instead she permits one of them to molest her, witnessed eagerly by his companions. Sex has no significance in this world, offering momentary pleasures that cannot compensate for the sterility of life. In another sequence Tülay visits Halit's poky apartment in the basement of their block and makes love to him: Demir-kubuz shoots this sequence clinically in a continuous aerial shot—we look down on the characters as if witnessing a surgical operation. Nothing can be heard save for the chirruping of birds outside. When they finish, they sit either side of a sofa with a large space in between, emphasizing their lack of emotional connection.

C Blok offers a bleak reading of a rapidly changing metropolis in which the quality of life declines as a result of modernization. Buying a luxury apartment with a Bosphorus view causes heartache rather than self-fulfillment (in contrast to what most television advertisements suggest).[2] Murat Gülsoy's short story "Hayatım Yalan" ("My Life's a Lie") voices the feelings of many:

> I live in Flat 12, Block B, Basın Housing Estate. . . . I talk about myself at great length. At first they listen to me, eyebrows raised, with a condescending look on their faces. But then they just say "rubbish" and walk away. I feel like running after them and pleading, but no, I can't bring myself to do it. I'm not an impor-tant person—that I accept. All the same, to be denied existence just like that

touches my honor. Everything has its honor: a stone, a tree, soil. Nothing can be denied existence. Nothing can be denied existence, as long as it exists. (258)

In spite of Gülsoy's narrator's protestations, it seems that estate residents have been denied existence. In *C Blok* Tülay and her husband Selim (Selçuk Yöntem) occupy separate spaces in their well-appointed living room: Selim mindlessly looks at the television while Tülay looks into the distance. Demirkubuz shoots them in close-up; they are as emotionless as the trinkets placed on the occasional tables separating them. The only snatch of conversation to break the silence occurs when Selim asks Aslı to bring tea. In a later scene Selim asks his wife if there is anything amiss; Demirkubuz has him address his lines direct to camera as if addressing the viewers. The emptiness of their marriage is emphasized through sonic contrast—while they spend their evenings in pin-still silence, Yeşilçam melodramas spout forth incessantly from the television, with the actors speaking at the tops of their voices. The gulf between fiction and actuality is palpable: Yeşilçam stories work toward a definite resolution, while Selim and Tülay inhabit a half-life devoid of moral certainty.[3]

Demirkubuz emphasizes his thematic points through a series of stylistic devices. The narrative unfolds in leisurely fashion through a series of continuous shots notable for a lack of movement. We witness the protagonists staring at one another or staring into the distance as if disconnected from the worlds they inhabit. Halit is frequently photographed in close-up watching Tülay getting in and out of her car, or Aslı going out and coming back from shopping. Using Laura Mulvey's framework in her seminal "Visual Pleasure and Narrative Cinema," we might perceive Halit as someone deriving sexual pleasure from the female form: curiosity without commitment, so to speak (25). Perpetually occupying the margins, he eventually gives up the struggle and is consigned to a mental home. Two visual contrasts draw attention to his plight; in the first, Demirkubuz intercuts a shot of him observing Tülay with a long shot of İstanbullus happily interacting in the harbor area of Eminönü. In the second the director intercuts two shots of Halit and Tülay with a close-up of Mustafa Kemal Atatürk's bust in bronze. The achievements of the Republic of Turkey's founder mean nothing to Halit, whose existence lacks meaning.

The action contains several tracking shots taken from inside a vehicle showing a road stretching forth into the distance or the buildings at the roadside flashing by as the vehicle speeds toward its destination. Such sequences underline the transience of existence; we are all traveling somewhere, and the journey passes so quickly that we should try and understand its significance. Yet this task proves impossible for many, as demonstrated through the repeated use of point-of-view shots taken from inside the vehicle showing the protagonists imprisoned behind their windshields. Occasionally Demirkubuz reinforces this notion by showing the windshields almost opaque with condensation, with a small slit through which the protagonists try to determine their way. Cars, like apartments, are customarily viewed as status symbols; in *C Blok* they restrict rather than develop human potential.

Set once again in İstanbul, *Üçüncü Sayfa* (*The Third Page*) rehearses some of the thematic points made in the earlier film. An establishing shot of Galatasaray's and Beyoğlu's teeming streets is contrasted with the central character İsa's (Ruhi Sarı's) prisonlike existence in a seedy apartment wherein most of the action takes place. His neighbor Meryem (Başak Köklükaya) is regularly beaten up by husband Yaşar (Şemistan Kaya): İsa regularly promises to "be there for her" but seems paralyzed when the occasion arises, leading Meryem to call him "a weak ass." The insult is a little unfair—as an inhabitant of a capitalist world İsa has become accustomed to not involving himself in others' problems. His inaction emphasizes the emptiness of the then-president Süleyman Demirel's claim (broadcast on one of the numerous television news bulletins seen throughout the film) that every Turk should "speak their minds according to legitimate rules" and thereby create a more just society.

İsa's lassitude is contained within a plot that contains repeated visual and verbal references to Yeşilçam. Leading man Cüneyt Arkın's rugged profile stares down from a poster on İsa's apartment wall, part of a huge collection of memorabilia that he has assembled. Meryem's two children are named Sibel and Can after the actor/singer Sibel Can; in a subsequent conversation they debate the merits of the celebrated actor/singer İbrahim Tatlıses. The name of Yılmaz Güney, the politically active director of realist classics such as *Yol* (*The Road*), also comes up. These allusions seem appropriate for a film in which İsa works as a bit-part player in a daytime soap focusing on the exploits of heroic İbrahim (Bülent Düzgünoğlu). Filmed cheaply with a skeleton crew and a camera operator sitting in a wheelchair, this production does not require the cast to learn their lines; a script girl shouts them out of shot and the actors repeat them.[4] To cut costs the producers recruit amateurs for the supporting roles; in one scene several of them (İsa included) are interviewed direct to camera. İsa has come to İstanbul from the provincial city of Çankırı, northeast of Ankara. He has no particular ambitions other than to be useful to his country in spite of his humble origins, just like İbrahim Tatlıses. The Yeşilçam references make some important points about the distance between art and life. While soaps can be wrapped up with a cliff-hanger at the end of each episode, real lives are messy.[5] This is one of the destructive aspects of a media-saturated world offering viewers images of perfection they can seldom achieve. Since *Üçüncü Sayfa* was released, most Turkish soaps have been transformed from daytime fodder into primetime winners; by 2013 they had become one of the republic's most successful exports to far-flung territories in the Middle East and South America. Writing in the Serbian journal *Balkan Insight*, the coauthors of an article suggest that they projected "an old patriarchal family model that appears dead in the Balkans but which is still alive in Turkey—on TV shows . . . [with] intriguing plot lines that involve whole families and the lack of violence and obscenities" (Hamzic et al.). Yet one Turkish newspaper reported two years later that life behind the camera was far from happy, with crews working fifteen- to eighteen-hour days and schedules frequently interrupted by accidents. In one mishap a crew member was run over and killed by a sleep-deprived truck driver during a break. In another a set designer died of heart failure after working forty-five hours in three days. In January 2015 the Ministry of Labor declared soap opera sets as dangerous workplaces ("Grueling Work"). Times might have changed but workers in the media industries are the victims of rapacious producers exploiting their aspirations to fame and fortune. This can destroy people's lives: at the end of *Üçüncü Sayfa* İsa observes that he had enjoyed "a life full of love" with Meryem, even though the two have never been physically close. Such hyperbole works perfectly well in the movies, but İsa cannot understand how fictional worlds differ from daily reality. Hence he cannot really understand when Meryem responds, "You did not ask me to wait for you," and ends the relationship for good.

Üçüncü Sayfa invites us to empathize with İsa's plight through a clever device in which the camera has been positioned inside or outside a room; when a door opens, one segment of the frame is filled with light, while the remainder stays black. This repeated image sums up his life as one of unremitting darkness punctuated with sporadic moments of happiness. As the film ends, İsa returns home from filming the soap; the screen goes black, followed by a shift to an exterior shot of him with a gun in hand. He bangs on Meryem's door and accuses her of "deceiving" him as she has found another man. He tries to shoot her in exaggerated fashion (recalling Yeşilçam) but lacks the self-confidence to go through with it. He turns to go, and the screen is once again plunged into darkness. Meryem opens the door, light floods in from outside and İsa exits for the last time. The screen fades to black once more. Life with Meryem represented İsa's final ray of hope; as he quits her apartment he is doomed to a life of unrelenting doom. The film ends with an epigraph, dedicated "To the defeated, to the forgotten, and to [the actor] Ajlan Altuğ," a member of the *C Blok* cast. Ordinarily this kind of message would communicate an optimistic message as the director pays tribute to those who have helped to realize his work of art. This epigraph strikes us as particularly ironic—although we have been exposed to the life of a defeated, forgotten person, he has now slunk back into obscurity. Most of the dispossessed share a similar fate in capitalist societies; although their lives might form a subject of passing interest, they are always flung back into the gutter.

Before and After:
Kader (2006) and *Masumiyet* (1997)

Although *Masumiyet* (*Innocence*) was released nine years prior to *Kader* (*Destiny*), the latter film forms a prequel to the former. While both contain social criticism, Demirkubuz shifts attention away to existential issues by suggesting that Anatolian humanism—which provided a source of spiritual as well as physical nourishment for centuries—no longer has any meaning in the contemporary Republic of Turkey. Güngör Dilmen's *Ben Anatolia*, cited in the previous chapter, ends with a climactic speech in which the female speaker claims that human beings' task consists of putting "the yarn of passion" into words to thereby "weave the human spirit," which is part of the universe but also contains the universe within it. Humankind exists with the deity in harmony, "Like the legendary phoenix / That catches fire from its own ashes; / To catch fire once again / From the sparks that spring out of your hearts" (242–43). The poet and academic Nail Bezel reemphasizes the link between humanity and the elements in the twenty-four-hundred-plus series of haiku, a selection of which appeared in English under the title *Word Seed on the Wind* (2007). One verse begins with the lines: "sky is sunny / water clear / earth green—" and ends with the speaker's observation that he should admit his grief to the elements, even if he does not really want to (8). Demirkubuz denies his protagonists the option of surrendering themselves to elemental authority; they are doomed to suffer in a postindustrial society. In *Kader* Bekir (Ufuk Bayraktar) spends most of his days minding his father's furniture store and his nights in a *kıraathane* playing cards. By chance he encounters Uğur (Vildan Atasever), a young woman from a violent family, in love with a habitual criminal Zagor (Özan Bilen). Bekir falls helplessly for her, traveling to İzmir and Kars in the east of the country in pursuit of her. The scenario is reminiscent of Yeşilçam, with its melodramatic emphasis on unrequited love, but there is no happy outcome. Instead Bekir inhabits a netherworld of sleazy hotels and backstreet clubs, cut off from his family and running the perpetual risk of attack from Zagor's friends. His only response lies in cursing his destiny, which forced him into a fruitless pursuit while making impossible promises to Uğur.

The impossibility of his quest is reinforced through stylistic devices familiar from other Demirkubuz films. One sequence begins with a close-up of raindrops falling on the sidewalk, and cuts to a pan of the deserted streets of Beyoğlu and a point-of-view shot of Bekir walking toward Uğur's home. Another sequence depicting Bekir's travels to İzmir shows him looking outside the window of a bus at the deserted road. The bus enters a dark tunnel; nothing can be seen except for sporadic glimpses of Bekir's expressionless face, a suitable visual metaphor for his current state of mind, as his fruitless pursuit of Uğur plunges him into despair. While traveling to Kars he slumps in an ungainly heap on the bus seat, his clothes dirty, face unshaven: Demirkubuz cuts to an exterior shot of the bus driving along another deserted road with snow-covered mountain peaks in the background. This is another pointless journey whose outcome we already know; destiny has played its part in forcing Bekir to travel.

Locations matter in this film. Uğur takes a singing job in the Paris Gazino—the name suggests sophistication and a high-class clientele. It is a seedy joint decorated in faded reds and yellows where apathetic clients loll in their chairs sipping rakı and listening to Uğur perform on a postage-stamp-sized stage. The threat of violence is never very far away, as Bekir discovers when two of Zagor's heavies stab him in the entrance hall. Having failed yet again to engage Uğur's affections, Bekir passes the night on a park bench by the seafront; Demirkubuz photographs him in close-up with the city lights in the background. In another shot we see the Kordon, İzmir's iconic seaside street of bars and restaurants, its lights glittering in the darkness, offering a glimpse of prosperity that he can never attain. The camera pans continuously through 270 degrees from the sea to the cityscape and back to Bekir's face, emphasizing his despair; nothing matters for him save for Uğur.

Kader takes pains to suggest that his life depends on a society in which gender distinctions matter. The world of the *kıraathane* in İstanbul is aggressively masculine, where teenagers like Kudret (Hikmet Demir) are routinely teased by the customers, secure in the knowledge that he can never hit back. His elder brother Cevat (Engin Akyürek) can; he takes revenge by repeatedly kicking Kamil (Çağlar Çorumlu). Strength matters in this world: when Zagor is released from prison, he comes to the *kıraathane* and has a violent argument with Cevat, culminating in Cevat's being stabbed to death. The only way women can compete with men is by adopting the same strategies: Uğur's mother (Müge Ulusoy) becomes involved in a three-way brawl with Uğur and Kudret while their father Şevket (Mustafa Uzunyılmaz), a stroke victim, looks on helplessly in the background. Most relationships are patriarchal, involving a violent male and a submissive female: when Uğur resists Bekir's advances, she threatens his conception of maleness. To let her go represents an admission of defeat, and thereby he runs the risk of being teased by his friends in the *kıraathane*.

Such notions are commonplace in a society that expects women to obey their fathers in the choice of marriage partner. When the protagonist of Bekir Yıldız's short story "Resho Agha" (1968) runs away after refusing to accept her elders' wishes, she is immediately denounced as someone who has "stained the family honor" and "turned into a prostitute" (270). Bekir grows up in the grimy, half-lit world of urban İstanbul, where apartment blocks sit side by side, permitting little or no daylight inside. It is thus not surprising that people are physically as well as emotionally constrained, as evidenced, for instance, in a shot of Bekir standing on his balcony surveying the city's slate-gray skyline while smoking reflectively. It is at moments like this that we should reconsider whether the protagonists are victims of fate or whether they make poor life choices. Demirkubuz refuses to provide easy answers. While Bekir's pursuit might be both foolish and unreasonable as he willfully neglects his wife and children, we understand the psychological significance of his quest as a means of confirming his masculine identity. Whether he should be blamed for his quixotic choice is beside the point; rather, we should reflect on his inability to cope with living in a world offering no prospect of personal salvation. Reminiscent of the absurdist dramas of Samuel Beckett, *Kader* focuses on individuals caught in hopeless situations.[6]

The Beckettian allusions recur at the end of *Masumiyet* in the form of an epigraph:

> You always tried
> You always lost.
> Never mind
> Try again
> But be a better loser.

The original source ("Ever tried. Ever failed. No matter. Try again. Fail Again. Fail Better") comes from the prose work *Worstward Ho!* (1983), a monologue on the continuum of existence whose speaker tries to recreate himself and, by inference, to imagine what the purpose of art might be. The work is a lexicon of negativism, of "less-ness" rather than growth, "the dimmest dim" (Beckett). The epigraph aptly summarizes the life of the older Uğur (Derya Alabora), who has spent her life shifting from place to place as a singer with her deaf-mute daughter Çilem (Melis Tuna). In a climactic scene she bemoans the fact that everyone treats her like trash: while the men in her life take the easy way out by committing suicide, she carried on, even though there is "nowhere left to go, nothing left to say." Demirkubuz underlines her plight through a recurring image of imprisonment. In the background of her hotel room, the bars across the window cast a threatening shadow on the opposite wall.

Masumiyet shows how impossible it is for people to determine their own destinies. The older Bekir (Haluk Bilginer) still pursues Uğur but has now become self-pitying, drowning his sorrows in drink and drugs. He passes the time by shooting at an empty rakı bottle or telling rambling tales in his hotel about his sham of a marriage or his involvement in petty crime. He is just "quietly walking" toward committing suicide, although it represents a cardinal sin for many İslamic thinkers. In the statements of *hadith* (the sayings of the prophet Muhammad) suicide is considered so ungodly that the perpetrator "will be in the [Hell] fire falling down into it and abiding therein perpetually forever" (*Salih-al-Bukhari*, 7:71:670). I find the sequence where Bekir shoots himself particularly disturbing, reminding me of the darkest moments in the aftermath of my operation when I feared I was no longer "masculine" enough to fulfill my responsibilities at home and at work. I felt at one with Bekir—a lost soul in an absurd universe.

Demirkubuz reinforces this notion at a structural level by introducing Yusuf (Güven Kıraç); recently released from prison, he travels to İzmir and there encounters Bekir. The plot follows a picaresque path similar to *Kader*: Yusuf travels to Ankara (where Uğur performs at another inappropriately named venue, the Kral [King] Club) and ends up back in İstanbul, where he continues searches in vain for Uğur. Ordinarily a picaresque work implies progress, from youth to age, rages to riches, innocence to experience. *Masumiyet*'s circular structure subverts the form to indicate the futility of Yusuf's life, a point emphasized through a deliberate recurrence of sequences also found in *Kader*: Uğur singing in a club, numerous tracking shots inside a moving vehicle showing the landscape flashing by, the climactic confrontation between Uğur and Bekir. We are reminded of how repetitive our lives are; there are no beginnings and endings, but rather, a perpetual sense of *déjà vu*.

The majority of the (male) guests in Bekir's hotel pass the time by watching Yeşilçam on television, fueled by endless glasses of tea provided by the manager (Doğan Turan). They show little or no desire for positive action but remain glued to the screen in silence. The manager views these nightly rituals as occasions not to be missed—at one point he tries to cheer Yusuf up by promising him another night of Yeşilçam, a pleasurable alternative to engaging with a brutal world in which Yusuf has been tied up and beaten on the soles of his feet by the police for refusing to divulge Uğur's whereabouts. One of these evenings begins with a clip from a classic involving leading actor Ayhan Işık in a court-room drama where the guilty have been sentenced and the innocent released. Such vehicles proved especially suitable for an actor whose black curly hair and pencil-thin mustache gave him a Clark Gable–like appearance (Raw, *Exploring*, 250–60). The action cuts back to the present as Uğur and Yusuf gently put Çilem to bed, closing the door silently behind them. The screen momentarily fades to black; a chink of light reveals Yusuf entering his hotel room followed by Uğur. There follows a climactic argument reminiscent of *Üçüncü Sayfa* wherein Yusuf declares his undying love and Uğur responds by dismissing his words as clichés suitable only for the cinema. The contrast between the worlds of Yeşilçam and the protagonists is palpable: whereas the Işık film depicts a simple choice be-tween good and evil, Uğur and Yusuf inhabit a bleak world where words can no longer be believed and everyone has to fend for themselves. Although *Kader* refers to the past while *Masumiyet* concentrates on the present, Demirkubuz indicates that temporal distinctions no longer really matter. The similarities between the two plots suggest a world whose inhabitants go through the motions of living until they pass away.

A Psychological Journey: *Bekleme Odası* (2003) and *Bulantı* (2015)

If *Masumiyet* forces me to reconsider myself and my mental state on account of Bekir's suicide, both *Bekleme Odası* (*The Waiting Room*) and *Bulantı* (*Nausea*) illuminate other aspects of my existence in highly suggestive ways. Demirkubuz plays the leading role of Ahmet in both films—a screenwriter (*Bekleme Odası*) and a university educator (*Bulantı*) unwilling (or unable) to devote himself to his work. The films offer an existential insight into what happens when someone believes that they no longer possess the transformative power to inspire those around them.

Bekleme Odası begins with the familiar clacking sound of a word processor, followed by a shot of the screen bearing the legend "Crime and Punishment." Almost as soon as it appears, Ahmet deletes it; the screen cuts away to a shot of him staring at the screen and smoking. To his left hangs a picture of Dos-toyevsky. The sound of a fly can be heard. Ahmet switches the reading lamp off and exits at the rear of the frame; after a while the sound of a flush can be heard as the screen fades to black. These few wordless moments rehearse the film's basic concerns: Ahmet lacks sufficient creative energy to follow Dostoyevsky's example and wastes as much time as he can. Beside his study desk a television shows a nature program where a leopard kills an antelope in a few brief moments. Animals don't need to think; they respond instinctively to their environment. By contrast Ahmet spends too much time thinking too precisely on the event.

The subsequent narrative unfolds in leisurely fashion by means of long takes with the protagonists moving slowly within each frame. One such sequence opens with Ahmet sitting on the sofa watching yet another nature program. His partner Serap (Nilüfer Acıkalın) enters and asks whether he is seeing someone else; Ahmet does not reply. A long pause ensues, followed by Serap posing more questions, to which he offers one-word answers while switching television channels to watch a live soccer game. In a matter-of-fact voice he admits to an affair and returns to the game as Serap exits whimpering. The scene ends with Ahmet walking through the entrance hall shrouded in shadows and sitting down once more in front of the television, apparently oblivious to Serap's departure from his apartment for good, plaintively asking as she leaves: "What did I do to you?" The answer is straightforward: absolutely nothing. The atmosphere in this sequence adumbrates that created in Cezmi Ersöz's epistolary novel *Derinliğine Kimse Sevgili Olamadı* (*Confessions of a Love Gone Wrong*) (2011), where the female lover admits to her one-time boyfriend: "Our love was washed away by the storms you yourself brewed. You tossed me here and there, among the waves of your fear, of your wounded past, of your shattered self" (71). Unable to write, Ahmet torments Serap with a mental storm—not violently, but through silence. We have no idea whether he is being sincere; in his writerly role he has been so accustomed to telling tales that truth cannot be separated from fiction.

Demirkubuz constructs this sequence in Pinteresque manner, wherein silence becomes more meaningful than words. The more Ahmet ignores Serap, the more we understand his desire to punish her for his own imaginative shortcomings. This sadistic streak runs throughout the film; later on he convinces local hobo Ferit (Ufuk Bayraktar) that he will soon be directing a screen version of *Crime and Punishment* and would like Ferit to play Raskolnikov. We are reminded of a similar moment in *Üçüncü Sayfa* where amateurs play supporting roles in the daytime soap. In *Bekleme Odası*, no such production exists: Ahmet plays on the younger man's dreams of stardom. He visits Ferit's meager home to discuss the project further and discovers that Ferit has been jailed for committing a petty crime. At this point we are reminded of Nick Carraway's description of Tom and Daisy Buchanan in *The Great Gatsby* (1925), which equally well applies to Ahmet: "They were careless people. . . . They smashed up things and creatures and then retreated back into their money or their vast carelessness, or whatever it was, . . . and let other people clean up the mess they had made" (chap. 9).

The parallels between Ahmet and Raskolnikov are obvious; both have imaginative ideas which could have come to fruition but lead to the destruction of others. They spend long periods "thinking," which they describe as "work" but nothing concrete emerges. Raskolnikov is a split personality—the root of his name, *raskol*, suggests this—oscillating between acts of extreme kindness and moments of cruelty based on the belief that good deeds can atone for a serious crime. Dostoyevsky invites us to reflect on the moral dimensions of murder based on the belief that some individuals are naturally capable of such actions and even have the right to carry them out. Ahmet lacks this depth of conviction; he is more likely to spend his time in front of the television, while insisting to his lovers that he has spent a hard day at the studio.

Bekleme Odası differs from other Demirkubuz films in the way it shifts attention away from the dispossessed and onto an apparently respectable member of İstanbul's artistic community. The director seems less preoccupied with social criticism and more interested in analyzing Ahmet's shifting states of mind. Asuman Suner describes the character as a habitual liar who does so "without a reason," as he drifts from relationship to relationship without committing himself to any of them (121). Suner's use of the term "reason" (and its implied opposite "unreason") seems a little incongruous: devoid of creative power, Ahmet finds himself overwhelmed by external forces—the four walls of his dingy living room, the insistent brightness of the computer screen, his girlfriend's insistent questioning—so that he ends up losing his self-confidence. This state of mind is not necessarily depressive (whatever that means) but rather a manifestation of "altered thinking." Chris Williams explains: "When someone feels anxious, panicky or phobic, how they *think* tends to change. . . . You begin to see everything in quite negative ways. . . . Your thinking becomes extreme, unhelpful and out of all proportion" (74, 76). It is only through his characteristic tendency not to tell the truth that we can appreciate the depth of Ahmet's mental turmoil.

It has become commonplace these days to describe most Turkish creative writers as social critics. Verity Campbell considers Orhan Pamuk an *agent provocateur* in his determination to expose the iniquities in contemporary society, while describing Elif Şafak as someone preoccupied with urban mores (55). *Bekleme Odası* reflects on the consequences of writers deprived of such powers— despite their ability to perceive the world differently, they are as much victims of a Fordist mentality as any other members of a capitalist society, as they are expected to produce a steady stream of work designed to consolidate their privileged status. At the end of the film Ahmet seems to understand this, as he faces his computer screen once more and begins the screenplay with the title "Waiting Room" and the following stage directions: "*Ahmet walks up and listens to the sounds of the night. He sits up and looks out of the window.*" This burst of creativity soon palls, as he hunches once again in his chair, a cigarette clamped between his fingers with the television quacking away in the background. Nothing, it seems, can alleviate his altered thinking; he writes to pass the time. The film's circular structure reinforces this impression; we end as we began with a shot of the protagonist trying and failing to work.

Bulantı (*Nausea*) begins with Ahmet kissing his wife Elif (Nurhayat Demirkubuz) and daughter goodbye as they embark on a bus journey. The *mise-en-scène* suggests doom, having been shot in washed-out colors from the inside of the living room looking outward. The sun shines brightly, but the net curtains and wooden frames of the balcony doors shut out the daylight. On the soundtrack a mournful melody slowly trills. As Elif exits, the screen fades to black and then into an exterior sequence shot from Ahmet's point of view as he watches his family leaving, their faces scarcely visible against the bus windows. It seems that permanent separation is inevitable—and so it proves, as Elif and her daughter are killed in a road accident. Thereafter Ahmet tries and fails to make sense of an existence devoid of meaning. He has a couple of brief flings with two young girls (Öykü Karayel, Cemre Ebuzziya), one of them his former student. While providing him with moments of brief sexual ecstasy, the love-making sequences are shot in such a way as to suggest imprisonment rather than liberation. Tight two-shots frame the lovers as they writhe in bed; later on the girls are shown in long shot preparing food in Ahmet's kitchen, their skinny torsos framed by the connecting door to the living room. Although not shot from Ahmet's viewpoint, these shots suggest remoteness; no one can ever get close to him. The only woman he can endure is his cleaner Neriman (Şebnem Hassanisoughi), who visits his apartment each day with her son. Unlike the girls, she does not threaten his sense of social identity.

Although not directly credited, the film recalls Jean-Paul Sartre's novel of the same name (1938) in its concentration on a protagonist becoming increasingly convinced that people, objects, and situations encroach on his ability to define himself, on his intellectual freedom, thereby causing nausea. A classic work of existentialism, Sartre's work was considered by his partner Simone de Beauvoir as a brilliant analysis of human consciousness and its relationship to reality (47). Demirkubuz uses familiar stylistic devices to emphasize Ahmet's listlessness—the use of the black screen, punctuated by shafts of light focusing on his resigned countenance—as well as repeated *leitmotifs* such as a an unanswered smartphone. The film contrasts his apparent confidence, as he lectures to a group of students about Goethe, with his inner turmoil, as evidenced in a dream sequence involving Elif and his daughter that culminates in the by-now familiar shot of Ahmet sitting inside his car looking out through a steamed-up windshield. The sequence ends with a shot of a pair of broken glasses denoting his inability to perceive the outside world (what Sartre might term "reality") with any clarity. As a teacher, especially in literature, he should possess sufficient breadth of vision to appreciate the authors he works with and communicate that enthusiasm to his students. *Bulantı* suggests he is merely going through the motions; the victim of a nausea that prevents him disclosing his innermost feelings to anyone, least of all himself.

He subsequently undergoes an MRI scan: we see his heart anatomized from a variety of angles. These shots sum up his current state of mind, as he is trapped within what Chris Williams terms "a circle of avoidance," leaving him to believe that he would be "a fraud" if he should give way to emotional thoughts: "Because of this, you might try desperately not to think of the thoughts" (126). In the initial months after my operation I felt the same as I consciously shied away from the reality that my voice had permanently changed. I shunned company and refused to answer any telephone, either my landline or my smartphone. Confined to my apartment, surrounded by pictures and other memorabilia, I felt claustrophobic and unable to communicate with anyone. Ahmet sits in his overstuffed living room shuffling idly through his contacts list on his smartphone. He rings one number but no answer ensues.

Eventually he discovers a means of recovering. He carries a candle from room to room of his apartment, placing his hand next to it. We think he might be snuffing it out (and thereby sealing his depressive fate), but instead he carries it to Neriman's apartment next door. For the first (and maybe the last) time he has set aside his social prejudices and actively sought human company. The candle continues to flicker as he buries his head in her lap and bursts into tears. For the first time in the film's one-hundred-minute running time, the camera abandons the two-shot and photographs the couple in wide angle with no door frames, impairing our view of them. They remain in the same position as the scene slowly fades to black. Thematically speaking, this sequence offers important pointers about how Ahmet can make sense of his future. A teacher by profession, he has at last understood the importance of *learning*; by opening himself up to others he can benefit from their insights as well as their succor in times of need. Such discoveries can lay the foundations for the creation of a community that can help individuals reconcile their personal with their professional lives. Ahmet has a long way to go, but at least he is willing to "take chances to express passions and hopefully find new ways to deal with nausea" (Nash 48).

More Dark Tales of the Soul:
Yazgı (2001) and *İtiraf* (2002)

Together with *Bekleme Odası*, *Yazgı* (Fate) and *İtiraf* (Confession) form a trilogy of "Dark Tales" (Demirkubuz's term) concentrating on the inner workings of the mind as it copes with inhospitable environments. Loosely based on Albert Camus's *The Outsider* (1942), *Yazgı* tells a story resembling *Bulantı*; a male protagonist experiences bereavement, has a casual affair, and spends most of his time trying and failing to adjust to the realities of his changed existence. This is no coincidence: Asuman Suner observes that "the sense of compulsive repetition" pervades Demirkubuz's work, creating "the impression that the characters are stuck in a labyrinth from which they cannot possibly escape. . . . Everything perpetually replicates itself. All the relations are the same; time and again, similar relations occur between different people" (Suner, "Horror"). Or more precisely, the *lack* of relations occurring between different people. Musa (Serdar Orçin) works in an open-plan office with Yavuz (Feridun Koç) and secretary Sinem (Zeynep Tokuş), who exchange few words with one another. The space is divided into small cubby holes by glass partitions, placing a physical as well as an emotional barrier between them. The boss Naim (Demir Karahan) has a separate room to conduct his extramarital affairs as well as make a clumsy pass at Sinem. Musa's alienation from his environment is total: when his mother passes away in her sleep, he does not appear in the least perturbed as he watches a Yeşilçam film on television while preparing a hot drink. Demirkubuz tracks to a close-up of the filthy cups and plates, the remains of his mother's last meal eaten the night before she died, and cuts to a shot of her corpse in bed. We witness another close-up of an ashtray overflowing with cigarette butts; the camera pans the dingy living room as we hear a reporter speaking on the television about recent violence at home and abroad and witness Musa looking out of the window through metal bars. Nothing, it seems, can release him from self-imposed imprisonment—not even the responsibility of giving his mother a decent burial.

Musa does not believe in anything or anyone; in one shot he stands on the curb of a busy İstanbul thoroughfare watching the cars and trucks thundering past in both directions. His countenance remains expressionless, as if unwilling (rather than unable) to cross to the other side. Unlike protagonists such as Ahmet (in *Bekleme Odası*), Musa's despair is so all-pervasive that he no longer cares about the distinctions between right and wrong, happiness and sadness, or love and hate. He represents what Talât Halman described in 2007 as the typical protagonist of contemporary Turkish fiction: "gripped by despair, alienated, gloomy . . . and . . . exiled from reality" ("Near Eastern," 68). Yet Musa is not quite detached from reality: after having served a four-year jail sentence for an offense he did not commit, he debates the moral issues of the case with a lawyer (Erol Babaoğlu). We learn that he considers himself neither guilty nor innocent; nor should he harbor any cause for complaint, as he admits that he wanted to commit murder for no apparent reason. The dialogue is comprised of a series of shot/reverse shot sequences, suggesting some kind of logic: perhaps Musa does embrace a certain worldview that no one actively understands. He delivers a soliloquy in voiceover at the end where he admits to reflecting on his mother's death and experiencing "a surge of excitement" as he did so. Such comments increase our interest—what should he be excited about? Perhaps he has discovered an alternative reality divorced from the workaday world in which he can communicate with his mother. His emotions are certainly *not* religious (earlier on he told us that his soul was empty), but they have enabled him to see light at the end of the despairing tunnel and thereby transformed what seemed like a "dark tale" into something with a partially happy outcome. Like Ahmet in *Bulantı*, Musa has found a means to cope with grief, not by releasing pent-up feelings but by creating a self-enclosed mental universe that no one else can penetrate. This is one of the basic advantages of a mindful view of the world: "to focus on the pain, rather than avoid it, to ride it, powerfully" (Sweet 17). In *Yazgı* Demirkubuz uses Musa's discovery of an alternate reality to reflect on the human condition as specifically applied to those living in contemporary İstanbul. The way to cope with daily life is to proceed outward from the imagination to the outside world. While most politicians would believe in the opposite (external reform promotes inner happiness), *Yazgı* shows that this is nothing more than an illusion. Humanity should acquire confidence in itself *before* reshaping the world it populates.

The title *İtiraf* is ironic, as it is precisely through the central character Harun's (Taner Birsel's) inability to confess to his past misdemeanors that lands him in emotional turmoil, as symbolized by his tendency to drive aimlessly through darkened roads, his side profile framed in close-up, intercut with point-of-view shots of the landscape obscured by the car windshield. As the action unfolds, so his behavior becomes even more unfathomable. Staying one night in an anonymous İstanbul hotel, he takes a shower, opens a can of beer and idly flicks through the television channels. He stares at the ground, and Demirkubuz cuts to a shot of him driving home that same night along the freeway. Arriving home in Ankara, he takes a quick peek at his partner Nilgün (Başak Köklükaya) sleeping soundly, returns to the living room, and tries to rest.[7] The jerky narrative style emphasizes his inability to settle, intercutting close-ups of his face with brief glimpses of the living-room furniture.

The most suggestive aspect of this sequence is the way our attention focuses on a reproduction of Vermeer's "Girl with a Pearl Earring" (ca. 1665) on the wall. It seems appropriate that this intertextual reference should crop up, particularly as Vermeer himself thought of the painting as one of a pair "painted in the Turkish manner" ("Girl with a Pearl Earring"). With her liquid eyes and painted mouth, the subject radiates purity, captivating everyone who looks at her; her skin is as unblemished as the surface of the large teardrop. Every aspect of the image sets Harun's guilt into sharper focus; he is neither pure nor unblemished and will never rid himself of the teardrops blighting his future until he faces the truth about himself.

We do not yet know what that truth is, but Harun's behavior becomes more and more unacceptable. He drags Nilgün out of bed, proclaiming that he cannot take "this" any more (what "this" represents is never explained), and accuses her of being unfaithful before leaving the room to watch another Yeşilçam movie on television. After a few moments he storms back in and tries to strangle her; she manages to break free and struggles into the bathroom gasping for breath, while Harun crouches like a frog on the bed. We subsequently overhear the sound of her throwing clothes into a suitcase prior to leaving for good. Throughout this painful sequence Demirkubuz contrasts the articulate dialogue of the Yeşilçam characters on television with Harun and Nilgün's inability to state precisely what they think. The strain of bottling their emotions up proves too great, causing Harun to veer between extremes—anger followed by childlike sobbing. He reveals the classic symptoms of manic depression, when "emotions loop back on themselves, having feelings about feelings, sometimes without limit. Feedback loops produce emotions that are experienced either as unbearably painful or out of control" (Scheff).

Demirkubuz underlines how the environment exacerbates Harun's condition. He is perpetually imprisoned in small rooms or poky balconies, looking despairingly out at the skyline like Bekir in *Kader*. The Republic of Turkey's capital was not so developed in 2002 as it is today (most of the concrete blocks and freeways that cover the landscape have sprung up in the past decade or so), but it was still comprised of anonymous-looking four- or five-story concrete blocks, creating a vista strongly reminiscent of Coketown in Charles Dickens's *Hard Times* (1854): "It was a triumph of fact. . . . It contained several large streets all very like one another, and many small streets still like one another, inhabited by people equally like one another who all went in and out at the same time, with the sound upon the same pavements, . . . and to whom every day was the same as yesterday and to-morrow" (88). Harun's imprisonment is repeatedly stressed through interior shots of him pacing up and down the excessively furnished living room of his upper-floor apartment, peering out of the window at the concrete mass that transforms itself into inky blackness at nighttime. Later on he travels to the poorer district of Mamak in an attempt to trace Nilgün (who has by now endured another failed relationship). He passes the cramped streets lined with mud-brick bungalows, whose inhabitants pass the time by sitting on the curb watching their offspring playing in the dirt. *Plus ça change, c'est la même chose*: all people look to escape their surroundings, but they lack the will to put their yearnings into practice.

The most effective form of liberation consists of a change of mindset similar to that experienced by Ahmet in *Bulantı* or Musa in *Yazgı*. We understand this more clearly when we discover the cause of Harun's mental anguish; he became involved in a complicated love triangle involving Nilgün and his erstwhile best friend Taylan, who later committed suicide. Initially Harun was content to blame fate for Taylan's passing; it is only when Taylan's family reject Harun's peacemaking efforts with an abrupt insult ("piss off!") that Harun begins to understand what to do. He buries his head in Nilgün's lap and bursts into tears, caressing her foot as he does so—a moment that adumbrates the film's final sequence when the two of them meet once again at Nilgün's house in Mamak. They sit either side of a rickety sofa as Harun asks Nilgün to accompany him to a new posting in Diyarbakır in the east of the country. Nilgün shakes her head, turns toward him, and observes trenchantly that "time is the only thing that passes. The past cannot be overlooked." Demirkubuz's camera tracks upward as the couple stare at one another wordlessly before the scene fades to black. The silence is important as Harun ceases to think of himself and opens his mind to others. This represents a considerable shift, as significant in its own way as Musa's decision to create an imaginative world of his own in *Yazgı*. Harun understands what true mindfulness involves—moving away from self-absorption and reflecting more deeply on one's position in the world. The process has nothing whatsoever to do with socioeconomic issues and everything to do with emotional well-being. In a deliberate confusion of life and art, Demirkubuz has Harun looking at a photograph of the dead Taylan, which just so happens to be an image of the director himself. The moment suggests Demirkubuz's willingness to judge his fictional characters as they try to establish a more coherent future for themselves. The ending of *İtiraf* embraces a world-view characteristic of Nâzım Hikmet toward the end of his life after decades spent fighting for political freedom:

I didn't know I loved as many things and I
had to wait until sixty to find it out sitting
by the window on the Prague-Berlin train
watching the world disappear as if on a
journey of no return.

("Şeyler Ben Sevdim Bilmiyordum"
["Things I Didn't Know I Loved"],
264)

Adaptations in an Unchanging World:
Kıskanmak (2009) and Yeraltı (2012)

Although inspired by various authors (Dostoyevsky, Camus, Sartre), most of
Demirkubuz's screenplays are original. The only two films directly based on
source texts are *Kıskanmak* (*Envy*), from a novel by Nahid Sırrı Örik (1946),
and *Yeraltı* (*Underground*), from Dostoyevsky's *Notes from the Underground*
(1864). The fact that these two are adaptations renders them slightly different
to the other works in the director's oeuvre, even though the issues raised are
very similar.

Initially it seems that *Kıskanmak* will project a more optimistic representation of life in the Republic of Turkey. Set in the Black Sea mining town of
Zonguldak in 1930, the action opens at the Independence Day celebrations (29
October) held in a large meeting room festooned with national flags and images
of Mustafa Kemal Atatürk, while guests from all social backgrounds sing, dance,
and partake of food and drink. Yet there are certain clues suggesting that all is
not well: spotlights shine on Halit (Serhat Tutumluer), his wife Mükerrem
(Berrak Tüzünataç), and local beau Nüzhet (Bora Cengiz) as their faces dart
about the room in a conscious attempt to be noticed in their well-tailored suits
and magnificent ball gowns. This is a stratified society in which everyone con-
forms to prescribed roles. Although Independence Day was initially conceived
as a communal celebration of republican identity, Zonguldak's bourgeoisie
will have none of it: class distinctions matter. The importance of this unwritten
social rule is emphasized in sequences taking place in Halit's coal mine as
workers carry out his orders and servants tend to his every whim. He has money
as well as status and wants everyone to know it.

Mükerrem wants for nothing except a purpose to her life. She lounges
about her overstuffed apartment reading style magazines and yearning to return
to İstanbul. The *mise-en-scène* denotes her mental state: metal grilles prevent
light shining in through the windows, while a giant drinks cabinet and bar at

the back of the room in best faux Art Nouveau style inhibits rather than permits movement. Demirkubuz cuts to a shot of her staring helplessly at the camera while the strains of Albinoni's "Adagio for Strings" can be heard, summing up her melancholy life.[8] Considered in relation to his earlier films, *Kıskanmak* indicates that loneliness and isolation is all-pervasive as well as transhistorical, blighting bourgeois lives as well as those of the dispossessed. It's hardly surprising that Mükerrem should seek solace in a clandestine affair with Nüzhet, even if that requires an elaborate pretense for her to go out at night. In Zonguldak women's place is firmly in the home. This arrangement might have continued smoothly (Halit is not above visiting a brothel for extramarital entertainment) were it not for Seniha's (Nergiz Öztürk's) presence in the house.[9] She fulfills a role as Mükerrem's friend and confidante, creating a feminine space within Halit's household where the two of them can knit, sew, and gossip. While gender divisions might be inflexible, it seems that resourceful women can exploit them. Yet the women's friendship proves wafer thin: once Seniha discovers Mükerrem's secret, she smashes a crystal bowl into smithereens, not only denoting her frustration but her determination to destroy the world that Mükerrem represents.

This is a significant moment, reminding us of other moments in Demirkubuz's oeuvre when characters deliberately destroyed their friends' lives (Harun and Taner in *İtiraf* is a good example). The director makes no judgment on their actions but expects them to face the consequences. Seniha is initially pleased with her plan, but as the action unfolds she becomes less and less convinced. She continually glances at a book of yellowing photographs; we find out that they are images of her late family who were socially and financially ruined when Atatürk came to power in 1923. Seniha's decision to ruin Mükerrem was prompted by the desire for revenge against those who had profited from the Republic of Turkey's social revolution. The dog-eat-dog view of life predominates, with only the fittest surviving. In a significant use of intertext, Demirkubuz shows Seniha sitting alone with a copy of *Crime and Punishment* in her hand—perhaps she considers herself a reincarnation of Raskolnikov meditating on the distinctions (or lack thereof) between right and wrong. Yet things do not turn out as she envisaged; forced out of Halit's house, she takes a job as a teacher in Trabzon, living alone with only her youthful learners for company. She sits in a darkened room surrounded by her family photographs, the embers of a fire illuminating her face. With the Albinoni theme recurring on the soundtrack, the action shifts to İstanbul as Seniha roams the narrow streets alone. Accompanied by a lawyer—especially hired for the occasion—she enters another darkened room caked with dust and waits for Halit in an attempt to engineer a reconciliation. Her hopes are dashed as he spits in her face and curses her for breaking up his marriage. The film ends with a repeated shot of her sitting alone on a ship returning to Trabzon; through another prison image suggested by a staircase, she sits down, her hair awry, and explains in voiceover how her life has been ruined by envy.

Unusually for Demirkubuz, *Kıskanmak* is a highly moral film suggesting that humanity often renders the world a more unpleasant place to inhabit, especially if their personal obsessions drive them to exploit others. We should be responsible for our own actions; the film's historical setting emphasizes the transhistoricity of this notion. Nâzım Hikmet makes a similar point in one of his late love poems:

> Should my journey end before I reach my city,
> I've rested in a rose garden thanks to you,
> Because of you I don't let death enter,
> clothed in the softest garments
> and knocking on my door with songs
> calling me to the greatest peace
>
> ("Senin Yüzünden"
> ["Because of You"],
> 239)

Yeraltı explores similar moral territory through the innermost thoughts of Muharrem (Engin Günaydın), an office worker pursuing a drab, monotonous life in a workspace recalling that represented in *Yazgı*. The basic scenario incorporates images familiar from other Demirkubuz films: the ashtray full of cigarette butts; a filthy frying pan with a half-eaten meal sticking to its sides; the flickering television screen showing nature programs, and (in one scene) Demirkubuz's *Masumiyet*. Muharrem has a cleaning lady Türkan (Nihal Yalçın) with whom he enjoys a close platonic relationship, to such an extent that she is the only recipient of his innermost thoughts. What differentiates *Yeraltı* is the way Muharrem also communicates with us through voiceover. While sitting at his desk idly contemplating his fellow office workers he reflects that: "A rational man cannot have pride if he's not merciless toward himself. . . . I despised myself hatefully." Later on he admits that "a secret fight [started] between myself and everything else," as a result of dealing with "fits of hysteria." He begins to "wander in dark places," "into the underground," both physical as well as psychological.

Narratively speaking the film analyzes Muharrem's progress as he discovers something about himself and his relationship to the outside world. He joins his friends at a dinner party held at the Tunalı Hotel in one of Ankara's more fashionable central districts, celebrating his friend Cevat (Serhat Tutumluer), who has just won the Best Novel Award for a quasi-autobiographical work "Boredom in Ankara." This is preceded by a shot of Muharrem's television at home broadcasting a nature documentary on "Hunters and Hunted"; the title foreshadows the development of the dinner party as the guests compete with one another for mental control of the proceedings. They toast one another in a mood of false bonhomie that contrasts with Muharrem's pent-up emotion as he grasps his wine glass and drinks. There is a brief lull, during which time Cevat and Muharrem stare at one another; Muharrem falls asleep and the remainder of the guests resume their revelries. This sequence exemplifies the title of Cevat's novel — *Boredom in Ankara* — as it depicts people passing the time by drinking without any real purpose in their lives. Muharrem adopts a course of action recalling Musa in *Yazgı* by creating an imaginative world of his own that no one can penetrate. He gets up from his chair and performs a solitary dance for the camera; no one takes any notice of him, but Muharrem does not seem perturbed.

Later that evening he checks in at a seedy hotel and encounters prostitute Fahise (Nergis Öztürk). The "Hunters and Hunted" theme continues as he growls at her like a predatory lion hunting its prey. Fahise is at first scared of him, but as the sequence unfolds she becomes more attuned to his worldview. She visits him at his apartment and expresses a yearning "to be a good person, but they won't let me." Precisely who "they" are is not specified, but it is of scant importance. Demirkubuz focuses attention on the odd couple — the leonine man growling at a woman sitting silently on his sofa. He shoots the action with a slightly tilted camera, suggesting psychological dislocation. Muharrem exits and showers, sniffing his armpits as he does so; covered with a bath towel, he sits down as Fahise exits silently. This moment seems characteristic of Demirkubuz, denoting the protagonists' inability to relate to one another at any level. Yet our assumptions are skillfully undercut by Muharrem's concluding voice-over describing his current state of mind: "[My] pain subsided, giving rise to a feeling . . . [I] had never experienced before. A strong, pleasant feeling like toothache. The reason for all the disorder. Change was not possible. [I] . . . could not become a different man." The film ends with him standing at his front door with an expression of intense relief. The sequence represents another important moment in Demirkubuz's oeuvre, with a male character finally coming to terms with the world around him by creating an alternative universe of the imagination both related to yet fundamentally different from the world he inhabits. Issues of madness and sanity no longer appear significant; it's more important to understand himself and the vagaries of his consciousness.

Muharrem embraces *Boredom in Ankara* in full knowledge that he cannot change it, but nonetheless discovers a way to work *through* it and thereby increase his self-esteem comprising "an internal judgement of your own worth based on your emotions. . . . The more open you feel, the more light you shine . . . [on] being and accepting yourself" (Sweet 48). The capacity for openness provides the basis for the SPN (scholarly personal narrative) underpinning this entire chapter. Exposure to Demirkubuz's quite sizable output prompts me to reflect on myself and how to cope with the task of adapting to my own world. He creates narratives of authenticity and connection, wherein the protagonists mostly try and fail to "heal the rifts that exist between their personal and professional lives. They want congruence. They seek wholeness" (Nash 99-100). Only Musa and Muharrem accomplish this task successfully by listening to themselves.

Yeraltı might best be described as a Dostoyevsky adaptation that retains much of the source text's plot—the dinner party, the encounter with the prostitute—so as to emphasize the importance of adaptation, understood as a process of regular adjustment to the exigencies of the outside world. In a 2011 interview during filming, Demirkubuz admitted that the experience of adaptation helped him to "start rediscovering the novel," especially when "stuck with problems in particular with [Muharrem's] narrative" ("Zeki Demirkubuz Adapts"). Through a comparison between screenplay and source text he came to understand that the protagonists and the viewers alike should be invited to participate in the adaptive process as a way of dealing with personal difficulties.

Fitting In

In an interview published in 2013, Deniz Bayrakdar claimed that Demirkubuz follows the example of many of his contemporaries in embedding "politics" in their narratives, more precisely defined as using stories as "cache to veil the politics of the [*sic*] everyday life. They hide politics behind the curtains of their rooms, in the television frames and at tables where no one speaks to each other" (Erdem). While such comments draw suggestive parallels between the personal and the political that undoubtedly have contemporary resonance in a rapidly changing republic, I think that they overlook Demirkubuz's overriding preoccupation with individuals' inability to relate to their environment both psychologically and spiritually. As with many quoted comments, we should treat most interviews with caution: perhaps the interviewees are restating what their interlocutors want. On Demirkubuz's website (www.zekidemirkubuz.com) there is a selection of articles dating from 2003-7 in which the director discusses his films. In an interview with the London *Guardian* (2006) he declared that his films were primarily about "pain, . . . with different characters working their pain through different situations. I try to make the same film over and over again. Changing subject is just opportunism to me, something that is done for political or financial reasons" (Gibbons). Speaking about the "Tales of Darkness" trilogy Demirkubuz describes himself as a skeptic who did not feel comfortable unless he asked questions: "This is why, even though I have a strong desire to believe, I am aloof towards concepts such as religion and faith. . . . I may be not someone who tries to explain himself or life with religion, but the feeling that comes along with the fact that some of the answers are missing is enough for me to carry a feeling about this religious essence" (Dadak and Aytaç). In 2006 he told Jamie Bell of *Sight and Sound* that in films like *Yazgı* and *İtiraf* he had taken "a human condition out of our lives and written a story about it," the sources of which originate from "life and literature, and my own inner darkness" (Bell).

Although he explores the dilemmas faced by male characters in a variety of situations, I believe that "politics" in Demirkubuz's terms is a complex construction. He does not use his films to make direct comments on corruption, as in Zaim's *Filler ve Çimen*; but the use of visual quotations from Süleyman Demirel and Tansu Çiller sets the action in its sociohistorical context of the late twentieth and early twenty-first centuries. Similarly, the use of gray, anonymous-looking tower blocks in *C Blok* (for instance) emphasize the negative impact of the Republic of Turkey's so-called economic renaissance on ordinary citizens. Nor am I convinced that Demirkubuz is an agnostic preoccupied solely with human beings' "inner darkness." He engages with existential issues, especially the complex question of how individuals struggle to find satisfactory answers to important ontological questions. In *Yeraltı* Muharrem makes a conscious decision to descend into the underground; there is no guarantee that he will discover anything there, but at least he tries to make sense of his life. The worlds depicted in Demirkubuz's films are harsh and indifferent, favoring the strong over the weak—hence İsa in *Üçüncü Sayfa* is always going to be frustrated, whatever he might believe. Other characters experience similar moments of "inner darkness," but often acquire the mental strength to resist it. Harun in *İtiraf* emerges from despair by coming to terms with his guilty past; Ahmet in *Bulantı* realizes that it is not a sign of weakness to give way to his emotions. This spontaneous act gives him a way into his tortured psyche.

What is most intriguing about Demirkubuz is his concentration on the issue of "fitting in." This is a complex concept that preoccupies social scientists as well as psychologists: Michael W. Taft wrote in 2012 that our "dark side" as well as our susceptibility to group pressure inhibits our self-fulfillment. This notion was picked up by Olaf Miller in a critical piece on Demirkubuz where he reflected on the director's preoccupation with "no" as "the essence of things, that which Demirkubuz's art makes visible th[r]ough its light, . . . spatial configurations, . . . rhythm, . . . not forgetting the actors' unique presences, which etch themselves into the celluloid" (71–72). Yet this assertion is not quite true: characters can discover their way out of their prisons, whether emotional or physical, once they appreciate their intrinsic worth and discover "the urge to cooperate," and thereby fit in, rendering "society [to] function more effectively" (Taft). Rather than exploring humanity's "dark side," implying the existence of a "light side," I would suggest that our desire to fit in with ourselves, and to use that experience to integrate with the world around us, has a personal as well as a social significance. We adapt to different environments—the rhythms of office life, the interpersonal exchange of the school or university, the daily business of running a home. Our public selves have to accommodate our inner yearnings; this is something that preoccupies most of Demirkubuz's protagonists as they deal with difficult or uncompromising situations. The task of reconciling private and public selves is complex and might never be resolved. Yet there are different ways of accomplishing that task, as Ahmet, Musa, and Muharrem demonstrate—either by acknowledging their emotions or creating imaginative lives of their own. Such successes might be temporary (there is no guarantee that anyone will feel the same even a week later), but the task of meeting diverse situations remains an ongoing one, both onscreen as well as in the world outside the movie theater.

3

Semih Kaplanoğlu

Reconciling Opposites

The most significant aspect of Semih Kaplanoğlu's directorial career is the extent to which he has been influenced by his previous vocation as a critic on plastic arts and cinema. Between 1996 and 2000 he had a regular column in the now-defunct daily *Radikal*. His preoccupations at that time were discussed in a foreword (published in 1990) to a catalog of paintings by Ayşe Erkmen. In the first paragraph he claims that "reality in life today is veiled, the corners are rounded off and it is alienated from mankind. . . . Modern man has been obliged to make do with the political rituals of indirect relations which narrow the scope of life and render it passive." Many creative workers have been "seduced by the channels of communication," to such an extent that their products are "mere marketable objects of value." The only means of survival is to "investigate truths which are heavily camouflaged and screened by habit, . . . to produce works of complexity, with an approach unique to themselves, . . . to experiment over and over again, with no aspiration to court posterity" ("Tractatus," 9–10). Erkmen's work achieves that task by "linking the created with the innate; the truth with the alternative self-engendered truth behind it; the rational with the irrational; the orthodox with the unorthodox; the exhibition hall with the outside worlds. She does this in the mind, in space, . . . in dimensions and in meanings" (11). The issues raised here have strong resemblances to those concerning other Turkish filmmakers about this time—frustration at the destruction wrought by capitalism, a desire to revive the social function of art, and a need to reacquaint individuals with the spiritual ability to appreciate what life truly represents. Such tasks require a unification of hitherto established binary oppositions to create new spaces for reflection.

By comparison with Zaim or Demirkubuz, Kaplanoğlu's oeuvre might seem somewhat sketchy. Since his first film *Herkes Kendı Evinde* (*Away from Home*) (2001), he has directed only four films—*Meleğin Düşüsü* (*Angel's Fall*) (2005) and the Yusuf trilogy of *Bal*, *Süt*, and *Yumurta* (*Honey, Milk, Egg*) (2007, 2008, 2010). He has subsequently coproduced two films, *Djeca* (*The Children of Sarajevo*) (2012) and *Mâsuk'un Nefesi* (*Breath of the Beloved*) (2014).[1] A new film *Tahıl* (*Grain*), with Kaplanoğlu as director/producer, is awaiting its Turkish release at the time of writing.[2] Other credits include fifty-two episodes as director of the soap opera *Şehnaz Tango* (1994–96). Yet his oeuvre demands our attention due to its stylistic qualities, with long takes and a significant absence of music that forces us to concentrate on the protagonists' relationship to their environment. While Zaim and Demirkubuz offer us snapshots of their characters' lives in urban or rural environments, Kaplanoğlu traces the life of a young man through the Yusuf trilogy, showing how past, present, and future should be approached as a living continuum; one cannot be separated from the others. Superficially this interdependent mode of thinking resembles that proposed by Western ecocritics such as Jennifer A. Machiorlatti: "[We are part of] a balanced relationship of the physical presence in this lifetime with the soul and spirit realms, coexisting with the living and the nonliving, the biotic and abiotic, the organic and the inorganic" (chap. 4). I contend that forging this form of "balanced relationship" is culture specific, requiring an extensive awareness of local mores as well as an acute understanding of the landscape and our position within it. Simply inhabiting a town or a village—even for several years—does not guarantee acquisition of such knowledge. We should listen to ourselves as well as others—all living organisms as well as humanity.[3] Through his films Kaplanoğlu invites us to follow a more mindful path through life, even if we do not relate to the worlds he creates on-screen.[4]

Heart's Wounds:
Meleğin Düşüsü (2005)

The plot of Kaplanoğlu's second film has been shaped by two leitmotifs, one aural, the other visual, both reminding us of the pervasive influence of the past. The first is the regular use of Edvard Grieg's elegiac melody "Heart's Wounds" (*Herzwunden*) on the soundtrack. Composed in 1881, this piece is both introspective and reminiscent, suggesting uncertainty about how to deal with past trauma. The second leitmotif is the regular appearance of a ball of twine, possessing both practical and symbolic value. When the central character Zeynep

(Tülin Özen) goes to pray, she takes a ball of twine to the mosque in case there is anything inside that requires repairing. The male protagonist Selçuk (Budak Akalın) takes advantage of the situation, as he takes some of Zeynep's twine to hold up his trousers in place of a belt. In the film's opening sequence Zeynep keeps tying some twine to gate posts as if trying to enclose a designated area of land; the twine keeps breaking, and she becomes more and more frenzied in her attempts to reattach it to the posts. The sequence evokes the myth of Theseus and the Minotaur, where Ariadne gives Theseus a thread (or a clew) to find his way out of the labyrinth, having put the monster to the sword. That the twine keeps breaking in *Meleğin Düşüsü* suggests Zeynep's inability to escape the labyrinth, whether physical or emotional.

Kaplanoğlu explores Zeynep's plight in subsequent sequences. Employed as a chambermaid in an anonymous-looking hotel, she spends her days changing the sheets, washing the bathrooms, and cleaning all surfaces. No one deigns to speak to her, not even the bellboy (Engin Doğan), who is seen crossing the frame carrying a suitcase while Zeynep labors in the background. The ambience is reminiscent of Zaim's *Filler ve Çimen*: drably decorated corridors with solitary armchairs placed in the corners, peopled by staff who are expected to remain unnoticed in the background. Zeynep's life of drudgery continues at home looking after her wastrel father Müfit (Musa Karagöz). Every night she prepares his evening meal and packs a lunchbox for the following day without a word of thanks: Müfit eats alone before watching television in the living room with only a beer bottle for company. Zeynep's plight is complicated by our knowledge that her father harbors incestuous feelings toward her; this is one of the "heart's wounds" she can never heal.

Kaplanoğlu follows his contemporaries in representing İstanbul as an urban dystopia. Through a series of long takes shot inside a suburban train looking outward, he contemplates forbidding landscapes full of anonymous apartment blocks and half-built offices. In an establishing shot around Eminönü harbor we witness Zeynep walking along through teeming crowds, seldom exchanging a word with anyone except for the occasional tradesperson—and then the conversation is confined to topics such as where people are going for their vacation. As in *Tabutta Rövaşata* Zeynep is imprisoned within continuous medium shots, the Bosphorus extending far behind her, suggesting some form of disconnection to the elements. She is seen walking the streets in a long tracking shot, passing some iron gates and subsequently taking the seafront road. As she hurries to her destination, an empty oil drum gently floats by, indicating how little respect humanity possesses for their world. Kaplanoğlu's representation is complicated by an establishing shot focusing on the Süleymaniye (1558) at dawn. A familiar site for most tourists, it sums up the city's reputation as an ancient site for people of different religious faiths. In *Meleğin Düşüsü* this shot fulfills a very different function: the Süleymaniye is seen from Zeynep's point of view as she opens the window, prior to leaving for work. The camera tracks right and downward to focus on a couple locked in a passionate embrace, followed by two shots intercutting Zeynep standing by the window with the risqué sight of the couple becoming more amorous as the female fondles the male's genitals. Evidently sexual gratification counts for more than religion.[5] Feride Çiçekoğlu's short story "Kimini Şahin Tırmalar" ("Some Get Clawed by Falcons") (1990) vividly sums up the landscape Kaplanoğlu creates:

> All foam and garbage. Fish caught in the garbage; on the pier . . . popular songs blasted at full volume, lahmacun with lots of onion, pickle juice, boiled corn, plastic slippers, cheap shirts.
>
> And then, crowds crushing one another, . . . serves them right, those who lag behind! . . . [Everyone] has no expectations from the future; [they] simply don't want to be bothered. (47–48)

In this world of unrelentingly limited prospects, Zeynep searches for a way out. She acquires a suitcase of clothing that once belonged to Selçuk's widow Funda (Yeşim Ceren Bozoğlu) and looks forward with relish to trying on some new outfits in the hope of assuming a new identity. Things are not that simple; as she opens the case, Grieg's "Heart's Wounds" melody can be heard once again on the soundtrack, reminding us of Funda's violent death in a car crash. Such knowledge affects Zeynep's behavior: Kaplanoğlu cuts to a shot of her seated on her apartment floor, rummaging through the clothes, followed by a point-of-view shot of her looking at sepia photographs of her past. After a short sleep she puts on Funda's jersey and undergarments and sits down to watch television. Müfit enters; she gets up from the sofa with a jolt and runs to her bedroom to put on her own clothes once more. With head bowed, she starts to prepare the dinner, hoping that her father will react to the sight of her in borrowed weeds. Drunkenly he gets up from the table and gives her a smack for her unseemly behavior.

This sequence can be deconstructed in several ways. We are reminded of the "heart's wounds" inflicted on Zeynep by Müfit, yet at the same time understand how an understanding of similar wounds inflicted by Funda's death makes Zeynep feel uncomfortable in the borrowed clothes. On a more ontological level we appreciate the impossibility of exchanging one identity for another; we should make the best of what we possess by recognizing the indivisibility of past and present, as Kaplanoğlu has suggested: "Time is not to be avoided, but something to come to terms with. . . . We live in an infinite present, which started at the moment of Creation" ("Cinema Militans"). The director acknowledges his debt to the twelfth century mystic Muhyiddin Ibn'Arabi, also known as Muhyiddin, the Reviver of Religion. One of Arabi's poems, "Listen, O Dearly Beloved," included in the *Kitab al'Tajalliyat* (*The Book of Theophanes*), sums up the relationship between time, humanity, and the Creation:

> I am the reality of the world, the center of the circumference,
> I am the parts and the whole,
> I am the will established between Heaven and Earth,
> I have created perception in you only to be the object of my perception
>
> ("Listen")

Superficially this might seem a touch narcissistic, where the speaker assumes powers not customarily associated with humankind. Yet this interpretation overlooks the presence of the Creator (as well as Mother Anatolia) in all things, helping us to appreciate the indivisibility between Heaven and Earth. Categories such as past or present, the self and the other, are mortal creations, designed to obfuscate rather than encourage our perception of universal truths. The contemporary novelist İskender Pala quotes the fifteenth-century Oghuz Turkish poet, writer, and thinker Fûzulî: "The universe is connected through and through with a single strand of your hair" (57).[6] Zeynep becomes dimly aware of this knowledge as she looks at the sepia photographs, understanding as she does so how they inspire her to continue in spite of the social restrictions placed on her.

Meleğin Düşüsü contains a climactic sequence beginning with Zeynep walking toward the camera, a quizzical look on her face as if searching for something or someone. The screen fades to black; after a few moments we witness her dragging her father's corpse into the living room and wiping his blood off the walls. Her face remains expressionless throughout as she calls Selçuk; the two of them place the old man in a rubbish bag and pitch it into the Bosphorus. In a lengthy take we see them looking on silently as the corpse bobbles on the surface for a few moments, then sinks to the bottom. Ethically speaking we should not condone Zeynep's action; despite his cruelty, Müfit does not deserve to be dispatched in cold blood. Kaplanoğlu complicates our reaction through a plot twist. Zeynep and Selçuk spend the night in a hotel room; as dawn breaks, she looks out of the window at the Kız Kulesi (the Tower of Leander) in the distance and strips off. She opens the balcony doors and steps outside, showing her naked body off to everyone outside. The shot of the tower suggests that Zeynep aligns herself with the Hero and Leander myth, wherein she is transformed from a chambermaid into a star-crossed lover. Her nudity denotes the desire for rebirth as she throws off the accoutrements of her previous existence and embraces the world anew. As she savors the morning air, apparently oblivious to everyone around her, the "Heart's Wounds" melody can be heard once again on the soundtrack.

What are we to make of the ending? We might deem it "morally ambiguous," but this judgment depends on our recognizing the distinction between right and wrong. In Kaplanoğlu's cinematic universe this does not exist, as he tries to reveal the beauty at the heart of the human soul that transcends the quotidian world "where truth is buried and everyone seems to be trying to make it even shallower [and where] . . . it becomes quite ordinary to kill someone or kill something — not just living creatures — but also ignoring the 'other' by dismissing thoughts, beliefs, and the rights of others" ("Cinema Militans"). Zeynep administers to Müfit a substantial dose of his own medicine — killing him is no different from the way he tried to kill her through mental and physical abuse. Once the deed has been done she can search for her inner truth.

Whether Zeynep's action can be justified is another matter. Ibn'Arabi's poem "Wild Is She, None Can Make Her Friend" creates a portrait of "one of the daughters of Rome" who "kills with her glances" and "has baffled everyone who is learned in our religion." The only way to resist her is to marshal "the armies of . . . [one's] patience, host after host" ("Wild Is She"). The act of killing transforms Zeynep into a "wild woman" who should be resisted rather than embraced; according to Ibn'Arabi's logic she has forgotten how reality exists as one in all humankind, male or female, young or old. To believe otherwise destroys the cosmic unity on the level of both Creation and Ghosts. Superficially *Meleğin Düşüsü* might end happily, but as the title suggests, Zeynep is doomed to end her days as a fallen angel.

Childish Dreams:
Bal (2010)

In terms of release dates, *Bal* is the last of the Yusuf trilogy; but as its subject matter deals with the protagonist's (Bora Altaş's) childhood, I have chosen to analyze it first. Once again Kaplanoğlu is fascinated by sound as a means of commenting on human life; in the opening sequence set in a Black Sea forest we hear birds singing in the trees; the scrape of human feet against tree bark; and the buzzing of bees. Cumulatively this soundscape suggests the harmony of nature that survives despite all attempts to disrupt it. It is our responsibility to accommodate ourselves to this order, not the other way around. Kaplanoğlu explicates this point through a lengthy shot of a verdant landscape with mountains in the background: Yusuf and his father Yakup (Erdal Beşikçioğlu) are walking home, but they resemble specks on the horizon, dwarfed by their environment. Thematically speaking we are on similar territory to that created by Derviş Zaim's most recent works *Devir* and *Balık*, in which human survival depends on awareness of the rhythms of the landscape. If these rhythms are disrupted, then the entire universe falls out of joint. Yakup discovers to his cost that the bees in the forest no longer manufacture sufficient honey to ensure his family's upkeep, driving him to take increasing risks by climbing trees in the forest.

As in *Meleğin Düşüsü*, *Bal* explores the effect of "heart's wounds" on an individual. Both Yakup and Yusuf are prone to epileptic fits that strike at unexpected moments. Yusuf suffers a further wound — an inability to express his feelings openly. When his mother Zehra (Tülin Özen) addresses him, he seldom answers; hence she asks the local imam to come and remove whatever spell has been placed on her little boy. The true explanation for Yusuf's disability proves more mundane; he suffers from a stammer that becomes worse during times of stress. Yet *Bal* suggests that spoken words represent a superficial means of uniting people; there are plenty of alternatives. Yakup and Yusuf mostly communicate in whispers; occasionally they are happy in total silence, as demonstrated in one sequence where they share an apple together. They find refuge from the world in Yakup's workshop — while the father sharpens his tools the son looks on in awe. Even when Yakup falls to his death out of a tree, the bond between himself and Yusuf remains as strong as ever: Yusuf can return to the workshop to experience once more the feelings of security and contentment. *Bal* communicates what Kaplanoğlu has described as "those experiences of humanity [that] were more in tune with the nature, spirituality, soul and creation of human beings" ("Cinema Militans").

Kaplanoğlu reinforces this point by ensuring that every sound assumes significance within the *mise-en-scène*: the crunch of Yusuf and Yakup biting into their apples, the hiss of the boy whispering into his father's ear, the rustle of leaves in the trees and the crack of Yusuf's feet on wet ground. The effect is to create an atmosphere of unity between humankind and the environment recalling Yaşar Kemal's words: "It was getting on for midnight. The murmur of the Savrun River filled the earth-scented night air. The Commissioner walked towards the sluice gates and the gleaming pebbles of the river bed crunched under his steps. No sound came from the sleeping town, except the whistle of the night watchman and the untimely crowing of a cock" (85). In this world, communication encompasses all elements, whether living or dead, animate or inanimate. It is part of Yusuf's achievement that he can understand this; he sits inside his house looking out of the window and listening to the rain plashing outside. This type of shot conventionally denotes imprisonment, as the protagonist is prevented from expressing him- or herself in the fresh air (as, for example, in Ang Lee's version of *Sense and Sensibility* (1995), where Elinor Dashwood (Emma Thompson) is confined to the family home to pursue ladylike interests such as sewing and socializing). In *Bal*, Yusuf's presence next to the window offers a positive representation of the boy's capacity for deep, meditative listening to his world. Kaplanoğlu likens his state of being to "*haal*, which is a state of consciousness just as in Sufi music . . . [that] is very local and very authentic but nevertheless has something universal about it" ("Cinema Militans").

By contrast Yusuf's life in school is one of endless torment. Unable to suppress his stammer, he experiences difficulties in reading out loud. Kaplanoğlu sums up his physical and mental confinement through a complicated aerial shot looking down at the class, with a bowl of buttons obscuring our view. Each time a learner accomplishes a task successfully, they are given a button as a reward. As he pins it on their lapels, the rest of the class applauds. Everyone aspires to possess one, as a means of self-affirmation. We gaze at the learners through the bowl, with Yusuf's eyes gazing winsomely through it, and understand how a meritocratic approach to education favors the strong.[7] Although the educator gives him a consolatory button despite his difficulties, we can empathize with Yusuf's look of disappointment.

The shortcomings of the Turkish education system have been explored in documentaries such as *İki Dil Bir Bavul* (*On the Way to School*) (2008), wherein an idealistic young educator finds it impossible to relate to his Kurdish-speaking learners in the east of the Republic of Turkey. Many educators (and learners) elsewhere experience similar problems in a one-size-fits-all education system, where learning by rote is favored above a person-centered approach. This kind of learning works to inhibit rather than enhance notions of psychosocial development that inform the structure of the Yusuf trilogy (Morsünbül 182). Yusuf has coped as best he can; at one point he willfully swaps his homework (written in a water-damaged exercise book) with that of his friend Hamdi, so as to avoid being scolded by his educator.

Scarred by these experiences and looking to nature for assistance, it's hardly surprising that Yusuf should end up as alienated from his surroundings as Zeynep in *Meleğin Düşüsü*. His plight is summed up in a sequence where he and Zehra visit a local market with music and dancing offered as entertainment. The camera pans the makeshift stalls offering fruit, vegetables, and homemade preserves: capitalism permeates even the most remote communities. In the background the car parks are filled with a variety of vehicles old and new. After the market has closed, everyone joins hands in a traditional dance, a time-honored celebration of family values. Several women encourage Yusuf to join in, but he goes missing, much to Zehra's alarm. Although the two are soon reunited, we understand the boy's mental isolation. He experiences similar emotions when left alone with his grandmother while Zehra goes to look for Yakup. Sitting cross-legged in a circle with her friends, the grandmother listens to a folktale about the angels before engaging in a collective act of worship. Left to his own devices outside, Yusuf sees the reflection of the moon in a pool of water, shimmering like a silver coin. He puts his hand into the pool, naïvely believing that he can somehow possess the image; after a second he removes his hand, the ripples subside and the moon reappears. The boy understands his limitations as a human being; he cannot assume control over the elements. Rather he should try to integrate with them in some way. Nâzım Hikmet's poem "Denize Hakkında" ("About the Sea") (1954) suggests how this process might be accomplished:

> [In the sea] *life bubbles up and dies down like the fawn*
> *on this unbounded, endless motion*
> . . . .
> Whether in moonlight or broad daylight,
> whether it's frothing or flat as a sheet
> to stand on the shore and watch it
> . . . .
> I must be at the center of its eye—
> with fishermen, say, of the nets
> . . . .
> I must be in the eye of it.

(164–65, italics in text)

Yusuf follows Hikmet's example; at the end he runs away from the camera into the forest. The button he received at school no longer matters to him; he wants to reunite with his father's spirit, which lives on through the elements. Thunder rolls as the little boy crosses the frame, looking for the spot where Yakup passed away. Darkness falls as Yusuf, having accomplished his quest, sits by a tree as the rain pours down. The leaves rustle; a bird can be heard singing in the distance as we listen to his regular breathing on the soundtrack while the screen fades to black.

Our experience of this sequence proves particularly satisfying, as it reveals how anyone's "heart's wounds" can be healed without causing harm to others. While Yusuf's reunion with Yakup might be brief, he can nonetheless experience the intense pleasure of engagement with the elements. Such moments only occur sporadically, but should be savored for their effect on the mind as well as the body. They cannot be articulated verbally, nor should they be. In their unification of inner and outer worlds they are quite literally inexpressible.

A Failed Poet:
Süt (2008)

One of the most memorable moments in *Bal* occurs when Yusuf sits at the breakfast table and Zehra places a glass of milk in front of him. Although reluctant to drink it, he looks up and drains it, clearly aware of how much it means to her.[8] In a dysfunctional family shorn of a father, it is important for the two of them to stay together, even if only a flimsy bond exists between them.

Milk unites mother and son once more in *Süt*, but in a more practical way. They have now moved to Tire in the west of the country—a largely flat rural area flanked by mountains. Yusuf (Melih Selçuk) helps Zehra (Başak Köklükaya) with the daily chores of milking their small herd of cattle and selling the product on the streets or going from door to door in local apartment blocks in the hope of attracting a regular clientele. Life is difficult: Zehra labors long and hard in the kitchen making cheese with only the television for company. Despite their determination to continue their way of life, it is evident that the rural values they uphold will be swept away by the inexorable progress of capitalism. Kaplanoğlu reminds us of this movement through long shots depicting the landscape being dug up in preparation for the construction of new apartments. Yusuf's friend Erol (Orçun Köksal) has found stable employment on a building site, preferring the security of a regular income to the more precarious life of a writer. Yusuf, on the other hand, continues his hand-to-mouth existence by driving around on an antiquated motorcycle that moves quite literally in fits and starts. On one occasion the cycle stalls and Yusuf is thrown onto the dusty ground, where he experiences another epileptic fit. With no one to assist him, he makes the best of a dire situation as he picks himself up and slowly wheels the antiquated machine homeward. As he moves slowly away from the camera we reflect on the hopelessness of his future, particularly when the apartments have been finished and new constructed, thereby reducing the traveling time between Tire and İzmir, the nearest big city.

Most of the villagers have an equally bleak future. Although the new apartments promise a better world for everyone, with improved accommodation and more efficient transport links, they condemn human beings to lives of perpetual isolation. When Yusuf returns to Tire from İzmir (having failed a medical for compulsory national service), he walks slowly through an ill-lit street flanked by half-finished apartments. In the background the screech of trains can be heard, mingled with the sounds of villagers wishing their friends and relatives good luck as they depart for the army barracks.[9] Yusuf's walk takes him past a basketball court where a teenager plays alone; the two exchange brief glances but do not speak. Yusuf grasps the handlebars of his motorcycle and walks on. Whereas the Black Sea community in *Bal* make a point of coming together for annual celebrations, the villagers of Tire studiously avoid one another. Writing in the *Guardian* in 2014, the journalist David Lepeska summed up the experiences of many people trying to adjust to a world newly dominated by capitalist values: "[They] feel overwhelmed and shunted aside by the ongoing makeover, which they view as focusing on profit for the privileged while ignoring the majority. . . . Turkey is undertaking gentrification by fiat and force — a top-down, lightning-fast version of a process that in mature cities [and towns] happens more organically" (Lepeska).

The adolescent Yusuf has learned to cope with this changing world through writing poetry; we witness him hunched over an old-fashioned typewriter placed by the window in his mother's house. The visual echoes of *Bal* are obvious: if the child Yusuf listened to the rain in the hope of recovering his father's spirit, the adolescent searches for inspiration from the elements. İskender Pala sums up the poetic mindset thus: "[They] must free [themselves] of reason and must bring [their] heart to the fore. If the mind holds sway over the person, the road to exaltation through love is closed" (137). Ideally Yusuf would like to emulate someone like Nazım Hikmet, who valued the natural world (likened to "a pot of honey") so highly that he was willing to go to any lengths to protect it "from pests of every species. . . . As long As I've got / honey in my pot, / bees will come to it" ("Benim Şiir," 3). Yusuf can certainly taste the honey pot and write poetry; the only snag is that no one wants to read it. Zehra chides him for spending so much time thinking, thereby consuming the family's limited finances. He shows his work to his educator Ali Hoca (Rıza Akın), but the now-retired pedagogue shows little response. In an extended two-shot inside a bar where the two of them meet, we watch a window cleaner working on the opposite side of the road while Yusuf mentions the poems in an offhand manner. Ali studiously ignores him and continues with a crossword puzzle. A disembodied arm appears at the top of the frame and places two beers on the table between them. Silence ensues: all we hear is the relentless quacking of a soccer commentary on television in the background. The action moves forward a few hours; by now Ali is very drunk, and Yusuf has the unenviable task of putting him to bed, covering him with a blanket just like he did to Zehra earlier on in the film.

Kaplanoğlu once again castigates the educational profession for their indifference toward learners young and old. Ali is just as culpable as the educator in the classroom forcing the child Yusuf to read despite his crippling stammer. Both embody capitalist values, which liken schools to factories producing generation after generation of supposedly educated learners while minimizing the personal element as much as possible. As a would-be poet, Yusuf is not a "useful" member of society and hence deserves to be ignored. Zehra thinks much the same: when a letter arrives for her son, she automatically assumes that it has been penned by one of his girlfriends. When the contents reveal that his poems have been accepted for publication by a small magazine, her face visibly falls. Literary fame is no substitute for potential marital stability.

Nonetheless, Kaplanoğlu emphasizes the importance of cultivating the poetic imagination, especially by those who truly believe in it. Yusuf's poem has been published in the magazine alongside a translation from the French poet Arthur Rimbaud (1854–91), who believed that poets were capable of understanding universal truths through "a long, prodigious, and rational disordering of all the senses." This could only be achieved through "faith and superhuman strength," helping poets to discover the unknown "more than any other man!" (Rimbaud). While Yusuf has not ventured so far along the poetic path, we understand his desires. Writing might be a painful process, but the process can help him toward a renewed understanding of himself and his relationship to the external world. He dispenses with his motorcycle and stands stock-still, listening to the birds singing and the rustle of leaves falling while watching the sunrise. A magpie flies across the frame, cawing furiously. Yusuf walks toward the camera, seemingly in complete harmony with nature, a state of grace achievable by anyone, as the poet Saït Faik suggests:

> Some days at dusk I would sit
> And write stories
> Like mad!
> . . . .
> I would jump into the sea
> And hear how I rend the water.
> I would see
> How my fall splashes water over the bridge.
>
> ("Geri Zaman," 190)

Visually speaking, the sight of Yusuf appreciating the sounds of nature recalls the ending of *Bal* when the child Yusuf walks toward the tree in the pouring rain. He has discovered how to unify inner and outer selves once more.

Sadly, the necessities of having to make a living assume more importance; the film ends with a sequence shot at dusk with miners finishing their shift, including Yusuf. Wearing a protective helmet with a powerful beam of light cast in front of him, he walks toward the camera once more. We are dazzled — so much so that we find it difficult to focus on Yusuf's face. In the background the rattle of the elevator taking more miners down to the coal face can be heard. The camera pans the dimly lit town before returning to a close-up of Yusuf smoking reflectively. His eyes droop slightly as he moves out of shot and the screen fades to black. This sequence serves as a powerful reminder of a world in flux; for all his poetic aspirations, Yusuf still embodies a world in decline. Imaginative identification with the environment cannot compensate for the decline of rural ways. While we sympathize with Yusuf's plight, the sheer emotionlessness of the sequence (comprised of two lengthy close-ups punctuated by a brief pan) indicates that the process of change is irreversible. Yusuf has no choice but to accept the practicalities of a world significantly different from the one he grew up in.

The Prodigal Returns:
Yumurta (2007)

Perhaps the relationship between past and present is not as straightforward as *Süt* would have us believe. *Yumurta* begins with a long shot of a wintry landscape with birds singing and dogs barking on the soundtrack. A middle-aged woman (Semra Kaplanoğlu) stumbles toward the camera, moves out of the right-hand side of the frame and walks on; the camera turns and pursues her. The sight of cypress trees, symbolizing the relationship between life and death can be discerned through the mist (Büker and Akbulut 21). We subsequently learn that it is Zehra making one of her final forays out of Tire before her premature death. This sequence reminds us of the importance of the elements, even in a changing world — despite the inexorable march of progress, we are swallowed up by the earth at the end.

At present, however, the mature Yusuf (Nejat İşler) does not appreciate this indisputable fact. Confined to an untidy secondhand bookshop, he smokes meditatively while dealing with a female customer (Tülin Özen). Leaning back in an armchair, he watches her without seeming in the least interested in her requests. We learn that he has chosen this vocation in İstanbul as a means of keeping body and soul together. He had his first poetry collection published several years previously, attracting good reviews; but now he has become one of that legion of forgotten writers haunting the restaurants, bars, and antique shops of the Beyoğlu district. The fact that he manages a secondhand book-shop should not be overlooked; having spent time and energy trying to cultivate an individual voice, he spends his time purveying other writers' voices in printed form. His creative endeavors, it seems, have been extinguished forever.

    Yumurta explores the issues—both psychological as well as social—consequent on the act of homecoming. A popular topic in Turkish cinema past and present, it provides the inspiration for Çağan Irmak's hit melodrama *Babam ve Oğlum* (*My Father and My Son*) (2005), to be discussed at greater length in the next chapter. Asuman Suner explains the attraction of this plot: "The enclosed world of the provincial town is comparable to the protective and embracing aspects of the childhood house. In this sense, Turkish nostalgia films are accounts of imagining the past as a period of collective childhood—that is, a period of the childhood of society as a whole" (*New Turkish*, 27). Kaplanoğlu adopts a skeptical stance toward the theme by showing Yusuf's return for his mother's funeral as a regretful rather than a nostalgic occasion, reminding him of what he could have done with his life if circumstances had worked more in his favor. Everyone who knew him as an adolescent goes out of their way to be friendly (emphasizing the strength of community values), but Yusuf rejects all their advances. He sits one day in a barber's chair having his mustache shaved off; the camera focuses on his reflection as he looks at himself in a mirror before leaving without a word. Kaplanoğlu cuts to a shot of him sitting alone at home, having eaten dinner served by Ayla (Saadet Aksoy), a family friend. As he chews each morsel, the sound of Ayla washing up can be heard. Yusuf rises, dons his sandals, and switches on the light, a direct reference to a similar moment in *Bal* when the child Yusuf annoys Zehra by switching the light on and off. Our response to the sequence in *Yumurta* is complex: while appreciating Yusuf's isolation as he returns to a world from which he feels per-petually excluded, the sight of an electric light being switched on and off reminds us of how the past inexorably shapes our present and future. We might be differ-ent from our past selves, but such differences might be ultimately insignificant. Oğuz Atay's short story "Unutulan" ("The Forgotten") (1975) likens this process of recovering the past to "digging for the details"—searching the recesses of the imagination for reminiscences uninfluenced by prejudice, public opinion, or am-nesia (123). Kaplanoğlu suggests that this process of recollection might not neces-sarily be restricted to the imagination: external forces can provide much-needed impetus as well. Yusuf learns that his father's memory has been canonized

through a plant—perhaps Zehra will receive similar recognition. Taken in isolation this might not seem especially significant, but the sight of the plant reminds
us once again of humanity's intimate connection to nature. Maybe we do not
need to rack our brains to excavate the past; it is already there.

The film has been interpreted by Hülya Önal as one of the first contemporary Turkish films to countenance "the possibility of a Sufi language that shows
that life and objects are in fact the realm of the imaginary and brings into view
the truth, i.e. what cannot be seen, through the main character Yusuf, attention
to the name itself, and the well scene appearing as a dream—referring to the
revival of Joseph who is thrown in a well" (214). I would not necessarily agree,
but in terms of action Yusuf begins the film at the bottom of a psychological
well but manages to emerge from it through a series of psychological confronta-
tions. One of these centers around the decision of whether to carry out Zehra's
dying wish to have a sheep sacrificed in the village of Birgi in İzmir province or
follow his instincts. The sacrifice goes ahead one cloudy afternoon, set against
the backdrop of a lake and the mountains in the background. All the towns-
women have gathered to mark the occasion: the sheep is brought in while Ayla
glances at Yusuf's apparently expressionless face. The sacrificial act takes place
off-screen—all we see is the flow of warm blood trickling on the ground followed
by a shot of Yusuf having his forehead marked by a sliver of blood. Kaplanoğlu
cuts back to a shot of the trees before ending with shots of everyone cleaning
themselves and preparing cuts of lamb for cooking. To outsiders, as well as
those more acquainted with urban rituals, the sacrifice might seem barbaric;
but as the Australian writer Lisa Morrow suggests, they are "intensely pious"
occasions designed for everyone, irrespective of social origin, who believes that
"their prayers will be answered." The ritual "hark[s] back to much simpler
times," when communities were more unified than they might be today (338–
39). The element of chance has been removed: "The ritual . . . seeks to extract
from the original violence some technique of cathartic appeasement" (Büker
and Akbulut 32). In *Yumurta* the element of catharsis is combined with nostalgia
(the blood on Yusuf's forehead recalls similar rituals taking place during childhood); Kaplanoğlu uses it to reiterate the link between humanity and nature.
Zehra might no longer be physically present but her spirit lives on in everyone
attending the ceremony that celebrates rather than mourns her passing.

Dimly Yusuf becomes aware of the truths he understood instinctively as a
child, which hitherto have been concealed beneath layers of disillusion. The
process of discovery is not easy; he talks to Ayla inside his car as the camera looks
through the windshield at the outside world, a shot emphasizing imprisonment,

psychological and physical. A similar type of shot recurs throughout Zeki Demirkubuz's oeuvre. Yusuf's mental recovery commences after attending a community wedding, where he witnesses the townspeople dancing and smiling without a care in the world. Although consciously separated from the celebrants, it is evident from his expression that he experiences a childlike pleasure in the ritual, an emotion aptly described by Saït Faik:

> Where golden evenings and blond children climb over
> Where birds chirp and all sorts of fruit is eaten,
> A country without boundaries or fences,
> Without fairies or jinns,
> Without chicken coops or houses,
> That is to say, without numbers.
>
> ("The Friend," 183)

The event impinges itself on Yusuf's consciousness, just like an unfortunate occurrence later on when a wild dog attacks him and refuses to let him go. The sun rises; the cock crows; the sheep bleat with bells round their necks to attract the shepherd's attention; and Yusuf wakes up with a start to find that the dog has moved off. This is a significant moment of self-discovery; despite the discomfort of the previous few hours, Yusuf understands his connection to nature. Selling secondhand books constituted a half-life compared with the pleasure of waking up at dawn on a deserted landscape. He walks away from the camera in a shot visually reminiscent of the opening sequence when Zehra ventured out of the town. Mother and son have been emotionally reunited for the first time since *Süt* concluded.

Returning home, Yusuf shares his breakfast with Ayla; she hands him an egg from the nesting box and he cradles it in his hands, recognizing it as a life form in embryo; "the symbol of the world, it unfolds life and the world" (Büker and Akbulut 25). Once it meant nothing to him; now it is something precious. Turning toward Ayla he continues to eat and drink silently as the screen fades to black. This moment underlines the importance of togetherness; that unspoken bond of friendship helping hitherto isolated individuals to cope with their situations. Moneymaking in İstanbul no longer has any significance compared with life's deeper realities. This might seem both idealistic and nostalgic, especially in rural cultures threatened by the onset of capitalist development (as represented in *Süt*), but Kaplanoğlu encourages us to savor the moment, that place where past, present, and future unite, rather than reflect on future consequences.

Communities Recovered:
Djeca (2012)

This transnational production directed by the Bosnian Aida Begić has Kaplanoğlu as one of a quartet of producers. Examining the daily struggles of Rahima (Manja Dikic) and her fourteen-year-old brother Nedim (İsmir Gagula) in post-civil war Sarajevo, the film creates a dystopia of dingy apartments, anonymous-looking concrete blocks, and mean streets peopled with shady characters. No one, it seems, has the power to stem society's gradual slide into economic chaos. Rahima works long hours in the kitchen of a local drinking club run by dictatorial owner Melic (Velibor Topic), who asks her to put in extra hours at very short notice. The fact that such decisions impact her family life is conveniently overlooked: Rahima can be readily replaced should she disagree. Begić's camera denotes the oppressiveness of this environment through a series of long takes wherein we witness every change in Rahima's expression as she struggles to survive.

The narrative unfolds in leisurely fashion — characteristic of most films where Kaplanoğlu has been involved — analyzing the protagonists in relation to their environment rather than concerning itself with plot. The camera moves slowly from room to room in Rahima's squalid apartment in a series of point-of-view shots; we share her frustration at her inability to keep the place clean and tidy. Meals are hurried affairs, eaten in the living room in front of the television — even before he has finished, Nedim gets up and resumes his computer games, leaving his mother to finish eating alone. Neither mother nor son can communicate with one another; they prefer to retreat into fantasy worlds with themselves at the center. Nedim stands in front of the mirror and rehearses the famous sequence from Martin Scorsese's *Taxi Driver* (1976) where Travis Bickle (Robert de Niro) holds a gun in front of him and hisses: "You talkin' to me? You talkin' to me?" This tough-guy image represents an attractive alternative to Nedim's lowly real-life status as a school student caught within a complicated web of money-making intrigues not of his own making.

Djeca returns to the subject of humanity's relationship to nature through Rahima's conversion to İslam, a decision that prompts certain members of her Christian family to accuse her of disloyalty. Even in the post-civil war era, religious differences matter. At a gathering marking the passing of a close relative, Rahima justifies her decision: was it political or simply a whim borne out of a desire to challenge parental authority? The answer is neither: Rahima made a purely personal choice that does not require any explanation. In an overwhelmingly patriarchal society where women — especially those in paid employment —

are regarded as fair game for exploitation, Rahima uses her religion to forge a personal connection between herself and the deity that no mortal can destroy. In times of stress, she feels she has someone to turn to for spiritual guidance.

Despite the film's overwhelmingly somber subject matter, we can still view its beginning and end in an optimistic vein. In the opening scene we witness groups of youngsters playing in Sarajevo's battle-scarred streets with the strains of Beethoven's Pastoral Symphony playing on the soundtrack. The same melody returns at the end when Rahima and Nedim are reconciled to one another, despite the threat of imminent arrest hanging over them. The edenic world of community, whether experienced through children of different faiths happily enjoying themselves or brother and sister deciding to face the world as one, has a powerful part to play in ensuring the survival of any society. Like Yusuf in *Yumurta*, we understand the importance of this dictum, irrespective of our racial, gender, or ethnic backgrounds.

The Music of the Spheres:
Mâsuk'un Nefesi (2014)

Written and directed by Murat Pay but produced by Kaplanoğlu, this film contains several intertexts that resonate for anyone interested in Kaplanoğlu's oeuvre. A straightforward tale about the power of education—so long as it is conducted in earnest, with a concern for learners' welfare—*Mâsuk'un Nefesi* focuses on Abdurrahman (Abdurrahman Düzcan), a learner at the İstanbul Conservatory who becomes fascinated by the *meşk* (traditional training in the recitation of the *mawlid*, the Nativity of the Prophet Muhammad). Initially he tries to find out more information from books alone, but he discovers the need for advice from a Hoca (Mustafa Başkan). After numerous fruitless attempts to organize a meeting (the Hoca keeps telling him to come back next week), they eventually meet in a local mosque. The two immediately forge a profitable working relationship; Abdurrahman becomes increasingly proficient through listening as well as practicing on every possible occasion—at home, on the train, on the ferry boat, at university, and in the local park. The film celebrates the strength of the oral tradition, handed down from generation to generation and involving people of all ages and socioeconomic backgrounds. Through the *meşk* Abdurrahman learns how to communicate with nature as well as the deity.

The film includes several shots of bookshelves in Abdurrahman's poky apartment and the secondhand bookshops he frequents in search of further information about the *meşk*, reminding us of the opening of *Yumurta* when

Yusuf worked in a bookshop to little or no purpose. The bookshelves serve a similar thematic purpose in *Mâsuk'un Nefesi*, as Abdurrahman searches vainly through several volumes in search of inspiration. Knowledge—especially that contained in the spiritual world—can best be obtained through interpersonal communication, so long as the participants remain open to one another's views. Another recurrent metaphor characteristic of Kaplanoğlu's work to appear in *Mâsuk'un Nefesi* is the electric light; despite repeated attempts to fix a light in his apartment, Abdurrahman cannot do so. It is left to one of his close acquaintances to fiddle with the fuse and thereby cast light on the bookshelves. Although lights help us to find our way around, they are artificial—unlike the divine light of the deity. Abdurrahman comes to understand this notion as he recites the *mawlid* both inside and outside the mosque.

As in the early scenes of *Yumurta*, *Mâsuk'un Nefesi* concentrates attention on the winding streets of Beyoğlu, full of apartment blocks with wrought iron gates reminiscent of prisons. The area might be fascinating for tourists, but it can also be incredibly confining. On at least two occasions Abdurrahman walks by the Bosphorus, the water stretching out behind him as far as the eye can see. Such shots emphasize the importance of self-development; the more attention he pays to the *mawlid*, the closer he feels to the elements surrounding him. Sitting on a ferry boat, he looks toward the land on the European side of İstanbul and glances downward toward the water. We feel that he has somehow possessed the Bosphorus and learned to appreciate its mysteries.

Abdurrahman's knowledge also gives him a renewed appreciation of the relationship between past, present, and future. He and the Hoca are continually photographed in exterior tracking shots as they walk toward the mosque. We do not always see them in full view; sometimes the gravestones and mausoleums get in the way. Such sequences emphasize how the living and the dead are spiritually connected through music and oral traditions. The Hoca received his knowledge from his ancestors and passes it on to Abdurrahman; in the future Abdurrahman will undertake a similar task to those younger than him.

Not much actually happens in the film: our attention centers on the *mawlid* and its effect on those attending the mosque as well as on Abdurrahman's developing spiritual awareness.[10] Kaplanoğlu has drawn attention to the role that sound plays in unifying image and soul ("Cinema Militans"); *Mâsuk'un Nefesi* achieves this effect by means of a static camera depicting human beings engaging in their daily acts of prayer or practicing the *meşk*. We listen to them rather than being distracted by the visuals—although we might not understand what it being said, we appreciate the effect the words have on individuals. The film sums up

Kaplanoğlu's interest in İslam—as Suner suggests, he is not preoccupied with an "İslamic message" (whatever that might be) but rather with examining the religion as experienced in everyday life by ordinary Turks; a sphere of spirituality and of a profound meaning of the faith ("Horror"). Kaplanoğlu himself has described the evolution of his state of mind during the new millennium as he grew increasingly uneasy with the established rational, secular, and materialist worldview he had grown up with: "The process of radical Westernization and secularization in Turkey had created a shallow intellectual environment alienated from its own cultural roots. It was during this time that Kaplanoğlu came to define himself as a faithful Muslim and chose to lead a life in accordance with İslamic rules. From then on, he embraced [the] Muslim faith to find a deeper meaning in life and cinema" (qtd. in Suner, "Aesthetics," 48).

A Journey in Microcosm

The experience of watching a Kaplanoğlu-directed or produced film can prove disconcerting in its emphasis on character and situation. Responding to a journalistic question posed in 2010 that accused him of being "affected and boring," the director replied: "There is nothing wrong with a little boredom. As a whole I am concerned with finding a rhythm between direction, camera, sound, etc. I strive to achieve a sense of harmony between all the elements that make up a film. This is in direct opposition to the speed of cinema, which is in fact dictated by the speed of modern-day life. By contrast, what is important to me is to find my own rhythm and my own pace" (Farzanefar).[11] In keeping with his views expressed during his time as an art critic, Kaplanoğlu strives for new aesthetic syntheses that transcend binaries—self versus other, individuals versus societies, spiritual versus corporeal, and so on. He asks us to respond to his work viscerally, not with the purpose of decoding its meaning (for example, by explaining symbols or visual metaphors) but, rather, treating it as a holistic experience prompting reflection on our relationship to the world.

Repeated viewings of the Yusuf trilogy have proved exceptionally therapeutic, as I have come to understand the presence of alternative modes of recognizing one's feelings and triggers and responding to them. Listening to the sounds of nature—rain on the windows or falling in droplets through the trees— can increase our understanding of the vastness of the universe. An appreciation of the strength of community values as communicated through rituals can encourage us to treat ourselves with caring and compassion and forge healing strategies when we feel distressed. This is how the adult Yusuf deals with the trauma of returning to his hometown in *Yumurta*; likewise Rahima and Nedim at the end of *Djeca*. Kaplanoğlu makes us aware that "[we] . . . are not alone. . . . [We] deserve to be happy, to have fun, and to feel" (Sutton 273).

On a personal level, Kaplanoğlu reminds us of humankind's capacity to appreciate entirely novel versions of our world—an *anima mundi* acknowledging the power of Mother Anatolia that enables us to reconfigure space in ways we have not previously entertained. Such worlds are not fantastic but grounded in the daily lives of communities in the Black Sea, the Aegean region, or the urban jungle of Sarajevo. All of us have the potential to develop our senses to a level that we have hitherto scarcely imagined and, thereby, to understand what one of neurologist Oliver Sacks's patients felt when she recorded her impressions of the world in epistolary form: "My new vision continues to surprise and delight me. . . . The snow was falling lazily around me in large, wet flakes. I could see the space between each flake, and all the flakes together produced a beautiful three-dimensional dance. . . . I felt myself within the snowfall, among the snowflakes. . . . I was overcome with a deep sense of joy" (142–43). Such feelings are paramount in the final moments of *Bal* when the child Yusuf sits alone under the tree in communication with his father's spirit. As an adult in *Yumurta* he only recovers this capacity for feeling once he has confronted the past rather than run away from it by returning to İstanbul. In a blog post titled "Movies That Make You Think," the writer suggests that the film is part of an analysis of male identities: stereotypically, Yusuf should become a breadwinner by returning from İstanbul and looking after his family. This might be true in material terms, but Kaplanoğlu is more concerned with the spiritual life—the capacity of all of us to transcend our often tedious personal existences and discover something more permanent beyond ("Movies").

The director's visions of joy transcend cultural and religious difference—non-Turkish, non-Muslim viewers such as myself can enjoy similarly transformative experiences, so long as we approach the world on its own terms as a place shared by all humankind.[12] In this kind of situation, time, space, and nationality are rendered unimportant; rather, we should lay ourselves open to new possibilities. The act of viewing and writing about Kaplanoğlu's oeuvre constitutes a microcosm of the psychological journey covered in this book—an opportunity to confront complex feelings produced by cultural and spiritual adjustment.

4

Çağan Irmak
Yeşilçam Revisited

Starting in 2000 I worked for a decade as a reviewer for *Theatreworld Internet Magazine*. I covered all productions at the Churchill Theatre, Bromley, and the Ashcroft Theatre, Croydon, both in south London; but my principal attention focused on the Turkish theater. I became a regular attendee at the Ankara Devlet Tiyatrosu (Ankara State Theater), interspersed with occasional forays to İstanbul as well as to local private (i.e., unsubsidized) outfits. As with all repertories, there were some good productions, others not so good; but I discovered very early on that the general acting style was very different from what I had experienced in the United Kingdom. Actors wore their emotions on their sleeves, declaiming their lines in ringing tones accompanied by the kind of expansive gestures reminiscent in the Western tradition of Victorian melodrama. During my doctoral thesis I remember watching several black-and-white movies starring the legendary British barnstormer Tod Slaughter, whose career spanned four decades from the twenties to the fifties. Several Turkish productions were staged in similar fashion: *Richard III* directed by Semih Sergen portrayed Gloucester as a ruthless villain hobbling across the thrust stage, taking the audience into his confidence through asides so as to drum up support for his schemes. The production was highly entertaining, but to my Western-educated eyes it seemed old-fashioned, paying little or no heed to the Stanislavskian approach to acting that continued to dominate the theatrical agenda in many countries. I collected my reviews and published them in Turkish and English under the title *Türk Sahnelerimden İzenimler/Impressions from the Turkish Stage*. Reading through them once more I discover that my most frequent complaint was that the actors tended to shout too much, thereby transforming plays of different historical periods and traditions into one-note productions.[1]

In my enthusiasm to highlight the allegedly low standards of the Turkish theater, I seldom considered why the Ankara State Theater embraced this approach. Was it a distinct house style, similar to the Royal Shakespeare Company's scholarly treatment of the Bard during the Peter Hall and John Barton era, or were there more culturally specific inspirations?[2] The answers to such questions eluded me until I encountered the work of the filmmaker Çağan Irmak, whose *Babam ve Oğlum* (2005) was a smash hit. As described by one blogger: "High on emotions, [it] makes you laugh and cry at the same time with equal zest . . . and makes one realize that eventually time is passing and people have to go to never come back. . . . Some critics have said that the movie is a bit too loud. But this could be a silo that one might get trapped in — [the] majority of Western viewers. Life too can be loud sometimes" ("*Babam ve Oğlum*"). The film's plot is unashamedly sentimental, as prodigal son Sadık (Fikret Kuşkan) returns to his hometown in the west of Turkey from İstanbul and patches up a long-standing quarrel with his father Hüseyin (Çetin Tekindor). As the story unfolds, we learn that Sadık has only weeks to live and that his son Deniz (Ege Tanman) will spend the rest of his life with his grandfather. Irmak explores the relationship between Sadık and Hüseyin as a way of foregrounding the importance of family values. With a florid musical score by Evanthia Reboutsika, the film tugs at viewers' heart strings in a way that might seem excessive to Westerners but certainly proved attractive to local filmgoers.

In a bold attempt to recreate the spirit of Yeşilçam movies of the fifties and sixties, Irmak consciously embraces the conventions of melodramatic modality and *özenti* (defined by historian Savaş Arslan as "a dialectical movement in which it is impossible to return to an originary self already lost in the process of modernization and westernization" [133]). *Babam ve Oğlum* offers an alternative to Kemalism (based on modernization, progress, and Westernization) by creating an alternative world comprising transhistorical elements — community, family, and tradition that might not physically exist but that assume significance in the collective imagination (Arslan 98). Whereas Westernization can be identified with rationality, Yeşilçam foregrounds sentimentality in which progress has been superseded by nostalgia for a more stable and less turbulent past.

Irmak's conception of filmmaking is very different from the directors so far discussed in this volume. His imaginative universe depends on binary oppositions; the sentimental world has to be set against the physical world — for example, the anarchy wrought by the 1980 military intervention forming a backdrop to *Babam ve Oğlum*. Although anything is possible in the realm of the imagination, its potential is limited: once the film has ended, we return to our quotidian ways of life. This worldview appears not only to reject the presence of an all-encompassing deity but also posits a conservative construction of humanity resembling that expressed by Puck at the end of Shakespeare's *A Midsummer Night's Dream*, wherein existing socioeconomic conditions should be resumed after a brief period of respite:

> If we shadows have offended,
> Think but this, and all is mended,
> That you have but slumbered here
> While these visions did appear
> . . . .
> Gentles, do not reprehend;
> If you pardon, we will mend.
>
> ("Epilogue," 1–8)

Change might be possible but should be gradual, paying attention to dominant sensibilities. For the Ankara State Theater—just like Çağan Irmak—this desire is expressed through a deliberately florid acting style that poses a temporary challenge to existing behavioral conventions. The directors emphasize the presence of alternative emotional constructions that defy the limits of (Western-inspired) reason; given the right circumstances, people can develop their imaginative potential; it is this vision of possibility, however limited, that renders the Ankara State Theatre so popular with playgoers of all socioeconomic backgrounds. Irmak has enjoyed similar success; unlike Zaim, Demirkubuz, or Kaplanoğlu, he has become a mainstream director alternating between big-budget cinema productions and regular forays into television, as a writer and producer as well as a director.

In trying to assess the impact of his work over the last two decades, we should bear in mind that Irmak's use of binaries is strongly reminiscent of Western directors working within the melodramatic genre—for example, Douglas Sirk. Mary Ann Doane suggests that Sirk explored its "radically democratic form" and its capacity to achieve "plenitude of meaning" by illuminating contradictions "controlled and contained through their narrativization" (71, 82). Inspired by Doane's analysis, I have divided the following discussion into three sections—sentimentality, the Gothic, and performance—in the belief that this is the best means of discovering how and why his oeuvre has been so financially and emotionally appealing to mass audiences.

Sentimentality:
Babam ve Oğlum (2006), Dedemin İnsanları (2011),
Prensesin Uykusu (2010), Unutursam Fısılda (2014),
Nadide Hayat (2015)

Irmak's treatment of sentimental themes recalls that of nineteenth-century novelists such as Dickens. Recognizing the social diversity of his audiences, he negotiates between their expectations, desires, and fantasies by presenting idealized images of the family (and, by implication, the nation). This strategy allows him to propose alternatives to dominant cultural values while ensuring that they are seldom fully explored; they often remain at the level of wish fulfillment (Wadsworth). In *Babam ve Oğlum* Hüseyin and Sadık are reconciled in a climactic sequence on the family farm; in a series of shot/reverse shots we learn why Sadık left home in the first place and his reason for returning. Irmak zooms in on Sadık's face as he finishes his soliloquy and tilts through 180 degrees so that the actors are photographed sideways. With violin music swelling in the background the camera shows Sadık bursting into tears and running out of the frame, leaving Hüseyin standing alone, unable to speak. The music diminishes, ending with one violin playing an insistent chord as the screen fades to black. By tilting the camera Irmak suggests that the family's entire world has been thrown out of joint by news of Sadık's terminal illness. Hence it is high time for father and son to reconcile their petty quarrel and bond together once more. This moment happens soon afterward in the local state hospital as Hüseyin takes Sadık's hand and admits: "It is important that sons remember their dads just the way they want." The notion of unity is reinforced by a shot of Sadık embracing Deniz. Nostalgia plays a significant part in bringing everyone together — as Sadık and brother Salim (Yetkin Dikinciler) sit together, they gaze at fading photographs of Sadık's late wife Aygun (Tuba Büyüküstün) and reminisce about happier times. Throughout this sequence strings can be heard on the soundtrack to emphasize its emotionality. Families should stay together; they might not be able to change the world, but they can draw strength from one another.

Achieving this kind of calmness might only be a pipe dream for most people, but it is worth contemplating. Irmak underlines the point by inviting us to recall a moment earlier on in the film when Sadık recalls the night of the military takeover (12 September 1980) when Aygun was due to give birth and Sadık could not find anyone to take her to hospital. Nor could he summon a doctor: she died in labor. For all his political determination to fight for his country's future he remains morally and emotionally isolated. Although we might share the family's happiness during their final reconciliation, we are simultaneously aware of the basic conservatism of Irmak's screenplay. The poet Gülten Akın once claimed that art should be an act of opposition, stimulated by a desire "to change life at a social or individual level," and should permit communication between people of different socioeconomic backgrounds, thereby forming "a universal — not national conscience, because, in my view, ordinary languages do not seem to be able to achieve this" (27-28). While *Babam ve Oğlum* stresses the importance of interpersonal communication, it suggests the impossibility of political change: the personal should take precedence over the political.[3]

We are given further insight into the film's lack of politics through Deniz's childhood reveries, as he imagines his father as a heroic Ottoman soldier evading kidnap by invading forces, or as a Kemalesque figure fighting for his nation's future during the War of Independence (1919-23).[4] The boy's fantasies contrast starkly with the realities of Sadık's existence as he is tortured in jail for his left-wing views. Times have certainly changed over half a century: whereas every Turk once fought on the same side, by 1980 it became impossible to separate friend from foe. Many so-called dissidents were imprisoned without trial by the military government. Yet Irmak shies away from exploring these issues and instead creates another sentimental fantasy in which Deniz carries a movie camera to record his life for posterity and points it at the ghost of his dead father. The two embrace as Sadık reassures the boy that such reconciliations can happen at any time if Deniz wills it. As a trumpet plays mournfully on the soundtrack, Sadık sounds a note of caution — as the boy gets older, he will require less paternal support. Deniz looks through the camera lens once more and sees Sadık and Aygun for the last time as he turns and runs into Hüseyin's arms while the screen slowly fades to black. This sequence once again emphasizes the importance of family over politics as a means of protecting Deniz from future harm.

Babam ve Oğlum is dedicated to Ö. Lütfi Akad (1916-2011), a legendary figure of the Yeşilçam era whose directorial career lasted from 1948 until 1974. The reference intensifies the film's aura of nostalgia; the desire to recreate the world of Turkish cinema's so-called Golden Age wherein order invariably evolves out of chaos.[5] This strategy depends for its effectiveness on an understanding of binary oppositions: the personal takes precedence over the political, while the past seems more attractive than the present. Nostalgia is an intriguing concept: Pam Cook reminds us that "it can be perceived as a way of coming to terms with the past, as enabling it to be exorcised in order that society, and individuals, can move on. . . . Nostalgia can form part of a transition to progress and modernity" (4). *Babam ve Oğlum* follows an opposite trajectory into the past: nostalgia represents an alternative to modernity, a sentimental throwback to a time of innocence when family loyalties counted for everything.[6]

Dedemin İnsanları (*My Grandfather's People*) (2011) makes a similarly nostalgic foray into the early eighties with Çetin Tekindor reprising his role as the patriarch of an extended family living in the Aegean region. Irmak photographs the action in a series of yellow and gold hues, evoking a world of perpetual sunshine as the family takes its annual vacation in a vineyard. They sit around the dinner table swapping stories and reminiscing; during daytimes they take picnics on the beach. This scenario contains political undertones: the family are Cretans who were forced to move from their homeland as part of the population exchange between the Republic of Turkey and Greece in the mid-twenties.[7] As a boy, Mehmet (Tekindor) experienced the trauma of finding a new home and learning a new language—over half a century later his grandson Ozan (Durukan Çelikkaya) has to endure racist insults from his classmates about not being a "proper" Turk. The boy considers himself a true nationalist, ever ready to salute soldiers in the street and sing the national anthem as a mark of true solidarity. His dreams are shattered by the 1980 takeover, as the army imposes martial law and bans all nonessential travel.

Irmak analyzes the kind of identity politics that characterized Derviş Zaim's *Gölgeler ve Suretler*: how can a family survive in a chaotic universe where former friends are now foes? Mehmet's son İbrahim (Yiğit Özsener) experiences this difficulty at first hand—as deputy mayor of the village where he is forced to submit to the authority of a demagogue (Zafer Alagöz) parachuted in by the military government. One-time friends are transformed into enemies, forcing İbrahim to resign. The only solution, as Mehmet suggests, is to set aside the political and embrace the person by trusting in "our people"—the family. This worldview underpins Gülten Akın's poem "Elegy for the Right Arm of Musa Akbaba from Lower Canbolat" (1983), inspired by an incident taking place three years previously when a farmer chopped off his right arm in response to losing his family business due to government "reform":

> [his] hand committed the crime
> No power is left to me but my own life
> What I let fall was mine, my own arm.
>
> (22)

The act of cutting his right arm cuts him off from his family, here represented as the innocent victims of the speaker's folly in supporting the government in the first place. In *Dedemin İnsanları* Mehmet does not want İbrahim to fall victim to a similar catastrophe; hence his sage advice.

At length Mehmet takes his own life by walking into the sea; as he does so a Greek song plays on the soundtrack as the camera tracks backward and upward so that he ends up as a speck on the horizon. Superficially this sequence recalls similar moments in Zaim's films where a character looks out at the water, as if yearning to reunite with the elements. In a moment reminiscent of *Babam ve Oğlum*, the older Ozan (Ushan Çakir) recalls how Mehmet's suicide helped him to grow up by reminding him of who "his" people were. No longer a boy pretending to be a "true" Turk, he decides to visit his father's homeland and thereby discovers traces of the family past in the form of dog-eared sepia photographs taken half a century ago. Once again Irmak creates a sentimental ending set against a background of strife. By walking into the sea Mehmet believes that he will create a better world for Ozan to inhabit. The film ends with a close-up of a beer bottle with a message in it bobbing up and down—a metaphorical reminder of how dreams can come true, so long as we believe in them.

By comparing this ending with that of Zaim's *Gölgeler ve Suretler* we can understand just how differently Irmak handles similar situations. Zaim has the child Ruhşar (Hazar Ergüçlü) reunited with father Salih (Settar Tanrıöğen) while performing a Karagöz in public. The fact that such an ancient popular art form entertains people, even during a period of political upheaval, emphasizes the notion of timelessness. Humanity can discover peace of mind if they detach themselves from worldly affairs and embrace spiritual peace. Irmak offers no moral or spiritual uplift but rather invokes binaries to enhance the audience's sense of well-being: fantasies are infinitely more pleasurable than unsavory realities. Gönül Dönmez-Colin's formulation, while not specifically applied to Irmak, seems especially apt: "*Fantasy films* and their subgroups . . . romantic fairy tales . . . create a world where the normal laws of physics and biology are suspended. If successful, they may offer a new form of reality and even serve as a social commentary" (129).

Both visually and thematically *Prensesin Uykusu* (*The Sleeping Princess*) (2010) strongly recalls Zeki Demirkubuz's oeuvre. Aziz (Çağlar Çorumlu) inhabits a gray concrete apartment block in Beyoğlu whose residents seldom speak to one another. Each day he commutes to his job at a university library where he tends plants in front of a filthy window with iron bars across it, stressing the prisonlike aspects of his existence. In a plot development recalling *Üçüncü Sayfa*, a single mother Seçil (Sevinç Erbulak) and her daughter Gizem (Şevval Başpınar) move into the apartment opposite that of Aziz: tormented by violent spouse Ersin (Baran Ayhan), Seçil tries her best to pursue a normal life as a hair stylist. Aziz befriends them both but finds conversation more difficult than he anticipates. Much of his leisure time is spent with his friend Neşet (Alican Yücesoy) among the down-and-outs living by the Bosphorus sipping tea (or something stronger) and complaining about life's exigencies. The vast expanse of water stretches out behind them, illuminated by the lights of the bridges connecting İstanbul's European and Asian sides.

The seamier aspects of Aziz's existence form a backdrop to the creation of a fantasy world. Gizem is rushed to hospital in a coma after hitting her head on the apartment floor; from then on Aziz maintains an almost constant vigil by her bedside, imagining her as the sleeping princess of the movie's title, lying on an elaborate four-poster bed with himself as the faithful servant. The film includes several animated as well as live-action fantasies wherein Gizem is transformed into a fairy with wings sprinkling dust on Aziz; Aziz protecting the little girl against the ravages of a nocturnal storm; or Aziz as a medium communicating with the dead. The inspiration for most of these imaginings springs from Gizem's journal, a potpourri of colorful drawings and prose where she imagines herself in a settled family environment with parents actively caring for her. In a climactic dream Aziz conceives himself as an ideal parent sitting under a tree next to Gizem, reading the journal and looking out at a calm blue sea.

Irmak's conception of childhood as mediated through Aziz's imagination is strongly reminiscent of Western Romanticism in the late eighteenth and early nineteenth centuries, which conceived of young people as the inheritors of a unique world uncorrupted by the ravages of capitalism, where

> The rainbow comes and goes,
> And lovely is the rose;
> The moon doth with delight
> Look round her when the heavens are bare,
> Waters on a starry night
> Are beautiful and fair;
> The sunshine is a glorious birth
> (Wordsworth, "Intimations," lines 10-16)

Aziz constructs this fantasy as a means of compensating for the emotional wounds inflicted upon him as a child; we learn how he was forcibly taken from his parental home and placed in an institution where his fellow inmates laughed at him and he wet the bed because of anxiety.

Prensesin Uykusu is less interested in contemporary İstanbul and more with the importance of the imagination as a means of compensating for life's vicissitudes. Aziz is a Walter Mittyesque figure using the sleeping princess story as a defense mechanism, an auxiliary construction centered on wish fulfillment, "carefully cherished by the subject and usually concealed with a great deal of sensitivity" (Freud 88). Yet such fantasies are not always private: as the action unfolds, Aziz and Neşet encounter Kahraman (Genco Erkal), a retired actor in Yeşilçam cinema who evidently worked with stars such as Belgin Doruk but now lives alone in a dingy apartment surrounded by memorabilia.[8] Like Mehmet in *Dedemin İnsanları*, Kahraman longs for death as a merciful release from torment, so that he can be reunited with his one-time colleagues from the cinema. The only way he can sustain himself is to share his recollections of Yeşilçam with anyone who is prepared to listen—as he lies on a hospital bed close to Gizem's private ward, he reminisces about the potential of the past to sustain him in the present. He does not need external stimulants (drugs, for instance); his imagination does the work for him.

Aziz experiences similar revelations as Gizem awakens from her coma. Using a handheld camera, Irmak intercuts close-ups of Aziz and Seçil's expressions with shots of a poster behind Gizem's bed of the Turkish band Redd, who had previously performed especially for the little girl's benefit.[9] The action shifts into another fantasy sequence involving a ghost (Işıl Yücesoy) and a kaleidoscope of fantastic creatures—fish, crabs, seahorses. Meanwhile the three mortal characters—Aziz, Seçil, and Gizem—link hands in a final gesture of reconciliation. We have traveled a long way from Western Romanticism in this sequence. It is not only children who enjoy privileged access to an innocent world of beauty and delight; adults can enjoy similar experiences if they believe in them sufficiently. They should have faith, not only in themselves and their imaginative potential, but in the possibilities of their dreams coming true. *Prensesin Uykusu* makes this point in numerous ways, both verbally as well as visually. The climactic sequences are usually shot in bright light, emphasizing the colors of the characters' costumes and facial expressions. The plot's basic implausibility is cleverly concealed through fast cutting and a repeated use of shot/reverse shot sequences concentrating on facial reactions, enhanced by a florid soundtrack (by Redd). Such cinematic techniques are the antithesis of those employed by Zaim, Demirkubuz, or Kaplanoğlu, all of whom favor long takes that force us to concentrate on every aspect of the *mise-en-scène* as well as the plot.

Unutursam Fısılda (*Whisper if I Forget*) follows *Prensesin Uykusu* by featuring a protagonist who was once a major figure in local popular cultures. While Kahraman was a film director, Ayperi (real name Hatice) (Hümeyra) pursued a career as a singer, first with husband Tarık (Mehmet Günsür) and subsequently on her own.[10] The plot bears strong links to *Babam ve Oğlum* in its focus on familial conflict: Hatice and sister Hanife (Işıl Yücesoy) have seldom spoken to one another as Hatice had stolen songs written by Hanife and recorded them under her own name as performer and lyricist. The action oscillates between past and present, concentrating on the sisters' school days, Hatice's meteoric rise to stardom, and her eventual reconciliation with her sister in retirement.

Irmak concentrates once more on fantasy worlds, but this time they tend to be destructive rather than life enhancing. Tarık regularly describes Hatice as his "fairy girl," placing her on an emotional pedestal as someone blessed with a wonderful voice and magnetic stage personality reminiscent of Judy Garland in George Cukor's *A Star is Born* (1954). Hatice takes the stage moniker Ayperi and savors the hedonistic life of a seventies star—a world of long hair, garish color, and limitless parties. Irmak includes several sequences of fictitious magazine covers showing Ayperi in fashionable outfits or new hairstyles being interviewed by everyone. She subsequently established herself as a Yeşilçam star, despite having to stand on a box during shooting to make herself taller. Surrounded by legions of adoring fans, she extracts full publicity value out of her charitable works, while taking care to ensure that there are plenty of photographers around to record her for posterity and thereby satisfy the rapacious instincts of her manager Kemal (Gürkan Uygun).

Ayperi's public persona is contrasted with Hanife's more mundane existence back home in the Aegean region. Dismissing her sister as a feckless publicity seeker, Hanife looks after her ailing father, who could never reconcile himself to Hatice/Ayperi's decision to elope with Tarık to İstanbul. Despite the demands placed on her, Hanife understands the importance of remaining true to her instincts—she has no cause to reinvent herself to satisfy an ever-hungry media.

Once again Irmak avoids exploring the protagonists' contrasting personalities in any great depth in favor of surface sentimentality. The older Hatice contracts Alzheimer's, forcing her to return to the family home: one night she goes missing and is found wandering in the street. The story somehow reaches the media's attention ("Seventies Star Found in Street") and a concert is arranged in Hatice's honor where she makes her final stage appearance. Hanife reveals that she has always loved her sister and opens the door to a locked closet filled with memorabilia from Hatice/Ayperi's past—pictures, magazines, cuttings, vinyl. She has been a fan who almost "died of love," pure, unadulterated devotion for her sister ("When Pop"). As Hatice totters onstage, Irmak dissolves to a group shot of the two sisters in their youth (as portrayed by Farah Zeynep Abdullah and Gözde Çığacı) with Tarık in the middle, followed by a further dissolve to the older Hatice tearfully exclaiming to a packed house: "I'll remember this moment! Life! Thank you so much!" Before she begins her first song, she summons Hanife onstage to face the public for the first time, whispering in her sister's ear as she does so to sing the lyrics if Hatice should forget them.

This sequence foregrounds the positive aspects of musical nostalgia as a means of healing familial conflicts and thereby enabling two aging women to face up to life.[11] The future might not be as exciting as the past for Hatice; but she can sustain herself with memories of the pleasure she gave to so many people (including Hanife). Now she understands how much she depended on her fans' support: life isn't just about sustaining a public image but encompasses more important realities. *Unutursam Fısılda* ends by emphasizing the importance of mutual love within the familial environment.

Nadide Hayat (*The Life of Nadide*) (2015) comes to a similarly sentimental conclusion in its treatment of an *Educating Rita*-style story of the eponymous hero (Demet Akbağ) who returns to university after a thirty-year hiatus to complete her degree. The task proves more difficult than she anticipates, as she is shunned by everyone, but she ultimately triumphs by revealing a hitherto untapped talent for deep-sea diving. Irmak's preoccupation with the seventies, so prominent in *Unutursam Fısılda*, resurfaces in a beach party sequence where the guests—Nadide included—dance and get drunk to the sound of Turkish hits from that period. The ending shows everyone reconciled to one another: Nadide opens a beachside restaurant with a ship's captain (Yetkin Dikinçiler) while her family dine happily there. Meanwhile two of Nadide's female fellow learners embark on a happy same-sex relationship. Nostalgia is conceived as a humanizing force rather than a bittersweet yearning for a past to which we can never return, as Alan R. Hirsch would have us believe (390).[12] Such yearnings can be satisfied so long as we learn to reconcile ourselves with our loved ones and embrace the world with renewed optimism. The innocent world associated with Yeşilçam cinema (in which good and evil are easily distinguishable) can be recovered if we desire it sufficiently, not only for ourselves but for others as well.

The Gothic:
Bana Şans Dile (2001), *Mustafa Herşey Hakkında* (2004), *Hayal-i-Cihan* (2006), *Kaçan Fırsatlar Limited* (2006), *Karanlıktakiler* (2009)

Melodrama and the Gothic have been synonymous in the popular imagination ever since the early nineteenth century when novellas like Mary Shelley's

Frankenstein (1818) caused considerable controversy with their blend of the supernatural and the horrific. Andrew Graham-Dixon argues that the Gothic not only explores hitherto untapped reaches of the human psyche but offers new possibilities for identity construction: what does it mean to be "male" or "female," or even "human," and should such categories be rethought? (*The Art of Gothic*). Second- and third-wave Western feminists seized on Gothic melo-dramas, especially those released during the classical era of the Hollywood studios, as examples of texts wherein "women play central roles, and it is their desires which are therefore seen to drive the narrative onwards. Thus, there is more room than usual for same-sex identification on the part of female members of the audience" (Tasker 89). Douglas Sirk's *Written on the Wind* (1956) enables viewers "to construct meanings beyond the confines of the individual commod-ity text" and thereby to look forward to "the rearticulation of class-difference and . . . new conditions for class-gender struggle" (Partington 63). The film contains a binary structure, with resistance posited as a liberating alternative to the confines of the gendered status quo.

Irmak's first cinema feature *Bana Şans Dile* (*Wish Me Luck*) (2001) offers a Turco-centric interpretation of this opposition set in a contemporary high school. Bahadır (Rıza Kocaoğlu) endures regular bullying—and at length takes revenge by holding up his class and their educator (Melisa Sözen) at gunpoint. The film engages with issues that Semih Kaplanoğlu would subsequently tackle in *Bal*—the repressive aspects of primary and/or secondary education, the re-fusal of educators to acknowledge their learners, and the basic cruelty with which learners treat one another whether inside or outside the classroom. Such criticisms are accompanied with a concentration on excess as Bahadır's class-mates are forced to disclose their inner thoughts to the people standing below their second-floor classroom—armed police officers, media personnel, and other hangers-on. This task is not easy, especially for those suffering from past traumas caused by sexual abuse from parents and/or other adolescents.

Irmak takes care to emphasize the learners' innocence: the parents are the guilty parties. Bahadır's mother (Aysun Metiner) spends most of her time looking for casual pickups rather than looking after her son, while Türker (one of the stars of the class) (Berke Üzrek) suffers regular beatings from his father for failing to meet impossibly high academic standards. Serkan (Mert Akça) is simply ignored at home. The film incorporates graphic sequences depicting the consequences of this neglect: Serkan becomes involved in macabre black magic rituals culminating in one of the participants being stripped naked on a patch of waste ground. Irmak's camerawork, comprised of frequent close-ups inter-spersed with zooms (a technique reminiscent of Yeşilçam) suggests a sadistic tendency to revel in his characters' sufferings. The only ray of optimism in an otherwise bleak environment is the educator's refusal to be intimidated by Bahadır's threats to shoot everyone. She empathizes with his turbulent mental state and takes charge of the situation; as a result the hostage crisis is peacefully resolved, although Bahadır is gunned down in the process. The educator crouches tearfully over his corpse, acknowledging as she does so the needless waste of human life. But perhaps Bahadır has found the emotional release he so desperately craved. In another fantasy sequence Irmak has him running across a deserted beach toward his younger self, the camera tracking him all the while, until he turns toward the sea and wades in as the screen fades to black (adumbrating the ending of *Dedemin İnsanları*).

In terms of gender construction *Bana Şans Dile* suggests that extreme circumstances free the educator from the constraints customarily imposed on her (for example, the belief that as a woman she should always remain subservient to her male principal), thereby prompting her to act on her own initiative. Yet the sentimental ending frustrates our hopes that the educator's assumption of an alternative role might be permanent; if Bahadır can only find salvation in death, then it follows that life (both for the boy and his educator) must be meaningless. Future possibilities are frustrated through another binary opposition.

Mustafa Hakkında Herşey (*All about Mustafa*) (2004) rehearses the plot of the alienated male trapped in İstanbul's urban jungle, subsequently explored in *Prensesin Uykusu*. This film bristles with prison images: iron bars across windows; shots of the eponymous central character (Fikret Kuşkan) driving in his car, photographed from outside; or lengthy tracking shots fixed on his expressions in close-up, as if Irmak were refusing to grant him any time or space away from the camera. The film uses Gothic themes to explore Mustafa's turbulent mind—for example, during the lengthy sequences where he kidnaps, imprisons, and ties taxi driver Fikret (Nejat İşler) to a chair on suspicion that Fikret had an affair with Mustafa's late wife Ceren (Başak Köklükaya). The subsequent action, where the two characters are imprisoned together, contains distinct echoes of Hollywood melodramas such as *The Defiant Ones* (1958): Fikret is threatened with a gun and later knocked out with a plank of wood, his limbs bound up, his face a mass of blood. In the end Mustafa forces the taxi driver to jump into a specially prepared grave, thereby completing the act of revenge for Ceren's extramarital liaison.

Irmak's treatment of Mustafa can be seen as an attempt to use the melodramatic genre as a means of exploring local constructions of masculinity. Sasha Torres wrote in 1993 that "the tension produced by the possibility that femininity will be diffused on to men forces . . . melodrama to reveal something of the ideological and representational states it tries to manage" (286). In mainstream Turkish society gender divisions are customarily perceived as unchallengeable: the man should always be the breadwinner protecting his family. Unable to conform to that social stereotype, Mustafa allows his emotions (associated with femininity in this binary scheme) to cloud his judgment and becomes a psychopath as a result.

Not for the first time, however, the film's social criticism has been blunted by sentimentality: in this case, through Mustafa's enduring attachment to his son Kerem (Arda Seçgün). Having spared Fikret's life, Mustafa returns home and embraces Kerem; the two sit beside a fir tree festooned with New Year decorations. We are asked to believe that he is not a bad person at heart; like Bahadır in *Bana Şans Dile*, he grew up in a dysfunctional family, with a father whose behavior was so violent that Mustafa eventually suffocated him to death by placing a cushion over his face. Evidently the strong man went too far. The psychological fallout inevitably affected Mustafa's adult life. It might seem perverse to associate violence with sentimentality, but as Elizabeth Barnes remarks with particular reference to nineteenth-century American culture, the two elements "work together to produce a more 'sensitive' citizenry. Aggression becomes a site of redemptive possibility because salvation is gained when the powerful protagonist identifies with the person he [*sic*] harms" (viii). Mustafa's abuse of Fikret constitutes a psychological process intended to exorcise the past trauma associated with killing his father. Once Fikret has been released, that process has concluded and Mustafa can be reunited with Kerem and die happily. The film ends with an epigraph ("For my father") suggesting some kind of directorial empathy with Mustafa. *Mustafa Hakkında Herşey* is a good example of a Gothic melodrama dealing with obsession linked to extreme psychological states arising from a highly gendered society.

Irmak's penchant for sentimentality has a lot to do with his experience as a television director. Perhaps uniquely among the subjects of this book, his work on various series (or *diziler*) has shaped his filmmaking style. Beginning with *Günaydın İstanbul Kardeş* (*Good Morning Brother İstanbul*) (1998–2001) and continuing with long-running hits such as *Çemberimde Gül Oya* (*The Rose and the Thorn*) (2004–5), and the reboot of *Çalıkuşu* (2013–14),[13] he has mastered the technique of making drama on limited budgets. The action customarily unfolds through a series of shot/reverse shot sequences linked by pans. Emotional extremes are denoted by zooms into the protagonists' faces accompanied by mood music. The lighting remains uniformly bright throughout, emphasizing a preference for character over situation. To sustain high viewer ratings, the majority of the plots focus on well-worn themes (love, family, and marriage) with situations influenced by Yeşilçam (for example, dominant fathers forcing their daughters into unwanted alliances, or lovers eloping in defiance of their parents' wishes). If they are set in the past, most *diziler* treat history straightforwardly: good characters with a patriotic belief in their country's future struggle against self-interested villains. These conflicts arise from the melodramatic notion of excess, which can be either beneficial (encouraging experiments with new things or forging healthy relationships) or destructive (as characters ignore their social responsibilities and pursue hedonistic desires instead). Barış Kılıçbay and Mutlu Binark argue that the popularity of *diziler* originates in the early nineties when the newly created private television channels established "a unique style combining already existing techniques and themes with narratives addressing the sentimentality of a Turkish audience. The majority of these programs revolve round individual stories of ordinary people" (140).

Two good examples of Irmak's television techniques can be seen in his contributions to *Kabuşlar Evi* (*The House of Nightmares*) (2006), a series of self-contained horror stories produced for Fox Turkey. *Hayal-i-Cihan* (*Cihan's Imaginary Life*) has the eponymous central character (Okan Yalabık) encountering a ghost from the past (Çetin Tekindor): through a combination of zooms and point-of-view shots, Irmak creates an atmosphere of menace as Cihan walks around the apparently endless corridors of the haunted house. We share his apprehensions about what might happen next. What eventually unfolds is a familiar tale of the ghost helping Cihan come to terms with his turbulent past and thereby face a more optimistic future (a plot line reminiscent of *Mustafa Hakkında Herşey*). *Kaçan Fırsatlar Limited* (*Escape Opportunities Limited*)—written by Irmak but directed by Ufuk Bayraktar—has successful executive Taner (Levent Üzümcü) subjecting himself to the authority of a mysterious organization (Kaçan Fırsatlar Limited) that controls his every move. Their leader Fuat (Ali Duşenkalkar), a sinister figure inhabiting a gilded office, takes pleasure in being able to possess other people's souls. Taner ends up mutilating himself for no apparent reason and gouging his eyes out as a self-punishment for not being able to "see" better. Once again Irmak combines violence with sentimentality in an attempt to warn viewers to remain vigilant and avoid the twin temptations of money and influence. The house of nightmares becomes a site of catharsis where Taner discovers the truth about his existence.

Violence also underpins the plot of *Karanlıktakiler* (*In Darkness*), a cinema release from 2009 where we find that Gülseren (Meral Çetinkaya) was raped as a young girl by a Kurd and subsequently brought shame into her family by producing a bastard child Egemen (Erdem Akakçe). The film is overtly misogynistic: Gülseren's sister (Şebnem Dilligil) is a shrew, the receptionist (Pınar Töre) is moody and unattractive, while Egemen's boss, an attractive and successful woman (Derya Alabora), cries at work over a hopeless love affair (140).

These stereotypes provide a framework for another analysis of the crisis of masculinity in urban Turkey. Like Mustafa in *Mustafa Herşey Hakkında* Egemen has become feminized in his behavior; as a gofer in an advertising agency, he carries out his boss's wishes to the letter in the hope of receiving compliments, while at home he remains subservient to his mother's will. This passivity renders him so abnormal (in Turkish terms) that the only acceptable way out is to quit the world altogether. Together with Gülseren he climbs aboard his motorcycle and speeds along a darkened road (recalling İsa and Bahar in Nuri Bilge Ceylan's *İklimler* [*Climates*] [2006]), the camera tracking them all the while as they curse any passersby unfortunate enough to stand in their way. The only way the protagonists can reconcile themselves with a hostile world is to quit it completely: the cycle moves away from the camera toward a precipice and they throw themselves into the sea below. Augustin Zarzosa argues that melodrama does not depict communities in turmoil but focuses attention on people within that community (88). Such techniques are certainly entertaining for filmgoers but are simultaneously distancing: we do not really care much about what happens to Egemen or Gülseren. This sense of detachment has been exacerbated by Irmak's use of binarisms that not only prevent interpretive subtleties (people can be both good *and* evil) but also negate any possibility for the characters' moral and/or spiritual growth. Unlike Kaplanoğlu—who invites reflection on the corporeal as well as the spiritual worlds—Irmak draws on Gothic themes to suggest (somewhat superficially) that we are independent beings determining whether we are happy or not without really considering where that happiness came from, or how it might be sustained in adversity. If we are not happy, then the only way out is to quit the world altogether and thence come to terms with past trauma. Yet it is obvious from the work of Irmak's contemporaries that the process of renegotiating past and future in relation to the present and future is perpetual—as our lives unfold, our perceptions change. Once we become aware of such changes, we acquire the kind of mindful ability to deal with past trauma that Irmak consciously overlooks. His characters can seem rather two-dimensional, lacking the kind of psychological subtleties that might sustain our interest.

Performance:
Ulak (2008), *Tamam Mıyız?* (2013), *Issız Adam* (2008)

In Irmak's defense, however, he has managed to produce at least three films that rework the melodramatic form to make some trenchant points about Turkish society past and present and the individual's place within it. *Ulak* (*The*

Messenger) (2008) is his only film to date set in the Ottoman era. It begins with a lengthy voiceover spoken by Zekeriya (Çetin Tekindor), a storyteller traveling from village to village attracting huge audiences comprised predominantly of children. His speech includes familiar clichés ("Once upon a time") and makes explicit references to Mother Anatolia and "the land itself" that she created. Evidently humanity as a whole is in poor shape ("What changed? What happened to us?"): Zekeriya's story explains why.

There follows a complex narrative describing Zekeriya's fortunes in one particular Anatolian village, while recalling the tale of what happened in the not-so-distant past. Through this strategy Irmak emphasizes the strength of the oral tradition as well as the importance of listening to the divine Word. Although he does nothing except tell stories, Zekeriya represents a threat to the village's stability; like the Pied Piper of Hamelin, he is popularly believed to have placed his childish audience under a spell so that they now ignore their fathers' bidding and, hence, challenge the patriarchal structure of society. The only way to remove that threat is to expel him. Even the *kıraathane* owner Dursun (Şener Kökkaya) has his suspicions. Village society is cruel, where female deviants such as Meryem (Hümeyra)—those who do not fit established gender categories—are kept in chains and spat on, and fathers routinely abuse their sons should their authority be questioned. Young Saffet (Ediz Erdem Uruş) experiences several panic attacks and eventually dies after a vicious blow to the head causes him to fall on a rock.

While it might seem that Irmak rehearses one of his familiar thematic preoccupations with dysfunctional families and their offspring, what differentiates *Ulak* is that there are possible solutions, as set forth in Zekeriya's tales. The curative potential is a long-standing advantage of the oral tradition, as Talât Halman reminds us: "Tales become tantalizing evangelical tools. . . . In a society where the rate of literacy remained below ten per cent until the mid-1920s . . . oral narratives played a major role in cultural transmission. . . . In them we find both a Realpolitik, with depictions of cynical oppression and the need to make compromises, and an *idealpolitik*, with virtually utopian dreams of justice, equality, and prosperity" ("Introduction," xii–xv). Ostensibly an apocryphal tale of divine transformation and redemption, Zekeriya's narrative uses autobiography to teach a moral lesson. He had a crippled son Mehmet (Yüksel Aksu) who could do little or nothing for himself until he learned to read and write. While books provided the boy with inspiration, they simultaneously rendered him an object of jealousy; the other villagers envied the fact that Mehmet knew more than they did and choked him to death in the belief that he posed a threat to the established social order. Whereas Zekeriya might have been devastated by his loss, books saved him. With their help he created the tale wherein those tyrants who murdered his son were exposed to God's wrath, while the community they inhabited was racked with plague. This is not a tale of revenge, but a salutary lesson designed to remind us of Mother Anatolia's perpetual presence and her dedication to maintaining the order of the universe. Zekeriya observes at one point: "Don't forget! Don't forget!" The *realpolitik* of oppression has been swept away and *idealpolitik* firmly restored.

A similar fate awaits those villagers who try to expel Zekeriya from their midst, proving beyond question that dreams can come true for those who believe in them sufficiently. The film's two narratives are fused into one: disease spreads through the village, claiming everyone in its path save for Zekeriya's young listeners, who walk slowly through the darkness toward a blue-gray light representing salvation, holding one another's hands for protection. The image emphasizes the strength of community in the face of evil, especially one that dedicates itself to God. The epigraph eulogizes all those children who "don't forget" and pursue their dreams regardless. Ataol Behramoğlu's poem "There's Something I Have Learned from What I've Lived" offers the requisite advice:

> There is something I have learned from what I've lived through:
> If you're to live, live big, as if you are mingling with the rivers,
>   the sky, the whole universe
> For what we call a life span is a gift to life
> And life is a gift to mankind.
>
>   (93)

It might appear that *Ulak*'s ending is as sentimental in tone as many other of Irmak's films. Yet we should not underestimate the film's uniqueness within the director's oeuvre; as in Zaim's *Cenneti Beklerken* Irmak collapses the distinctions between past, present, and future to make a powerful statement on the link between inspiration, knowledge, and power. True awareness originates not from brute force and ignorance but from an awareness of the divine presence in all things, a notion as true in today's Republic of Turkey as it was in preliterate times. *Ulak* emphasizes the enduring power of the oral tradition, especially when practiced by professional storytellers such as Zekeriya: "When they [the storytellers] describe a mountain, you feel the mountains. When they tell a story about a girl, you suddenly find yourself in love with that girl" (Brunwasser). The film emphasizes the importance of such modes of performance that require considerable acting abilities so as to permit access to divine knowledge and subsequently renew our faith in ourselves and our place in the world.

Tamam Mıyız? (*Are we OK?*) draws on the relationship between two male protagonists—Temmuz, a sculptor (Deniz Çeliloğlu), and İhsan, a limbless teenager (Aras Bulut İnyemli)—to make a powerful statement about prevailing attitudes toward disability.[14] İhsan's father Serhat (Uğur Güneş) considers his son a freak of nature, while his mother Feride (Zuhal Gencer Erkaya) is zealously overprotective. Initially it seems as if Temmuz simply feels sorry for the boy, as he volunteers to read stories out loud on selected afternoons; but their friendship changes abruptly when İhsan asks Temmuz to help him commit suicide. We return once again to the familiar thematic territory explored in *Karanlıktakiler*, where a male misfit looks for escape from social imprisonment. But here Irmak springs a surprise by showing the protagonists' interaction developing in unexpected ways. İhsan firmly believes in the afterlife; by ending his time on earth he will answer Mother Anatolia's calling and reunite himself with the elements. This belief sustains him to such an extent that he exclaims at one point, "Life is wonderful." Initially Temmuz cannot understand this view; but as the two come to know one another better, he likens his young friend to Aries, the god of war—someone who always knew his own mind. This is an important development; for the first time Temmuz abandons worldly thoughts (for example, his lack of professional success as a sculptor) and commits himself to a transhistorical mode of being that unites past with present. His artistic output improves significantly; whereas his works were previously inanimate lumps of clay, their faces staring blankly into space, they now assume a life of their own. Like Zekeriya in *Ulak*, Temmuz discovers his own form of performance technique to move his intended audience. A recent guide to contemporary Turkish sculpture identifies the following intrinsic themes in many artists' works—the malleability of memory and time, the defiance of the human spirit, and a personal exploration of what the mirror sees in the human face ("10 Turkish Contemporary Artists"). Temmuz's sculpture of İhsan encapsulates all these values, while translating the boy's love of the afterlife into tangible form.

From then on it is only a matter of time before the two implement İhsan's wish. Temmuz takes İhsan up a tower outside İstanbul in a sequence visually reminiscent of *King Kong* (1933). Together they survey the cityscape and liken themselves to Sisyphus, the King of Ephyra forced to roll an immense boulder up a hill only to see it roll down once more. Once they might have shared his unfortunate fate; now they have reached the top of this particular emotional hill. No longer constrained by worldly affairs, they can jump into eternity. Irmak's camera encircles the tower with the two men perched triumphantly at its peak. İhsan cries: "I'm the king of the world!" and the two make the ultimate leap as the screen fades to black. As the title suggests, they are truly okay, having made peace with themselves and their world. The film contains several spiritual moments where the protagonists envision alternative modes of existence. Sitting in the family back garden on a glorious summer's day, İhsan projects himself imaginatively into an idealized world where anything can be achieved, including suicide. Later he admits to a desire to recreate that moment in James Cameron's *Titanic* (1997), where Leonardo DiCaprio stands triumphantly on the ship's prow and salutes the entire world. The sequence is of paramount importance to İhsan's psychology; hence his elation in the final sequence as he stands at the top of the tower and reenacts DiCaprio's gestures. The Hollywood dream has now transformed itself into reality.

İhsan's joy brings the shortcomings of his previous life into sharper focus. Serhat is a professional scrounger, perpetually willing to sacrifice his family's integrity for a few extra lira to spend on drink. Perpetually conscious of his emotional inadequacies, he vents his frustration on Feride by beating her. While there is a certain degree of poetic justice in watching him being outwitted by his son, we are made palpably aware of how violence still pervades certain sections of İstanbul society. Hence it is hardly surprising that İhsan should yearn to escape his environment. Yet *Tamam Mıyız?* does not offer death as a pleasurable alternative to life; rather we are asked to look beneath life's surfaces and search for beauty—that indefinable quality that nurtures the spirit and brings us closer to nature and the deity. Temmuz and İhsan discover it through different forms of performance, through sculptures, reenacting *Titanic*, and jumping off the tower.

Issız Adam (*Alone*) (2008) looks at the pitfalls of public performances, especially those undertaken for material or personal gain. Alper (Cemal Hünal) is a successful chef in central İstanbul, running his own restaurant and attracting favorable reviews in the media. Yet his personal life is both morally and spiritually bankrupt, inspired by the need to prove his manliness. Surrounded by seventies memorabilia in his apartment, he appears superficially to be a familiar Irmak character believing in the power of nostalgia to recreate a long-lost world. We soon discover that his love of retro-pop has a more sinister purpose as a means of softening up his female conquests and thereby bedding them more quickly. Clothes-shop owner Ada (Melis Birkan) is one such victim, despite her awareness of his true intentions. This ritual of finding a girl and dancing with her, followed by the sexual coda at home, is as meaningless to Alper as the sessions spent with neighborhood whores where he indulges his passion for S&M.

The film contains sequences that might be viewed as savage pastiches of moments in Irmak's earlier work. If *Ulak* reveals the power of books to inspire the soul, *Issız Adam* shows their fundamental irrelevance in Alper's existence. In one sequence he dashes into Homer Kitabevi close to the Galatasaray Lisesi in Beyoğlu and buys a copy of Thomas Hardy's *Far from the Madding Crowd*; the fact he cannot remember the exact title emphasizes the educational gulf separating him from his intended conquest. He subsequently dashes after Ada, whom he had previously seen trying and failing to purchase the title at a local secondhand bookstore. For him books have no real function except as weapons in his attempts to add to his list of conquests.[15] This materialist outlook is brutally summed up in a telephone conversation with one of his whores that opens the film:

ALPER: You feel this kind of stuff before?
WHORE: Sure.
ALPER: Good. Clean and confidential. My partner wants to wear a basketball cap and slacks. That doesn't bother you, I hope.
WHORE: Okay, no problem. My only condition is I won't go with him. Otherwise, like I said, I am up for anything.

It seems somehow appropriate that he should drive a flashy Mercedes that remains ostentatiously parked outside his restaurant; this represents another manifestation of a surface lifestyle where outward show matters most. Ada embraces a similar worldview through her decision to run a clothes store dedicated to children's costumes. Whenever any bourgeois İstanbullu wants to show off at a birthday party, she can rent a cowboy or a ballerina's outfit. As the youngsters preen themselves in front of a mirror, we cannot help but conceive of them as representatives of a society dedicated to outward show. No one—not least Alper himself—is willing to make the effort to discover emotional or psychological depths within themselves.

While *Issız Adam* is Irmak's most socially critical work, it is not without its melodramatic elements. Alper is portrayed as an out-and-out villain devoid of any redeeming qualities. He dumps Ada with ruthless abruptness claiming that he needs to be alone; the fact that he cannot find a new girlfriend and ends up yearning for her to come back is beside the point. He learns nothing about himself or those around him; he remains a narcissist obsessed with performance. He stares blankly across the Bosphorus in a trancelike state, unable (or unwilling) to reunite himself with the natural elements. True to the film's melodramatic structure, Ada becomes the victim; she visits Alper's childhood home in Tarsus, southeast Turkey, with his mother's (Yıldız Kültür's) blessing and steals a seven-inch single from his collection of fairy tales being read aloud.

This becomes a nostalgic reminder of happier times for her, while reminding us once more of the power of stories to stimulate the imagination.

Nonetheless, Irmak is obviously proud of his film; in an epigraph he dedicates it to his audience, who have been invited to reflect on Alper's and Ada's performances and consider whether there are any more profound, satisfying lifestyle choices. In light of other films in the Irmak canon, as well as through Ada's experiences, the answer is palpably obvious.

Trial and Error

The experience of watching Irmak's films is a salutary one. Although much has been published about the so-called "New Turkish Cinema" of Zaim, Kaplanoğlu, and Nuri Bilge Ceylan, there remains a slew of mainstream films, conceived on bigger budgets and distributed to multiplexes throughout the Republic of Turkey, that to date have received scant critical analysis.[16] Yet they remain enduringly popular at the box office. This is definitely the case with Irmak, ever since the runaway success of *Babam ve Oğlum*. His record should not be underestimated; by keeping his name in the public gaze through film and television work, he attracts the kind of funding that enables him to release one film a year, not to mention additional work in *diziler*.[17] Irmak is a filmmaker much in demand, a reincarnation of the Hollywood studio workers of the past who moved seamlessly from project to project with little respite in between.

Of course Irmak's substantial output might be viewed more cynically as the work not of an auteur but "a director-for-hire that a studio [or financier] can depend upon for a more controlled approach. These filmmakers, often classed as 'journeymen directors,' are regarded as competent, if somewhat unspectacular, movie makers . . . [whose] films may lack style and personality but . . . tell a solid story and make a solid buck while they're at it" (Oden). Turtletaub rather than Quentin Tarantino; Taylor Hackford rather than Steven Spielberg; Irmak rather than Ceylan. I think it would be wrong to place Irmak in this category; with most of his films being self-financed, he has enjoyed perhaps more artistic independence than several of his more well-known contemporaries. His films possess a unique style and personality, but perhaps more elaboration is required.

Superficially Irmak's melodramas have strong thematic links to the cycle of Hollywood products that dominated the studios in the middle of the previous century. The content can be sentimental, Gothic, or nostalgic, evoking past worlds that could be attractive or unpleasant, while prompting us to reflect critically on gender constructions within present-day societies. Yet we must also bear in mind that Irmak's work owes a lot to the distinctly non-Western

Yeşilçam cinema, the majority of whose products appeared at a time when the fledgling Turkish film industry not only established itself as a major art form but acquired a definite identity as well, with its own set of conventions appealing to all socioeconomic groups. Some contemporary writers deplore its legacy: Feyza Hepçilingirler's *Kırmızı Karanfil Ne Renk Solar* (1998)—translated into English seventeen years later as *As the Red Carnation Fades*—has the central character complaining: "In our youth, why did we always let our dreams be shaped by those silly films? We fell in love, not knowing what would happen after the film ended. The films never showed what happened after the happy ending, and we always wondered about that, as if the joy of marriage would go on forever. Why did we deceive ourselves like that? . . . Now that I am in my thirties, haven't I managed to escape from the influence of those phony films?" (229–30). While Yeşilçam's days are long gone, the films' legacy lives on through the television *diziler* as well as in certain forms of live theater (the Ankara State Theater being a prime example), proving that there is still a formidable demand for this type of material. Any Western filmgoer approaching Irmak for the first time has to make an imaginative leap into the past and understand the director's uncanny ability to keep local cinematic traditions alive and fresh for his audiences.

Having said that, I must acknowledge a certain difficulty in evaluating his films. Perhaps I am too steeped in Western film cultures that traditionally view melodrama as a mainstream genre with subversive potential. That distinction does not really apply in the Turkish context: far from being subversive, Yeşilçam offered the pleasures of familiarity with little concern for originality as understood in the Western sense (Ulusay 7). This does not mean that directors did not make significant social or political points in their work; but perhaps it is not valuable to scrutinize their films for "hidden" or "implicit" meanings. Everything remains on the surface. When that surface is so excessive in terms of acting style or content, it can seem so oversentimental that I wince with embarrassment— the legacy, perhaps, of my natural English reserve, sharpened through nine years of public (i.e., private) education in a single-sex school.

On the other hand, Irmak at his best can communicate something of the uninhibited joy people experience while discovering an imaginative world that brings them closer to nature, a world aptly summarized by Hepçilingirler's narrator: "For the discerning eye, there was a pass shaded from luscious to grass green, there were waves on the top right, . . . and in the lower left there were white houses like fields of daisies that contrasted with the waves, and great care should be taken with the shore, as every inlet and promontory must be stitched in like the edging of lace" (266). By savoring such environments to the full, individuals become more mindful, enabling them to appreciate beauty for its own sake and revel in the joys of reading books. There is something hugely uplifting about listening to Çetin Tekindor's Zekeriya in *Ulak*, or sharing İhsan's enjoyment of his exalted state at the end of *Tamam Mıyız?* I feel I have acquired a wider perspective and a broader idea of the role of human beings in the universe so that they can see their own role, a feeling commonly associated with Sufism (Lago 89). Searching for such moments provides the main impetus for watching Irmak's films; while I might be unsuccessful in my emotional quest, the pleasure of participating in an interpretive trial and error is perpetually enticing. Not only do I discover something about myself, but I understand the difficulty of acquiring the kind of inter- or cross-cultural competence that might help me to understand better how and why Irmak's films are so enduringly popular with Turkish audiences, despite many years of residence in the Republic of Turkey.

5

Tolga Örnek

Retelling Stories

In the late nineties I made my first visit to the battlefields of Gallipoli near the town of Çanakkale. Hitherto most of my knowledge of the campaign originated in Peter Weir's 1981 film *Gallipoli* in which the Anzacs, led by a youthful Mel Gibson, had been thrust into a conflict not of their own making and experienced unbelievable hardship. They become resentful of their British commanding officers while simultaneously cultivating a newfound respect for "Johnny Turk." Weir indicates that the campaign played an essential part in formulating a distinct Australian identity existing independently of the demands of Empire that had hitherto played an important part in ordinary people's lives. This theme was taken up in Russell Crowe's take on Turco-Australian relations, *The Water Diviner* (2014). As I strolled through the battlefield I became aware of a feeling I had never previously experienced: the ghosts of the fallen soldiers on both sides seemed strangely alive. I was no longer just a tourist but a historical wanderer beginning to understand that sense of utter despair experienced by everyone involved in a military stalemate costing thousands of casualties. I was not reenacting history (like those fond of reenacting the American Civil War) but rather experiencing a confluence of past and present. Some of my fellow travelers scoured the terrain in search of relics from a conflict that ended eighty years previously; I felt that to do this represented a form of desecration in an area that should be left untouched, a harrowing testament to the sheer futility of war. Perhaps I was overreacting; but my experiences that day played a major part in my subsequent understanding of Turkish history, both ancient and modern.

In 2005 Tolga Örnek's feature-length documentary *Gelibolu* (*Gallipoli*) debuted at Turkish theaters. Its box-office performance was surprisingly good, especially for a factual piece, attracting audiences from all socioeconomic backgrounds who wanted to be reminded of the pre-republican period when Mustafa Kemal was a general in the Ottoman army defending his territory against European invaders. I admired Örnek's determination to retell the story from the soldiers' perspective as they were drawn into a battle that, from the Allied perspective at least, was particularly ineptly managed, with little or no prior research being conducted into the size of the Ottoman army or the harshness of the terrain that they proposed to occupy. Hence it was hardly surprising that they experienced an ignominious defeat. Örnek's documentary is only incidentally preoccupied with military history; instead he examines the hardships of fighting in extreme weather conditions, with soldiers on both sides having barely enough supplies of food and water. Fresh produce was scarce, sometimes nonexistent; infectious diseases ran riot, killing almost as many men as those unfortunate enough to fall on the battlefield.

Structurally speaking *Gelibolu* is an empirical film that marshals its historical evidence—extracts from soldiers' diaries, expert commentaries, and historical recreations—to make trenchant if slightly contradictory points about the wastefulness of a war that nonetheless helped to overcome cultural and religious differences. No one, not least the ordinary soldiers with little or no experience outside their small towns (in Britain, Australia, and the Ottoman Empire), should have had to fight such a pointless and bloody battle. By doing so, however, everyone acquired a form of intercultural awareness that they would never have experienced if they had stayed at home. Such issues of national, local, and familial identities are addressed throughout Örnek's oeuvre. His first film, a documentary on Atatürk (1998) surveyed the leader's career while underlining his importance to the republic's future. Another documentary on Mount Nemrud (2000) showed how Hittite cultures continue to shape contemporary political and diplomatic thought. Örnek's debut fictional work *Devrim Arabaları* (*The Cars of the Revolution*) (2008) told the story of the creation of the first Turkish-made automobile, while making pointed criticisms of the dead hand of bureaucracy that stifles creativity. The thriller *Labirent* (*Labyrinth*) (2011) aims similar barbs while recognizing the efforts of individuals to try and get things done. Örnek's latest film to date, *Senin Hikayen* (*Your Story*) (2013), uses the romantic comedy form to emphasize the importance of the family as the bedrock of a stable society. His films appear to avoid the existential preoccupations characteristic of the other directors hitherto surveyed in this book.

Or perhaps not. Çağan Irmak's *Ulak* has the central character Zekeriya telling his tales to different communities and thereby increasing their sense of historical awareness. It does not matter whether they are true or not; they provide life lessons for listeners by emphasizing past mistakes while offering infinite possibilities for the future. Örnek situates his films squarely within that oral tradition; he tells stories about people from different socioeconomic backgrounds in an attempt to understand where they came from, while mapping out the journeys they might choose to pursue in the future. He avoids classification as a political or didactic filmmaker but considers himself an artistic wanderer exploring the past through the lives of individuals, part of a larger imaginative community encompassing creative workers as well as filmgoers both inside and outside the Republic of Turkey (Raw, "Tolga Örnek," 341–43). Örnek draws on his talents as a writer and director to prompt reflection on the narratives we tell ourselves as well as others. Through the experience of watching we understand how our lives comprise a continual process of narrative making (Bruner 93) as well as construct what Benedict Anderson has memorably termed "imagined communities" (6–7) based around concepts such as nation, family, or community. There is often perpetual tension between our individual sense of identity and community loyalties, emerging from our understanding of the relationship between past, present, and future. It is this tension that preoccupies Örnek throughout his work, despite the apparent diversity of subject matter.

Rethinking National Myths:
Gelibolu (2005), *Atatürk* (1998), *Devrim Arabaları* (2008)

To understand the point of *Gelibolu* we need to know something about the competing mythologies that have emerged since the conflict ended just over a century ago. For Britons it represents a low point in an otherwise distinguished military history. In a largely enthusiastic survey of Winston Churchill's political career, the current British Foreign Secretary Boris Johnson acknowledges that the, then, first lord of the Admiralty made some serious tactical blunders on the basis of impetuous judgment and inadequate information: "We have no alternative but to give the Dardanelles a 'Fiasco Factor' of 10 and a 'Churchill Factor' of 10, since it would certainly not have happened without him. It could have worked, . . . but the mesmerising disaster convinced many people that . . . he was positively unstable in his vanity" (209–10).[1] Those involved in the conflict, such as Compton Mackenzie, insisted that the Allies would have triumphed if they had really wanted to. Most members of the governing coalition were more preoccupied with the Western Front (9–10, 282). The BBC-financed drama *All the King's Men* (1999) tells the story of the Sandringham Company led by Captain Frank Beck (David Jason), which landed on the Gallipoli peninsula and were subsequently enveloped by a mist, never to be seen again. Forty of the original one hundred and fifty soldiers survived and were eventually shot by the Ottomans. The film represents the company as the proverbial lambs to the slaughter, lost in an alien landscape.

Australasian views of the conflict have been significantly shaped by *Gallipoli*, as Weir's long-time cinematographer Russell Boyd (interviewed by John C. Tibbetts) indicates: "Gallipoli, in Australian folklore, represents coming of age to Australia, where a lot of young men went to war thinking it was going to be a great adventure. In fact, a lot of them didn't come home. . . . We were a bunch of farmers before then, but after that we were part of the rigors and fatalities of war" (227–28). On 25 April 2015 tens of thousands of Australasians congregated at Gallipoli for a service marking the centenary of the landings. The then–Prime Minister Tony Abbott remarked that the Anzacs were the "founding heroes of modern Australia. . . . They lived with death and disease because that was where their duty lay. . . . The Anzacs represented Australia at our best" ("Gallipoli 2015").

Turkish filmmakers have represented Gallipoli as a turning point in their national history, as their defense of their territory helped to strengthen the desire for reform. The 1964 Yeşilçam epic *Çanakkale Aslanları* (*The Lions of Çanakkale*) cast stage star Cüneyt Gökçer as Mustafa Kemal triumphantly leading his forces to victory against overwhelming odds. More recently Yeşim Sezgin's *Çanakkale 1915* (2012) celebrated the achievements of the entire nation, as everyone—men, women, and children—played their part in the war effort. Success in battle was based on shared purpose: inspired by Mustafa Kemal, everyone ensured that Anatolia would not be overrun. This representation has been challenged in recent works. Ayşe Çolakoğlu, writing in 2008, describes the Ottoman army's "hopeless nausea" as they fought: "They were dirty beyond recognition and they would go without for days. Fatigue ran in their veins instead of blood." Corpses lay "under the scorching sun, . . . a great pile of bodies" that was so big that it was often difficult to distinguish the living from the dead. One member of the walking wounded finds it "impossible to open his eyes. . . . He could feel his feet and his hands but it was as if he was in a grave with a pile of earth on top. . . . His ears were clogged or maybe the dead didn't hear" (91–92).[2] Leylâ Yıldırım's historical novel *Orada Herkes Ölüyor* (*Unfulfilled Promises*) (2015) looks at how the conflict erases the faith in the deity's power to protect individuals from harm; her protagonist Gül falls in love with an enemy soldier but finds herself both ostracized as well as having to cope with the pain of not knowing where he actually is. The strain involved, in addition to the conflict between personal desire and national and familial dishonor, proves shattering for her.[3]

Örnek takes all three culture-specific representations and sets them side-by-side in a documentary focusing on the ordinary soldiers' experiences of the conflict. We hear the observations of British private Joe Murray and officer Guy Nightingale, Ottoman officer Selâhattin Adil, Bill Ledley from New Zealand, and Australians Oliver Cumberland and Ellis Silas, a British émigré who joined the Australian imperial force as a signaler and recorded his impressions in words and pictures, later published as *Crusading at Anzac: Anno Domini 1915* (1916). *Gelibolu* begins with an epigraph describing how all these soldiers lived "in the shadow of certain death," and throughout the ensuing action Örnek creates a series of memorable images reinforcing this message. They include bullets being fired into the sea; tracking shots set in deserted trenches showing empty kit bags hung carelessly on the walls; or close-ups of disused guns once used to defend the Ottoman positions on the beachheads of Çanakkale. This was a battle that no one really won—although the Ottomans successfully defended their land, they did so at a terrible human cost. Örnek uses close-ups of archival photographs showing the dead lying on the battlefield accompanied by extracts from Joe Murray's diary describing the sheer hell of advancing into a solid wall of enemy fire in the certain knowledge that one was going to die. The Ottoman trooper İsmail Hakkı describes the horrific sight of human flesh flying into the sky, while Silas takes note of the mangled heap of bodies piling up in no-man's land separating the two lines of trenches. Jeremy Irons's sonorous narration (Zafer Ergin's in the Turkish version) emphasizes the sheer futility of the struggle.

Örnek relates the conflict to the passing of time. A shot of a full moon forms the prelude to archival footage of Allied troops landing at Suvla Bay with extracts from Oliver Cumberland's diary on the soundtrack. Later Örnek pans the afternoon sunlight shining on the now-deserted peninsula as we hear about soldiers cut down like cattle as they vainly tried to negotiate the treacherous stretch of water between their landing craft and the mainland. The sun sets slowly in the west as we learn about Mustafa Kemal's herculean feat of defending his lines with only four thousand fit men facing an Allied force comprising three times that number. As the conflict intensified, so the carnage increased: Örnek shows the consequences of the battle at Conk Bayırı Muharebesi (Chunuk Bair) by means of a slow pan of the fields at dawn, the sun rising over a forest that now covers the ground where the two sides once fought.[4] On the soundtrack we hear Ottoman soldier Mehmet Tevfik's desire to give up his earthly existence and sacrifice himself to God. Through such strategies we are made aware of the unchanging nature of the universe—dawn breaks, the sun shines, and darkness falls irrespective of the human struggle unfolding in a small corner of northwest

Turkey. If the generals had been less obsessed with dreams of national (as well as personal) glory and devoted themselves to otherworldly issues, then perhaps the carnage might have been avoided.

Despite the somber mood, *Gelibolu* ends with a tentatively hopeful message, communicated through a sequence when Bill Ledley's recollections are heard on the soundtrack describing the sight of a pair of ladies' white gloves lying on the battlefield adjacent to a pile of corpses. Örnek cuts to a close-up of the gloves as Ledley describes how they remind him of his family back in New Zealand participating in formal dances. Life continues as normal away from the theater of war; perhaps it is time to set aside petty squabbles over territory and learn how to coexist, as one might do at a ball where most of the guests are total strangers. Such moments of peace occurred regularly during the battle; at one point both sides agreed on a temporary ceasefire, giving them the chance to collect their dead comrades' corpses and bury them as decently as they could. During one such period of respite an anonymous soldier (christened "Ernest" by the Anzacs) went across no-man's land to collect tins of bully beef from the Anzacs in an attempt to improve the Ottomans' daily diet. As the conflict dragged on, so the respect between the two sides increased: Örnek includes a shot of an Australian newspaper headline ("Farewell to Johnny Turk") published the day after the Anzac withdrawal began on 15 December 1915. The need for increased cross-cultural understanding, both then and now, is highly significant. While *Gelibolu* pays tribute to Mustafa Kemal's achievement, the action also suggests how leaders on both sides deluded ordinary soldiers into believing that the conflict would be speedily resolved. It is a testament to the strength of their spirit that British, Anzac, and Ottoman forces came to realize that they were all in the same boat, so to speak. Guy Nightingale, who had embarked for Gallipoli with the unshakeable belief in Allied superiority, came away from the war with a firm belief in "live and let live. Turkey for the Turks." İsmail Hakkı vowed not to fire another bullet "without good reason."

Örnek combines several narratives—not only those of eyewitnesses to the conflict, but also comments made by a variety of experts, including Nigel Steel of London's Imperial War Museum, Robin Prior (then of the University of New South Wales but now based at Flinders), the author Les (L. A.) Carlyon (who published a Gallipoli history in 2012), and the New Zealander Christopher Pugsley, who worked in the Department of War Studies at the Royal Military Academy, Sandhurst.[5] Viewers are invited to reflect on these plural narratives (including the commentaries) and make up their own minds about the significance of the conflict. Örnek does not take sides; he expects us to conduct our own processes of narrative making, while bearing in mind the importance of listening to others. In terms of subject matter *Gelibolu* is very different from other films hitherto discussed in this book, but nonetheless invites us to make parallel reflections on the relationship between past and present.

Örnek's boldness in tackling contentious subject matter cannot be underestimated. In his debut feature *Atatürk* (1998), he questioned the master narrative that continues to dominate Turkish cultures, even after nine decades. The presence of Atatürk in pictures, buildings, in the media, and through a proliferation of academic studies can appear disconcerting to the first-time visitor (Akçalı 1–23); and it takes a long time to understand how Kemalist ideology continues to play an important role in formulating political, cultural, and educational policies, however much the lawmakers might disagree with it.[6] Örnek's contribution to this narrative focuses on the ways in which Atatürk transformed his country. Narrated in portentous tones by the British actor Sir Donald Sinden (1923–2014), we learn how the Ottoman Empire was once the "most glorious" and "most feared" power in the region. By the late nineteenth century a succession of corrupt sultans had reduced it to a tin-pot dictatorship memorably described by Tsar Nicholas I of Russia in 1853 as "the sick man of Europe." From a young age Mustafa Kemal harbored the desire to restore his country to global prominence under a different national flag: "He was born an Ottoman, but he would die . . . a Turk!"

Örnek contrasts Atatürk's liberal, Western ideology with the absolutism characteristic of the Ottoman élite, which "chained all free thought." At military school Mustafa Kemal learned about multiculturalism through exposure to Rousseau, Montesquieu, and the poet Namık Kemal. Ayşe Sarıalp Cebesoy, the niece of Mustafa Kemal's close acquaintance Sarıalp Cebesoy, recalls that by the outbreak of the First World War Mustafa Kemal considered himself "the savior of the country" with a clear mission to eliminate corruption and radical İslamist thought. Although still subject to the sultan's bidding, his writings repeatedly invoked "the will of the nation," differing radically from that of the rulers. By the time of Gallipoli, Mustafa Kemal was ready for action: Örnek deliberately compares him to ancient heroes such as Jason or Alexander the Great.

With the help of comments from renowned Ottoman historian Stanford Shaw (1930–2006) and psychologist-turned-historian Vamık D. Volkan (1932–), not to mention Atatürk's adopted daughter Sabiha Gökçen (1913–2001), we learn about Mustafa Kemal's grasp of local and international politics as well as his inspirational leadership qualities. Örnek quotes the famous occasion when he was wounded in the heart area by Allied shrapnel, but saved by a watch hanging from his neck. Volkan believes that this incident inspired in Mustafa

Kemal's mind the belief that he was immortal; the gods had preordained his inexorable rise to power.

By focusing on the origins of the republic as an alternative to years of Ottoman neglect (described in Sinden's commentary as "lethargy"), *Atatürk* challenges the belief that we should rely on Mother Anatolia to help us make sense of the world and our position within it. Atatürk's defeat of the Ottomans severed the link between religion and the state and thereby "opened the road to civilization"—in other words, the adoption of Western-influenced morals and methods. Donald Everett Webster (1901–2003) taught at two American secondary schools in the republic in the first decades of Atatürk's rule and later served as cultural attaché to the US embassy. His book *The Turkey of Atatürk*, published immediately before the outbreak of the Second World War, chronicled Atatürk's achievement in creating a republic from scratch. In Örnek's film he recalls Atatürk's desire for all people to be "educated and open" by discussing hitherto contentious subjects (especially politics and religion) freely and intelligently without fear of censure. Atatürk revered educators and set aside considerable funds to send them to Europe or the United States so that they could absorb the latest thinking in their subjects and subsequently disseminate it among their learners.[7]

Yet perhaps he was not quite as altruistic as he claimed, despite the paeans of praise heaped upon him by Sinden's narration ("For Turks he is immortal. They turn to him for sustenance"). We learn a lot about his complicated personal life—after marrying Latife Uşaklıgıl in 1923, he divorced her two years later. The circumstances surrounding the breakup remain publicly unknown. Atatürk had abandoned former lover Fikriye Hanım for the marriage; he sent her to Switzerland out of harm's way, and she eventually committed suicide.[8] Örnek suggests that Atatürk put that misfortune behind him, just as he did with the divorce, concentrating on matters of state instead; but we get a sense of the lengths to which he would go to protect his public image. Lovers were banished or kept secret; ex-wives conveniently forgotten; he wanted to be identified as "father of the Turks" rather than a family man. Privately he lived a solitary existence, despite the presence of several adopted daughters in his palace at Dolmabahçe in İstanbul. His excessive fondness for alcohol resulted in cirrhosis of the liver, and he died aged only fifty-seven on 10 November 1938. Several senior authorities berated Örnek for concentrating on Atatürk's personal life, but the director defended himself in the belief that he created "a fuller picture of the man through serious [material] both political and personal" (Raw, "Tolga Örnek," 341).

Örnek remains determined to tell different stories about a subject. As in *Gelibolu* we are presented with a variety of historical narratives mediated through scholarly comment, reminiscences, and reconstructions. We should weigh up the evidence and make up our own minds about Atatürk's reputation: should we embrace the dominant construction or create alternatives of our own? We might wonder whether his reforms, although far reaching in their consequences for the republic's future, were inspired by the desire for dictatorship rather than democracy. The columnist Mustafa Akyol, writing in the English language *Hürriyet Daily News*, observes that Atatürk "never competed with his opponents in free and fair elections. He rather relied on arbitrary courts which executed an estimated 5000 of his dissidents." In Atatürk's defense, we might interpret his policies as similar in orientation to those created by other authoritarian revolutionaries at that time such as Lenin in Soviet Russia or Josef Pilsudski in Poland (Akyol). Like the shah of Iran during the "White Revolution" of 1963, Atatürk's view of Westernization was advertised as a step toward modernization, but it also represented an attempt to strengthen support for the ruler among the peasants and working classes. In terms of personality, the two leaders could not have been more different: Atatürk was a strong and forceful leader, while the shah was perpetually haunted by his father's absolutist beliefs.[9] Yet there remain certain parallels between the two rulers in the ways in which their approach to Westernization suppressed the past in favor of the present, causing considerable resentment among many socioeconomic groups.

Örnek poses a psychological question: can we ever discard the past, understood not so much as a collection of events but rather a mode of representation; of communities held together by rituals—social, religious, or otherwise? Ernesto Spinelli avers that the past is not only "a meaning giver" for our experience but also symbolizes something "far more plastic and dependent on the present (as well as future expectations)" (193). *Gelibolu* shows how the events of a conflict taking place nine decades prior to the film's release continue to shape people's reactions, especially to the issue of integration between members of different cultures.[10] Örnek's *Devrim Arabaları* deals with similar issues. Based on actual events that took place in 1961 shortly after General Cemal Gürsel's (Saït Genay's) inauguration as president, the director examines the efforts of a group of engineers under Gündüz's (Taner Birsel's) stewardship based in Eskişehir, central Anatolia, to create the Devrim (or Revolution) automobile. The name was deliberately chosen to evoke a spirit of hope and anticipation associated with Atatürk's coming to power, but it refers as much to the engineers' never-say-die spirit that sustains them throughout the apparently impossible task of completing the project in only 130 days. As Gündüz points out: "This is a matter for believing . . . [that it is] a matter of honor for us now." That honor is not only personal but patriotic as well—to quit would be to betray their country as well as Atatürk's memory. The dictatorial memories of his rule have been erased; what matters more is the way in which a commitment to Kemalism binds people together.

Although optimism flourishes in the microcosm of the engineers' factory, it certainly does not prevail in society at large. *Devrim Arabaları* follows several recent films by other directors in its stinging criticism of the government and its machinery as fundamentally self-interested. In 1959 (two years before the action of Örnek's film takes place), the historian Kemal H. Karpat had this to say about most *memurler*, or civil servants: "[They] enjoyed a relative bounty amid general privations. . . . The government was quite legitimate in protecting its own personnel, but by doing so it acted as though its interests and survival were above and unrelated to those of the people. . . . The present-day bureaucracy . . . still possesses the power, owing to its long-entrenched habits and skill, to mould the policy of any government to accord with its own mentality and views" (130). Spearheaded by career bureaucrat Sami (Uğur Polat), the government machine tries its utmost to derail the Devrim project. They deem it too expensive for further funding, a drain on the republic's already precarious finances; when this strategy fails, they create a series of petty obstacles (including the demand that the engineers should build a second automobile at short notice). Still the group presses on, forcing Sami to engage in direct action by emptying the gas tank of the automobile scheduled to ferry President Gürsel in a public ceremony covered by television and radio. Through a contrast between the bright daylight shining through the factory windows and the dingy ambiance of Sami's office, Örnek reinforces our negative impression of the bureaucracy, which even has the temerity to write a letter proclaiming that "the automobile is a Pink Dream" even before the project has come to an end. It's hardly surprising that Latif (Selçuk Yöntem), one of Gündüz's senior engineers, should remark that "no success goes unpunished" in government circles, so that they would be unlikely "to allow a car named Revolution to be on the streets anyhow."

Latif's comment reveals an underlying skepticism about the efficacy of Atatürk's reforms. Accustomed to being told what to do, the bureaucracy looks out solely for itself; nothing matters other than to maintain outmoded procedures and receive a monthly paycheck. In truth, there was not too much difference in efficiency in the civil service in the Ottoman and republican periods. Hence the popularity of Ahmet Hamdi Tanpınar's satirical novel *The Time Regulation Institute* (1954), which focuses on a fictitious department devoting its entire energy to regulating all clocks by Western standards. The work continues to capture the *zeitgeist*: a new English translation by Maureen Freely and Alexander Dawe appeared in 2014.

The engineers' efforts are contrasted with the birth of Nilüfer's (Seçil Mutlu's) first child. Örnek stages a series of sequences involving her husband Necip (Onur Ünsal), almost beside himself with worry, who walks up and down in the hospital waiting room awaiting news of his wife's progress. Taking a welcome break from their labors, his fellow engineers make every effort to calm him down. A nurse enters with the news that mother and child are both fine; Necip bursts into tears of ecstasy while his colleagues embrace him. The action switches back to the factory, as the Devrim takes its first hesitant test drive, with the engine cutting out in the middle of it. Taken together the two sequences make a pointed criticism of humanity's perpetual search for material progress: vast sums have already been spent on the project and still the finished product has its teething troubles. By contrast, the nine-month gestation period for a child is straightforward, a source of happiness not just for the parents but for work colleagues as well. Expanding the family increases community strength, as summed up by a local axiom that translates as: "Children make the family's kettle whistle" ("Birth Traditions").

Eventually the project founders in the wake of a catastrophic ceremony when President Gürsel's automobile cannot move because of lack of gas. The media have a field day with headlines such as "[the] Revolution has suddenly stopped," or "the Revolution Broke Down." We are painfully aware of the political fallout from this event: the cream of the republic's industrial talent tried and failed to build "like a Westerner" and thereby proved that Atatürk's reforms had run out of gas too. No one, it seems, has either the strength or the willingness to embrace the progressive spirit, as one of the engineers rather bitterly observes: "[When] the Revolution stopped at least people [sh]ould give it a push." Yet individuals are not so easily suppressed. As the engineers congregate for the final time, they embrace each other in a reaffirmation of unity stimulated by a sense of inner pride in themselves and the community they represent. Gündüz offers them a final payment (courtesy of the government), but they refuse it in the belief that the memories of working together cannot be measured in material terms. The strength of communities is not confined to just rural districts (as in Kaplanoğlu's *Bal*) but prevails everywhere, so long as people sustain them. Sometimes such communities extend across time and space, embracing spiritual as well as political matters—for example, among those who respect Atatürk's reforms as well as those committed to Mother Anatolia. *Devrim Arabaları* ends with Gündüz placing a label "Made in Turkey" (in English) on the windscreen of one of the Devrim automobiles, followed by a coda set in the present day where the aging Necip (Haluk Bilginer) returns to the now-derelict factory in Eskişehir and drives the automobile—now preserved as a museum exhibit—out of the gates. The tagline "Made in Turkey" not only refers to the Devrim but more importantly to the community spirit associated with the project.

The three films—*Gelibolu*, *Atatürk*, and *Devrim Arabaları*—cumulatively offer a series of pointed comments on the early years of the republic. While recognizing Atatürk's achievement on the battlefield and in the political arena, they emphasize the importance of maintaining loyalty, community, and cross-cultural understanding. Örnek makes us aware of the apparently limitless possibilities of storytelling; we do not have to accept the official versions of history handed down to us in schools and other institutions but can work from the bottom up and listen to the words of ordinary people. We learn to trust in ourselves rather than swallowing official interpretations of the worlds we inhabit.

Lessons from the Ancients:
Mount Nemrud: The Throne of the Gods (2001) and *Hititler* (2003)

While Atatürk will forever be associated with Westernization, the origins of the Republic of Turkey can be traced back through traditions, ancient as well as modern. Örnek's documentaries on Mount Nemrud and the Hittite civilizations provide further insight into the permanence of community values and their connection to spirituality. *Mount Nemrud* tells parallel stories about Western-inspired excavations of the ancient site as well as the rule of the Commagenian Antiochus I (?-38 BCE). The archeological tale is a familiar one of European experts colonizing Nemrud throughout the late Victorian era as they discovered "the surprise of a lifetime."[11] By the late forties when the American Theresa Goell (1901-85) began work there, the ethos had shifted somewhat; while funded largely by institutions from her home country, she collaborated with local archaeologists in joint ventures. Örnek underlines the synthesis of East and West that not only increased the efficiency of Goell's projects but helped to discover an infinite number of finds. The archaeologists achieved what the Allies and the Ottomans had singularly failed to do in 1915: to maintain a harmonious relationship through dialogue rather than conflict.

Achieving cultural syntheses also underpinned many of Antiochus's projects. Örnek reenacts one of the battles he fought with rival tribes; the screen dissolves into a fire image followed by a shot of the rivers around Mount Nemrud, suggesting his desire to win in the hope of preserving the natural order of things. He instituted a bold project designed to unify the Hittite peoples by casting himself in a godlike role and building monuments designed to honor his memory. The parallels between Antiochus and Atatürk are obvious: two nation builders laboring long and hard to strengthen their territories against possible invasion from others. If the realization of that objective involved despotic methods, then the ends justified the means. Örnek's visual imagery, especially the focus on Nemrud as it stands today, silhouetted against the clear cold light of an eastern Turkish spring, underlines the efficacy of Antiochus's policies by suggesting an elemental force that resists any attempts at colonization. Murathan Mungan's poem "Doğu Dağı" ("Eastern Mountain") sums up the experience thus:

> You know,
> That rekindling light is the East
> From fire and blood it greens
> It yellows
> Into three colors
> The saga scatters on your anvil
> An old necessity
> From the way the East was created.
>
> Some mountains are born blacksmiths
> Anvil and hammer
> Scythe and mace
> They've got the know-how
>
> The kite rips, the landmine stirs
> A person grows.
>
> (127)

The poem associates human development with the elements that create shapes over time, just like a blacksmith. Our capacity to reshape this landscape is infinite, so long as we remain mindful of our relationship to it.

Örnek shows how Antiochus took this dictum to heart as he embarked on his "life's project" to create something intangible in the site that could never be discovered by archaeologists of the future. This might seem odd—especially for someone so preoccupied with ostentatious displays of power—but seems entirely appropriate to his self-designation as a god blessed with knowledge that no mortal could possess. The film's commentary makes his objective clear by emphasizing that Antiochus's legacy in Nemrud has "yet to reveal all its secrets."[12] Consequently what we are left with is a film that begins by embracing Western colonialism (as mediated through the archaeologists' discovery of the site) and ends up by exposing its limitations. No one, it seems, can provide answers to questions such as, was Antiochus buried inside Mount Nemrud? or what became of his tomb chamber? In 1999 Sencer Şahin of the University of Ankara conducted intensive scientific research on the site, but even such methods failed to produce tangible results. We need to approach the site on its own terms as "a gift from the past which we should try to maintain and preserve as much as possible."

Mount Nemrud makes some fascinating points about the limits of empirical historical inquiry. The efforts of Goell, Şahin, and others have offered new insights into ancient societies, inviting us to draw transhistorical parallels between Antiochus and Atatürk. On the other hand, Örnek makes us aware of the importance of contemplating the presence of Mother Anatolia's knowledge in Mount Nemrud, accessible only to those with the willingness to accept it on its own terms without the need to explain it. The novelist Buket Uzuner terms it "poetic Anatolian knowledge [including] . . . the ideas of tolerance and patience, . . . the deep cultural inheritance from Kaman [shaman] tradition" (81). Transhistoricity is identified with an instinctive appreciation of this inheritance and how it impacts our lives today.

Hititler develops the issues raised in *Mount Nemrud* through the drama-documentary form. Structurally speaking, both films resemble one another: *Hititler* begins with an account of late nineteenth- and early twentieth-century excavations before showing a copy of the Treaty of Kadesh adorning the entrance of the United Nations building in New York. Past and present are unified to suggest the Hittites' understanding of diplomacy as a means of overcoming armed conflict while ensuring no loss of face among the participants involved.

Örnek concentrates on the religious aspects of Hittite life: the gods who subsequently morphed into Zeus and Jupiter; the monarch's dual role as ruler and chief priest, divinely appointed to bless the land and ensure victory in battle; the regular enactment of fertility rites ensuring that women produced as many children as possible; and the construction of status designed to reinforce the monarch's divine status. *Hititler* also underlines the potential of storytelling to unify society through mass education: tales were handed down from generation to generation, providing moral lessons as well as promoting reverence for the past. We are reminded of history's enduring significance—not just facts, but the stories of gods and their acolytes that provided the cornerstone of Hittite cultures. Örnek continually emphasizes the point through reenactments, showing successive kings kneeling in front of a multitude of shrines and seeking advice about their future courses of action.

The film spends a long time analyzing the Battle of Kadesh (1274 BCE) that took place between the forces of the Egyptian empire under Rameses II and the Hittites led by Muwatalli II. Unlike *Gelibolu*, which dramatized history through static shots of kit bags and trenches, *Hititler* spares no expense in filling the screen with images of molten metal, reenacted sequences of troops from both sides fighting desperate hand-to-hand combats, and computer-generated images of battle in the background. The Hittites march boldly into battle followed by chariots studded with sharp weapons glinting in the sunlight. Yet Örnek does not glorify conflict for its own sake, as he shoots these sequences in washed-out colors resembling archival footage. At the end of the conflict his camera pans the scene of utter devastation, with rows of corpses lying on top of one another. Such images expose the falseness of Egyptian reports that describe Muwatalli refusing to fight "for fear of his majesty [Rameses II]. . . . His majesty halted in the rout, then he charged into the foe, the vanquished of Kheta, being alone by himself and none other with him. When his majesty went to look behind him, he found 2500 chariotry surrounding him. . . . Said his majesty to them [his troops], . . . 'The vanquished chief of Kheta is in the land of Aleppo; he has fled before his majesty, since hearing that, behold, he [Rameses II] came'" ("Egyptian Account," 137–41). Örnek shows not only that the battle was much bloodier than the Egyptians claimed but that the Hittites had much the better of the skirmishes, as witnessed through their tablets celebrating the nation's achievements in repelling potential invaders.

Eventually the two nations signed a historic peace treaty at Kadesh in 1259 BCE. Örnek cuts to close-ups of the two copies currently preserved in the Temple of Karnak at Luxor and the İstanbul Archaeological Museum and follows by a cut back to the Hittite capital of Boğazköy. The narration — by Irons in English, Cüneyt Türel in Turkish — informs us that as a consequence of the treaty the city transformed itself into a major regional center. The new Hittite king Hattusili III (played by Haluk Bilginer) emulated Antiochus's achievements; by the time he passed away in 1236 BCE he had created a slew of historic monuments, elegant squares, a workable drainage system, and a series of apparently impregnable city walls. The people marked his death with a public display of grief recalling the response to Atatürk's demise in 1938: Örnek emphasizes the solemnity of the occasion through a slow dirge played on a violin (by Tamer

Çiray), with the camera pulling outward to reveal an orange sunset. Hattusili's funeral marked the end of the Hittites' day; from now on the race would enter a period of inevitable decline.

Politically speaking the Treaty of Kadesh allowed for the consolidation of not one but two great nations—the Egyptians as well as the Hittites. Present-day politicians—especially those who impelled the Ottomans and Allies to fight in the First World War—might have been better advised to learn the lessons of history. This is the main purpose behind *Hittitler*; it is certainly not a pacifist film, but it rehearses the notion that negotiation rather than aggression is the best means for leaders from different cultures to coexist with each other. By retelling this ancient story, Örnek offers an implicit comment on the limits of patriotism. The Hittites' faith in their future sustained by divine encouragement inspired them to create great cities such as Boğazköy. On the other hand, the monarch had to look after his people to ensure the race's future, hence the desire to sign the Treaty of Kadesh. While both *Mount Nemrud* and *Hittitler* create stories about top-down rather than bottom-up modes of operation, with the monarch firmly in control of the people, they nonetheless suggest that we could do no worse than understand ancient modes of governance, especially their peace-loving instincts and religious tolerance.

Dreams and Dystopias: Kuruluştan Kurtuluşa Fenerbahçe (1999), Senin Hikayen (2013), Kaybedenler Külübü (2011), Labirent (2011)

Soccer has always been an essential aspect of Turkish popular cultures. I was regularly kept awake at nights by the sound of cars packed with supporters hooting their horns in celebration of a win, no more so than in 1999-2000 when Galatasaray from İstanbul beat Arsenal on penalties to win the UEFA Cup. Aslan Amani describes the status of the sport in the republic as "a major social force transcending, crisscrossing, and at times, reinforcing gender, ethnicity, ideology and other fault lines." The major teams, including Galatasaray, attract a multicultural following with huge levels of support among Kurds in the southeast of the country. The club runs initiatives designed to attract younger followers—male and female alike—to their stadium. While the major clubs are not free from institutional and financial chicanery, they try to establish "space[s] of freedom and experimentation" as well as reinforce positive images of the nation's present and future (Amani). Published in 1989, the poet Tarık Günersel's collection *Muhafızgücü 1, Hayalgücü 0* uses the score of a soccer match containing deliberate wordplay (the phrase literally translates as *Rearguards 1, Power of the Imagination 0*) as a basis for a series of dazzling verbal experiments exploring the possibilities of the language to express complex and frequently contradictory emotions. Soccer becomes the pretext for the poet's analysis of humanity in relation to the environment in what he himself terms an "envirocentric" form (qtd. in Katapish 27).

Örnek's documentary *Kuruluştan Kurtuluşa Fenerbahçe* (*From Creation to Independence: Fenerbahçe*) takes up some of these ideas and presents them in a narrative centered on the first two decades of the twentieth century, culminating in the War of Independence and its aftermath. The club began life as a multicultural institution dominated by British expatriates based in the İstanbul district of Kadıköy. In the first few years of existence Fenerbahçe performed indifferently, finishing in the lower reaches of the newly established league of eight teams; but by the outbreak of the First World War they had transformed themselves into a championship-winning outfit, with a tightly knit structure attracting the best young talent from all over the country. The thematic links between the club's story and Mustafa Kemal's rise to power are obvious: Fenerbahçe performed a unique service for the newly emergent nation in training young men, giving them the sporting as well as the social abilities that would prove invaluable on the battlefield. As the conflict wore on, so soccer became less important as a popular pastime; but Fenerbahçe continued to attract talent from junior clubs and give them a crash course in the importance of national unity. Ethnic origins did not matter: if the players were good enough, they would be fast-tracked into the first team. The club's efforts were rewarded at the end of the war by regular visits from Mustafa Kemal, who recognized their achievements both on and off the field. Success followed success; in 1918 and 1919 they staged challenge matches against visiting foreign opponents from Britain and elsewhere, winning them handsomely. Örnek sets these achievements in context through reenactments, showing the team in action as well as showing short sequences more suited to a spy thriller, where individual players performed acts of sabotage against the Ottoman oligarchy in the service of the emergent republican nation.

Following the victory at the Battle of Sakarya (1921), the republic was established while Fenerbahçe's players returned to full-time soccer. In the wave of patriotic fervor that ensued, the club established its Articles of Inclusion and celebrated its newfound status with crushing victories over a British Combined Services team. The film adopts a triumphalist tone: Fener's victory represents an affirmation of the republic's status as an independent nation overcoming a once-dominant Western colonial power. Their players are accorded heroic status;

just the kind of people to implement Atatürk's secularist vision of nationalism and disseminate it through sporting encounters.

It might seem rather curious to compare the celebratory *Kuruluştan Kurtuluşa Fenerbahçe* with the more somber *Senin Hikayen*, a sweet-and-sour domestic tale of an upper-middle-class mother Meral (Nevra Serezli) diagnosed with terminal cancer who survives just about long enough to enjoy the early years of her grandson Derin (Derin Örnek). Produced by Çağan Irmak's company TAFF, the film contains melodramatic elements hitherto uncharacteristic of Örnek's work as well as more recognizable intertextual references. Derin's father Hakan (Timuçin Esen) endures similar agonies prior to his son's birth as Necip in *Devrim Arabaları*. His wife Esra (Selma Ergeç) experiences contractions at home: Hakan runs abstractedly round their apartment collecting clothes before bundling his wife into the family car and speeding toward the hospital. He paces up and down the waiting room while Meral sneaks into the delivery room to witness the birth: Hakan enters later on but finds the experience almost unendurable and seeks consolation from his close friends. Örnek draws attention to the value of community as a means of coping with unexpected surprises, especially during times of stress.

The film's melodramatic elements can be seen in the way Örnek contrasts Hakan and Esra's idealized existence with Meral's painful passing. With a Dean Martin song playing on the soundtrack, we witness a montage showing the parents playing with the infant Derin, putting him to bed and walking happily in the park at weekends.[13] The light remains uniformly bright, suggesting a perfect world. By comparison, Meral's last days in hospital unfold in claustrophobic, dimly lit rooms, with the elderly lady perpetually gasping for breath. The *mise-en-scène* recalls Irmak's *Prensesin Uykusu*, with her family crowded round the bed hoping she will make a miraculous recovery. Fate dictates otherwise: to the sound of a dirge played on violin and piano, Meral slips away. Hakan moans: "What will I do without you?" and embraces Esra as the screen fades to black. Even the most well-intentioned souls are not immune from death.

This rather labored sequence prepares the ground for the *dénouement*, which further reveals the director's preoccupation with storytelling and its consequences. Meral's husband Orhan (Saït Genay) gives his son a scrapbook with accompanying commentary: the story of Hakan's life from birth onward. Close-ups of fading black-and-white photos are linked by a series of dissolves to Hakan leafing through the scrapbook accompanied by Meral's voiceover: "I love you forever. . . . Welcome to your story, my son." Some pages have been left blank, giving Hakan the chance to continue the tale with Derin as the subject this time. Meral's vocal intervention indicates the link between story-telling and immortality: although physically absent, her presence lives on through words as a way of encouraging Hakan toward self-knowledge by revisit-ing the past and evaluating it in terms of present and future. Perhaps most significantly this scene confirms the strength of the family as the bedrock of a stable society, where social and moral lessons are handed down from genera-tion to generation. Nilüfer Pembecioğlu comments: "Families . . . have 'mutual interests.' They try to be involved in one another's life trying to have an impact on each other. . . . It is easy to teach something . . . within a family system" (153). Such "mutual interests" are shared by the nation, which likewise depends on notions of stability handed down from generation to generation. If Fener-bahçe soccer club set an example of creating harmony in the public sphere during the early twentieth century, the modern-day nuclear family as represented in *Senin Hikayen* has been equally assiduous in the private sphere through story-telling. Once again Örnek reflects on the consequences of patriotism: while belief in the nation will always be intrinsic to the republican Turkish identity, it should always be accompanied by a concern for humanity.

Kaybedenler Külübü (*The Losers' Club*) sets up an antithetical situation: two supposed thirtysomething losers (Nejat İşler, Yiğit Özsener) host a late night radio show (titled *The Losers' Club*) on a local independent station, Kent FM.[14] Broadcasting from Kadıköy, their show comprises a series of pseudophilosophi-cal musings interspersed with overt sex chat. The inspiration is straightfor-ward: unable to fulfill anything in their daily lives, the two men find their only outlet through radio. Örnek creates a visual dystopia to sum up their existences; they broadcast from a dingy studio in an anonymous-looking apartment block, while spending much of their leisure time looking for casual pickups in local bars. Having reeled in their nightly catch they return to an apartment strewn with beer cans and empty takeaway food cartons and smartly repair to the equally seedy bedroom, where the groans of sexual pleasure can be clearly heard. Meanwhile their feckless flatmate Murat (Rıza Kocaoğlu) sits sprawled in an armchair watching nature programs on the National Geographic Channel, with animals engaged in similar acts of coitus.

These sequences are reminiscent of Zeki Demirkubuz's work (especially the National Geographic Channel reference), while the protagonists' amoral outlook on life recalls that of Alper in Çağan Irmak's *Issiz Adam*. Yet the major irony of *The Losers' Club* is that the presenters' idiosyncratic blend of philosophy and obscenity transforms them into cult figures. The film is full of reaction shots from a cross-section of listeners including suicide candidate Hakan (Giray Altınok), an aging singleton (Erdal Küçükkömürcü), and a group of female university learners in a cramped dormitory. Örnek emphasizes the stability of this community through repeated shots showing the listeners going about their nightly business but unified by their pleasure in listening to the program. Catapulted into the public eye, the presenters are losers no more: young women queue up to spend the night with them, and they become the center of attention in the sweat-filled nightspots of Kadıköy.

The question of celebrity and its potentially destructive outcomes has been addressed in Irmak's *Unutursam Fısılda*, as Ayperi/Hatice enjoys a meteoric rise to fame yet finds herself increasingly isolated in a manipulative world. *Kaybedenler Külübü* takes the issue of celebrity to make a pointed comment on the effects of isolation and alienation in contemporary Turkish urban cultures. The figure of the (invariably male) individual at odds with the world is a familiar one (as we have seen throughout this book): Örnek turns that convention on its head by suggesting that alienation is nothing more than a performance designed to attract attention. Like a wannabe on a talent show, men of a certain age and outlook increasingly cultivate an image of themselves designed to be media friendly and thereby advance the cause of capitalism ("Celebrity and Development"). While Kent FM's controller Aslı (İdil Fırat) might object to some of the explicit material broadcast on air, she will not suspend her presenters knowing full well that her ratings would suffer significantly.

Throughout the film Örnek exposes the falseness of the protagonists' public image. Mete (Özsener) is not a loser at all but a middle-class graduate living in a comfortable apartment with his devoted mother (Serra Yılmaz), who willingly prepares breakfast for him at all times of the day. Kaan (İşler) falls in love with Zeynep (Ahu Türkpence), who introduces him to a more emotionally fulfilling lifestyle. In a dénouement strongly reminiscent of *Issiz Adam*, Kaan faces the decision of whether to sustain the increasingly tiresome pose as a loner or marry Zeynep. The confrontation between the two takes place beside the Bosphorus with the flowing waters clearly visible at the rear of the shot, reminding us of the timelessness of the elements. Kaan opts for the single life—not necessarily willingly but out of a myopic duty to maintain his constructed public persona (how can a loner be seen to fall in love?)

We are encouraged to reflect on the shortcomings of stardom in the Turkish context. In the seventies, Yeşilçam stars were idealized, their screen personae offering behavioral ideals that ordinary people tried to emulate. Türkân Şoray, Belgin Doruk, and Fatma Girik offered contrasting visions of femininity, while Ayhan Işık and Tarık Akan were rugged yet mostly evenhanded in their dealings with the opposite sex. *Kaybedenler Külübü* treats stardom as little more than a series of empty rituals depriving individuals of the capacity to determine the course of their lives. There is something highly uncomfortable about two thirty-somethings pretending that their existences lack meaning at the expense of their listeners and their lovers.

At length Mete and Kaan finish their radio careers. In another sequence comprised of split screen shots, we see them thanking their listeners for being so loyal, then getting up from their chairs and quitting the studio for good. The sounds of a seventies Turkish pop song describing the pain of love can be heard. The film ends with a pan of Kadıköy at night, the streetlights twinkling like stars. Superficially the ending might indicate a change of heart in the protagonists as they discover just how much they have become victims of their celebrity. Yet Örnek refuses to offer clarification; for all we know they might sink back into obscurity, unwilling—or unable—to acknowledge the confines of their new existence. Bethany Usher's recent article draws our attention to the loss of social standing and position that occurs within a group when celebrities no longer occupy the public sphere: the use of the past tense ("weren't you on television/radio once?") drawing attention to their fall from grace (306–21). This decline is endemic in capitalist societies, which continually embrace the new and innovative while casting anything considered *passé* into oblivion.

For those who are prepared to work at it by embracing community narratives, life can be emotionally and personally fulfilling, even after death (as in *Senin Hikayen*). For those embracing self-interest, success is inevitably achieved at a high price as individuals are trapped within labyrinths of their own making, with little or no power to control their lives. I use the term labyrinth deliberately, as it offers a way into *Labirent* (*Labyrinth*). A political thriller with distinct echoes of Ridley Scott's *Body of Lies* (2008) as well as the Turkish-made *New York'ta Beş Minare* (*Five Minarets in New York*) (2010), Örnek's film examines the personal and professional lives of secret service agents Fikret (Timuçin Esen) and Reyhan (Meltem Cumbul) as they struggle to outwit a terrorist leader (Altan Gördüm) determined to blow up one of İstanbul's Bosphorus bridges. The film tackles issues close to the director's heart, especially that of cross-cultural understanding: Fikret has to collaborate with MI5 agent Hugh Spencer (Martin Turner) but, in the belief that the relationship might invariably sour, feels that he cannot trust the Briton. As long as Western business and political interests are satisfied, the British remain friends; in other contexts the two nations would be at loggerheads with each other. At length Hugh appreciates Fikret's integrity and agrees unconditionally to share secrets, but we are left feeling that old-fashioned diplomacy as practiced in the ancient world (and discussed in *Hittitler*) no longer carries any weight in the post-9/11 era.

Even the belief in the republic as embraced by Atatürk seems to have evaporated, despite the pictures adorning every wall of Fikret's workplace. His superior Serdar (Erdal Küçükkömürcü) turns out to be a double agent, passing on vital information to the terrorists while still protesting his lifelong commitment to the secret service. When his treachery is discovered, Serdar insists that it was due to concern for his family; if he had not acceded to the terrorists' wishes, they would have committed cold-blooded murder. Even if that were true, Örnek suggests that patriotism can be bought and sold like any other commodity in a capitalist world. Family values still survive, but inevitably occupy an insignificant place in the agents' lives. Reyhan has a young daughter but cannot find sufficient time to look after her owing to the pressure of work. Matters eventually come to a head in another confrontation sequence taking place by the Bosphorus, as Fikret moves close to Reyhan and the two hold hands for the first time. Through bitter experience they have come to understand the importance of their personal lives over and above their commitment to their jobs. Yet Örnek refuses to grant us a happy ending: Fikret is fatally wounded in the climactic shoot-out, leaving Reyhan inconsolable with grief. The action shifts to an award ceremony; beneath another portrait of Atatürk, Reyhan receives recognition for her bravery in bringing the terrorists to justice. Professional lives, it seems, will always triumph over familial desires.

Labirent shows how the power of storytelling has also been corrupted by capitalism. Zait (Ümit Kurt) infiltrates the terrorist network and is thereby accommodated into "the Islamic family," committed to restoring the Caliphate and ridding the Middle East of "the evil Americans." Death possesses no particular significance: suicide bombers like Zait make the ultimate sacrifice for the greater good while receiving Allah's blessing for their efforts. In Irmak's *Dedemin İnsanları* death is perceived as a merciful release from suffering by the elderly Mehmet as he walks into the sea to reunite with his Cretan ancestors. This is developed by other creative artists: Haydar Ergülen's poem "Kayip Kardeş" ("Lost Brother") (2008) emphasizes the need to achieve a state of being (or nonbeing) where "the soul coincides" with "the many / lost brothers I have on this path" (177). In *Labirent* death has become politicized as young people are brainwashed into the belief that being a suicide bomber will initiate a regime change. Zait cannot reconcile himself to this responsibility and therefore becomes a legitimate target for revenge. The only means to secure protection is to work as Fikret's informer. Örnek includes a sequence in a quiet İstanbul backstreet where Zait, almost paralyzed with fear, looks to left and right before agreeing to talk in Fikret's car. The conversation unfolds breathlessly before Zait opens the door gingerly and walks into the shadows once more. If stories should bring people of different ages, classes, and religions together, Örnek shows the opposite: unless the terrorists' followers embrace the cause without question, they should be exterminated as soon as possible. This story suppresses rather than encourages free will.

Yet perhaps the unimportance of individual lives is inevitable in a dog-eat-dog world where human lives are readily expendable. Fikret and his fellow agents raid an anonymous apartment; it is a sunny day in early spring with the trees in full blossom. The agents proceed warily through the rooms until Fikret's colleague Bülent (Sarp Akkaya) enters the bedroom and is blown to bits by another suicide bomber. Örnek slows the pace of the action right down to show Fikret's horrified reaction, as he steps back and utters a scream reminiscent of a wild animal. The need to eradicate terrorism no longer has any meaning in a world where a promising agent has been needlessly slain. After Fikret's death in similar fashion all that is left of his memory is a hastily engraved headstone and a clichéd newspaper obituary reminding readers that the nation should be proud of his efforts.

Labirent is at heart a pessimistic piece showing how human values have degenerated in the eight decades since the period covered in *Kuruluştan Kurtuluşa Fenerbahçe*. Young men living in the First World War were prepared to give their lives in the republic's service, in the belief that what they were doing was vitally necessary for the public good. Likewise, playing soccer, especially against foreign visitors, had a competitive edge, an opportunity for republican citizens to show that they were equal to, if not better than, the established colonial powers. By the new millennium such self-sacrifices had been devalued to such an extent that Serdar was prepared to sacrifice his country in exchange for money. While terrorist groups still encourage their members to fight for a cause, they do so by deliberately trying to maim or kill their enemies. This was not the case during the Gallipoli campaign, for instance—although two armies were determined to win, they had an enduring respect for one another's integrity. Now agents such as Fikret come to understand that their causes—the nation's future, for instance—are not worth fighting for.

Polysemic Tales

One of the enduring clichés claimed by all directors is that they are primarily storytellers. Writing about Wim Wenders, Michael Rabiger and Mick Hurbis-Cherrier emphasize his preoccupation with "Developing empathy with the characters and knowledge of them in their unfolding difficulties, and [he] tries profoundly to understand them. It is a part we all play in life, so it feels familiar, and it is a role that every director must actively adopt in making films" (Kaelan). While such positions are identifiable in Örnek's oeuvre, we must also remember that he draws on a highly culturally specific oral tradition of community storytelling that disseminates familiar myths and legends while giving them a contemporary spin. His choice of subjects is ideal for this purpose as a way of assessing the effectiveness of Atatürk's reforms and his status as a republican icon, for example. This is quite a delicate matter, especially for one's first major feature. A decade later the journalist and filmmaker Can Dündar released *Mustafa*, a film that made similar claims about Atatürk's loneliness, his drinking habits, and his womanizing. The reaction was swift and sudden: Türkcell, the republic's major mobile phone operator, withdrew its sponsorship of Dündar's project in the belief that it might reduce the company's customer base. Two professors filed a court case claiming that Dündar had deliberately tried to "evade Atatürk's responsibility" ("Atatürk Film").[15]

Despite the possible risks (that include the possibility of not securing funding for future projects), Örnek has continued to reflect on familiar stories that continue to have a significant role in Turkish life. He maintains a lasting interest in the plight of individuals trying to cope with an increasingly materialist society, where possessions, celebrity, and social status matter more than personal happiness, patriotism, or respect for the past. While remaining aware of individual shortcomings (especially during the Gallipoli campaign), Örnek emphasizes that we should learn from the past, not only socially but politically: the Hittites understood the value of diplomacy, which explains why the Treaty of Kadesh is carved into the United Nations building. Out of the carnage of Gallipoli there emerged a newfound tolerance for other cultures, existing alongside the desire to create a new republic among the ashes of the Ottoman Empire. The consequences of ignoring these notions are chillingly set forth in *Kaybedenler Külübü* and *Labirent*, both of which are set in an İstanbul riddled with isolationism and fear of the other.

Stylistically speaking, Örnek's cinema has more in common with Western or other cinematic traditions, especially when compared with Zaim or Kaplanoğlu.[16] As befits someone trained in film studies at the American University in Washington, DC, he opts for briskly paced narratives full of close-ups, shot/reverse shot sequences, and pans. Occasionally he employs more sophisticated devices such as split-screen techniques to emphasize the simultaneity of action in a fast-paced world. We are given little chance to contemplate aspects of the *mise-en-scène*: narrative matters most. Nonetheless, I would suggest that Örnek's style is eminently suitable for explaining his preoccupation with storytelling. By analyzing his historical documentaries—supposedly based on empirical evidence—our imaginations are stimulated as we reflect on how the past still matters. We might not necessarily be very interested in Hittite cultures or the minutiae of Fenerbahçe soccer club's past glories, but we can draw some significant life lessons from both films about the importance of diplomacy and teamwork as pillars of a stable society. Through exposure to culturally specific material we can learn to reflect both spiritually as well as critically on our relationship to the world, by considering how what we said or did yesterday might only bear a tangential relationship to what we say and do tomorrow. To understand this principle constitutes a fundamental aspect of psychological adaptation. Örnek's films are not just about the republic past, present, or future; they concern us all.

6

Nuri Bilge Ceylan

Rediscovering Anatolia

Of all the filmmakers discussed in this book, Nuri Bilge Ceylan is by far the best known. His personal website (nuribilgeceylan.com) lists twenty-four books in English and Turkish containing critical discussion of his films on subjects covering non-American westerns, Asian cinema, the cinema of the "East," and cinema as weather. His international reputation was established with *Uzak* (*Distant*) (2002), which won the Grand Prix at the 2003 Cannes Film Festival and subsequently accrued a total of forty-seven awards, the most ever won by a film in the entire history of Turkish cinema. Ceylan's next film *İklimler* (*Climates*) (2006) won the Fipresci Prize at Cannes, while *Bir Zamanlar Anadolu'da* (*Once Upon a Time in Anatolia*) (2011) scooped the Grand Prix once more. *Kış Uykusu* (*Winter Sleep*) (2014), costing a mere $3.7 million to make, won the Palme d'Or.

Although releasing only seven feature films plus one short in a twenty-year career, Ceylan has evolved a style of filmmaking centering on images rather than narrative: viewers concentrate on every aspect of the *mise-en-scène* including landscapes, light, and sound. Like Semih Kaplanoğlu, Ceylan began his career as an artist and photographer; after having worked in the commercial sector, he acted as cinematographer on his first three features before forging a successful partnership with Gökhan Tiryaki. His films are characterized by long takes, featuring static compositions or slow zooms, creating self-contained universes. Asuman Suner believes that "[he] offers a peculiar blend of documentary-style realism and highly aestheticized visuals. Depicting tiny details of everyday life, his films contain very little overt action, . . . [creating] real as well as imagined journeys of homecoming and leave-taking" ("Home, Belonging, and Other Aspects," 124–25). Ceylan's style has spawned a host of imitations: reviewing

Ali Aydın's debut feature *Kuf* (*Mold*) (2012), I commented on the director's preference for "lots of lengthy shots in which very little actually happens. We observe characters moving within the frame, or talking to one another. . . . This is a deliberate technique designed to focus attention on characters in relation to their environment" (Raw, "Criticism").

A new release from Ceylan attracts considerable publicity. *Kış Uykusu* was the first to boast a major star—Haluk Bilginer—who accepted the lead while running his own company (Oyun Atolyesi) in İstanbul. Having won the Palme d'Or, the film attracted congratulations from the, then, prime minister and president, Recep Tayyip Erdoğan and Abdullah Gül. Ceylan responded by dedicating the prize to the Republic of Turkey's youth who "lost their lives" in their demonstrations against Erdoğan at İstanbul's Gezi Park in 2013. The director did not mince his words: "If it was Japan, the PM would resign. But not in Turkey." One journalist concluded that while freedom of speech "is still a sensitive issue, . . . Ceylan uses family drama as a metaphor for Turkey. . . . The main problem lies in the widening gap between the generations . . . and the deepening misunderstanding between old and young" (Poirier). Such observations did no harm to the film's box-office performance; it was the biggest grossing work in the director's career and made the transition from art house to mainstream release by playing in most of the multiplexes in city malls countrywide.

We need to be patient when watching a Ceylan film.[1] His focus on images encourages us to reflect on our existences: do we spend too much time pursuing our materialist dreams of wealth and prosperity and thereby forget our link to nature? The point is metaphorically stressed in his early films through images of tortoises and the characters' responses to them. In the short *Koza* (*Cocoon*) (1995), Ceylan contrasts the reptile's behavior in a storm with that of a youngster (Turgut Toprak), who runs for cover while the tortoise crawls into his shell, which provides camouflage as well as shelter. The tortoise remains close to nature while humanity dissociates itself from it.[2] In *Kasaba* (*The Small Town*) (1997) the youngster Saffet (M. Emin Toprak) resents the tortoise's proximity to nature, prompting him to turn the animal upside down, its shell on the ground, rendering it helpless. While Ceylan does not advocate a return to nature, he encourages us to be mindful of our connection to Mother Anatolia. Set in the historic region of Cappadochia, *Kış Uykusu* includes several shots of the central character Aydın (Bilginer) driving across the snow-covered plains, his car a speck on the horizon. Likewise *Bir Zamanlar Anadolu'da* includes several pans of the Anatolian landscape: the headlamps of the cars in the background resemble safety matches almost invisible to the naked eye. We are neither superior nor inferior to other living creatures — something we can only understand if we focus more closely on our environment by listening to birdsong, or the wind rustling through the trees, or the crack of twigs beneath our feet. Although Ceylan cannot be described as an eco-filmmaker,[3] he is nonetheless preoccupied with the balance between economic, social, and environmental issues. In her 1991 novel *İki Yeşil Su Samuru* (*Two Green Otters*), the novelist Buket Uzuner likens her two principal characters to otters (endangered species in a pollution-laden world) — an essential part of the environment with their intelligence, gregariousness, and curiosity. They should be preserved to sustain the natural balance of the universe (*İki Yeşil*, 234–35). One character observes that "Water, air and soil interact with each other, and in the same way oceans and continents are all dependent on each other. There isn't a living organism on this planet that is immune to the problem: no matter what race or creed or gender or which language they speak" (235). Once we have grasped that basic truth, then we can reflect on our ontological status by examining "every aspect of . . . life . . . to reevaluate our concepts of family, mother and father, . . . women and men and everything else for that matter, . . . to rethink them and come up with new norms to work together in a new harmony" (251). Such concerns are shared by Ceylan and his contemporaries including Demirkubuz and Kaplanoğlu: what distinguishes Ceylan is the breadth of his vision, as the action of his films shifts from the country to the city and back again. He offers snapshots of an environment undergoing profound socioeconomic change, while inviting us to reflect on our position within it. His films are at once local yet global in their concerns, which accounts for their extraordinary popularity both inside and outside the Republic of Turkey.

Aubade:
Koza (1995)

Financed by TRT, the national television and radio broadcasting company, *Koza* begins with a series of black-and-white views from the past before cutting to a long shot of an elderly man (Mehmet Emin Ceylan) lying on the ground listening to the birds, the water, and the wind. The action shifts to a view of urban İstanbul with a boat crossing the Bosphorus — a shot familiar from Zaim's oeuvre that draws attention to the centrality of water to our existence. Yahya Kemal's poem "Açık Deniz" ("Open Sea") offers some thoughts on the subject:

> Waters that are beyond the sad boundaries flowing
> Murmured in my memory with that emotion:

I knew what was infinity beyond the horizon.
One day I said no more love or country for me.
Passing from land to land I went for a long journey.
I went to the very spot that's land's extremity.

("Açık," 31)

Ceylan's shot of the Bosphorus links up with another shot of an elderly woman (Fatma Ceylan) sitting in a boat looking pensively out to sea, followed by a close-up of a duckling struggling to swim for the first time. Whatever the demands of daily life among mortals, they pale into insignificance compared with the rhythms of nature that continue throughout space and time.[4]

Ceylan sets this tranquil scene alongside interior shots of the woman imprisoned in her house looking wistfully at the trees slowly blowing in the wind outside. The old man lies on a truckle bed in a darkened room. This is the cocoon of the film's title, a manufactured form of isolation that restricts personal and emotional development. By night the couple sits by the fireside without speaking to one another; all we can hear is the metronomic click of her knitting needles and the rustle of pages turning as the old man reads his book. The camera cuts to a close-up of the old man's grizzled features and the old woman dozing. Time passes; but it seems as if they have not grasped how much of their lives they waste by sitting alone at home. A shot of a headstone reminds of death's ubiquitous presence. Written in the late fifties, Özdemir Asaf's poem "The Departed" reminds of what follows:

It is a night from you towards you.
The passing is what you've lived, not understood while living,
The remaining is perhaps a verity,
Lost like a pin, broken as a glass.
The coming seems that which you expected
And the departed, the sweetest, the warmest, the grandest.

("Departed," 27)

The action shifts to morning, a cock crows, and the dawn chorus commences. There is no movement indoors: the couple sleeps until the old man awakens slowly and looks out the window. Ceylan cuts to a close-up of the woman pretending to doze—as she does so, a tear rolls slowly down her cheek as she understands the shortcomings of his existence but remains powerless to resolve them. The action moves forward to later in the day as raindrops trickle down the windowpane, making it seem as if nature empathizes with the woman's plight. Once the rain has passed, the couple walk slowly away from the camera in an otherwise deserted exterior landscape. In a piece of open ground they light a fire and warm their hands. They have managed to escape from their cocoon but seem unable to align themselves with nature. Visually speaking they recall two Beckettian characters awaiting death with no visible emotional reaction.

Koza ends with a montage of shots previously seen in the film: the woman sitting on the boat; the man warming his hands; the woman beside the barred window; and the rain plashing on the window. The action fades to black without any apparent *dénouement*, thereby reminding us that life has no beginning, middle, or end. What we are left with is a kaleidoscope of melancholy memories. Only when we make the effort to escape from our physical or mental cocoons can we understand Mother Anatolia, symbolized in Ceylan's film by the sight of a single bird feather falling slowly to the ground and blown away by a gust of wind. The protagonists' plight resembles that voiced by Orhan Veli Kanık in the short lyric "Separation," where the speaker's social condition prevents him from communing with the world around him:[5]

> I stand behind the boat, watching:
> I cannot jump into the water; the world is lovely:
> I am also a man, after all, I can't cry.
>
> (96)

The Anatolian Trilogy:
Kasaba (1997), *Mayıs Sıkıntısı* (1999), *Uzak* (2002)

To understand Ceylan's preoccupations in all three works, we should remind ourselves of his previous career as a photographer. Together with his sister Emine, he has endeavored to capture the uniqueness of Anatolia in a variety of projects. Published in 1987, Emine's book of images contains a preface written by Ceylan where he admits that both of them are "passionate dreamers" looking for "a secret compartment where they [extreme emotions] cannot reach. . . . This compartment is always alert; . . . it rushes out of its cocoon and getting hold of things, repairs the wounds and slyly prepares her [Emine Ceylan] anew for life" ("Introduction," 4). Working with Mother Anatolia creates "a voyage of discovery," both psychological and geographical, in search of this "secret compartment." Emine's collection begins with a series of views (taken four years previously) of their childhood home of Yenice near Çanakkale: rolling landscapes stretch into the background flanked by mountains, while the villagers pursue time-honored vocations such as looking after their sheep, picking produce, or preparing family meals. Another photo superimposes Emine's face on a snow-covered view of the mountains with the clouds forming an imposing backdrop, emphasizing her connection to nature. A "Portrait of Zalha" (Emine's title) has a head-scarfed young woman staring at the camera lens with a panorama of the village behind her. "On the Road" depicts another young woman, a suitcase to her right, standing on a deserted mountain path. The images denote that once the "secret compartment" has been uncovered, we can connect opposites—past and present, city and country, tradition and innovation, or migration and stasis. We might not be able to reconcile such opposites, but we at least understand that they are part of Mother Anatolia's world and also affect our own lives. Ceylan offers a similar set of photographic images in Tanıl Bora's *Taşraya Bakmak* (*Looking at the Countryside*) (2005), a travelogue chronicling the author's progress around central Anatolia. Rural life might be stagnating, especially in a country so committed to capitalist modernization and migration to the big cities, but it still offers those who grew up in that world a form of stability.[6]

His first full-length feature, *Kasaba*, cowritten with Emine, offers further variations on the theme. The small town is not just a place but also a state of mind: the fount of tradition, family, and community loyalty. The anthropologist Mahmut Makal observed as long ago as 1954 that "the age we live in demands them [new ideas] and we listen of course, but it is the other thing [religion] that really matters. . . . You're a decent, honest, truthful fellow but you need to put yourself right with God, as you have with us. . . . The long and short of it is that they [Turkish villagers] don't in the least understand what is meant by freedom of thought, and freedom of belief" (104–5). The perceived lack of freedom is stressed in the film's opening shot set in the local school, a dilapidated structure wherein learners recite their daily oath of loyalty to Atatürk (without in the least understanding its meaning) and subsequently listen to their educator describing the rules of effective social life. The sequence adumbrates similar events in Kaplanoğlu's *Bal*, where youngsters are subjected to rote learning that takes no account of individual personalities. In *Kasaba* the learners endure further humiliation as their educator sniffs them to ensure that they have taken a bath and not brought anything unhealthy to school for lunch. Asiye (Havva Sağlam) is picked out and told off. Ceylan contrasts the artificial atmosphere of the classroom with the landscape; snow trickles down the windowpane as the educator looks outside, wishing that he could be somewhere else. On the window sill a scrawny plant struggles to survive—a suitable metaphor for an environment in which independent spirits are crushed rather than allowed to grow naturally. The leisurely pace of rural existence is stressed by means of a series of lengthy takes showing deserted streets with a stray dog, small children playing in the background, the village elders passing the time of day outside their mud-brick residences, and newly killed lambs being roasted on spits prior to a festive occasion. Such rituals seem timeless, conjuring up a world that the British film critic Robin Wood (writing in 2006) believed was characteristic of a society whose inhabitants are "trapped, . . . controlled, and belittled by a system (family, nation, religion) that doesn't work and has never worked" (59).

In truth, Ceylan's villagers have little cause to think for themselves; they conceive of the world as timeless, revolving around the seasons rather than being affected by individual decision making. In class the learners' attention centers on a feather floating slowly downward, a reminder of the birds' perpetual presence outside the classroom (as well as Ceylan's use of a similar image in *Koza*). In another lengthy shot we hear the wind howling as the camera tracks left to show two telephone wires with pelicans perched on them. Two small children eat plums while sitting in a graveyard; Ceylan cuts to a close-up of a gravestone, followed by another close-up of a donkey tied to a stake with flies buzzing about his ears. Despite our wish to "escape" the restrictive system (in Wood's terms), we encounter a similar fate. Hence it is better to accept rather than subvert the timeless rhythms characterizing life in an Anatolian small town. Faruk Nafiz Çamlıbel's poem about the sun and the seasons sums up this worldview:

Spring Sun
With southerly winds trees loosen their tongue;
Against the sun fresh flowers are hung.
The sun seems dreamy over the lawns as a youngling
Balmily making his way for his first meeting.

Summer Sun
Lover and beloved lie in the shade,
Beneath the pine spreading on unseen muslin,
Sun, on the opposite shore, resembles a maid
Bathing half-naked to quench her passion.

Autumn Sun
Leaves seem sweethearts set apart,
Water the last flap of a wing broken.
Sun leans its forehead against the horizon
Even as a widow laments the idle summer depart.

Winter Sun
Two mortals are yesterday and tomorrow,
Twin brothers are death and famine.
Sun is a lonesome spirit on the brazier low
Of an old man looking wan and warm.

(174–75)

Taking such traditions into account, the plight of Saffet (M. Emin Toprak) should be approached with a certain degree of skepticism. In one shot we observe his torso filling the frame, the sky in the background amidst a dozen chairs carrying customers on a carnival ride as they shout with delight. The dreamlike ambiance is suffused with color, noise, and light, contrasting with the darkening clouds reflected in the water of a well. Yet Saffet seems not to take much notice of his environment: "I've got no home, no friends, no job. I'm a loser. You're fed up with my discontent. I've no talent for anything. I'm like a useless cigarette butt. My best years were wasted in this town. My manhood and my heart are melting away before my eyes. There were deeper ties holding me . . . when I was away in the [military] service—the scent of pine, oaks, quiet mornings, stray dogs. . . . What's wrong with wanting to go someplace when something serious is going on?" He considers himself a prisoner of changing times: as village life continues to stagnate, he is caught between two worlds— the rural past and the industrial present—with no freedom of choice.

In a later sequence Saffet's family gather in a clearing around an open fire. Dede (Emin Ceylan) reminisces about the past, while his spouse (Fatma Ceylan) worries about the shortage of cherries. The action shifts to a quick shot of clouds in the sky and a snake crawling through the undergrowth. As night falls Dede talks about his military exploits in the Republic of Turkey and India, before launching into a rambling tale about Babylon ("the cradle of civilization") and Alexander the Great, in the belief that such stories might draw his family together (like Zekeriye in *Ulak*). No such miracle happens here, as the conversation dies and Ceylan's camera switches to quick shots of Saffet smoking languidly in the shadows, crickets chirping in the background. Dede's son Emin (Sercihan Alevoğlu) picks up the conversational threads with a lengthy digression on the advantages of leaving one's hometown for a university education in the metropolis. We are reminded of other protagonists (Ahmet in Demirkubuz's *Bulantı*, for instance) who have pursued such career paths and how barren their existences actually are. Emin suffers the same fate: despite his fine words, he is emotionally and physically paralyzed.[7] The Chekhovian echoes of this sequence are obvious (the Russian receives a cocredit for the screenplay along with Ceylan and his sister). The family in *Kasaba* fails to acknowledge how traditions collapse in front of their eyes: talk provides a means to avert despair.

We are invited to look beneath the surface through a dream sequence involving the boy Ali (Cihat Bütün) as he falls asleep while listening to the adults prattling with one another. He sees himself asleep in bed, with his mother tucking him up, which is followed by a shot of pigeons sitting on the window-sill outside. Ceylan cuts to a shot of the tortoise turned upside down, feebly moving its legs. Ali sees his mother once again performing *namaz*, the prayer ritual undertaken five times a day; he wakes up in a cold sweat and notices that his mother has assumed a body position strangely reminiscent of the tortoise. The final image depicts the upturned reptile once more. Guilt has overwhelmed him as he understands the consequences of his past action. What began as a childish prank turns out to be a crime against nature. Ali has failed to recognize the importance of Mother Anatolia to human existence; the sounds, sights, and smells of all creatures, the dawn chorus, the sunrise and sunset, and the sky alternately light and dark. To enjoy such sensations cannot guarantee survival, but it helps us to forge a deeper relationship to our universe, transcending material concerns.[8]

By comparison Saffet's mental anguish seems superficial, and so it proves in a *dénouement* emphasizing the importance of forging close links to our environment. As the thunder rolls in the background, Dede shuts himself up in his house and thereby cuts himself off from nature. Meanwhile Asiye exits the house and crosses the now-deserted landscape. She plays with her hairband and puts her hands in a pool of water, creating ripples as she does so. Ataol Behramoğlu's poem "The Song of Time Passing" uses repetition to denote the spiritual effect of understanding our proximity to the elements:

> The days they flow flow yes they flow
> They flow yes they flow days of my youth
>
> The wheels they spin spin yes they spin
> They spin yes they spin days of my youth
>
> The belts they pass pass yes they pass
> They pass yes they pass days of my youth
>
> And time it flows yes it flows
> They flow yes they flow days of my youth
>
> (70)

The image of reconciliation between humanity and the environment contrasts with the basic scenario of *Mayıs Sıkıntısı* (*Clouds of May*), where aspiring filmmaker Muzaffer (Muzaffer Özdemir) returns to his hometown of Yenice from İstanbul with the intention of making a documentary, with his parents (M. Emin and Fatma Ceylan) in leading roles. Suner notes that the film provides a "self-reflexive exploration of the theme of homecoming," with Muzaffer, "a young director, just like Ceylan himself, returning to his hometown to make a film about it" (126). Although the self-reflexive elements are significant, Ceylan appears far more interested in the difficulties experienced by the visual media in their attempts to communicate lived experience. At best they can only play what Uzuner terms an "as if" game, whose elements only pretend to be authentic: "To behave AS IF you're happy, to act AS IF you're just, to talk AS IF you're honest, . . . to show emotion AS IF it was red, to cry AS IF you were a crocodile, and so on" (*Balık*, 35). The shortcomings of this approach are emphasized when Muzaffer looks for Pire Amca (a villager playing himself) in the hope of persuading him to perform some traditional dances for the benefit of the camera as well as to speak about his past life. Pire dutifully recites the script but does not appear to understand what he is expected to say: dissatisfied with the old man's efforts, Muzaffer and his brother Saffet (M. Emin Toprak) pay their respects and leave. In truth Pire has some profound observations to make about his past, the shortness of life, and death's omnipresence, but Muzaffer clearly isn't interested as he idly plays with some nutshells while waiting for the old man to finish. All he cares about is reproducing the superficialities of rural life—those quaint rituals that might interest urban cinema audiences. Ceylan underlines the futility of Muzaffer's enterprise by contrasting his efforts with an expansive pan of the landscape, capturing some of its ontological mysteries.[9]

The director's criticisms resemble those made by his contemporaries: the television quacking relentlessly in the background with no one watching indicates the extent to which people take the media for granted. The efforts of Muzaffer's father to recite the script recall the sequences in Demirkubuz's *Üçüncü Sayfa* where the actors are seen rehearsing and performing a soap opera. Muzaffer calls "Action!" and Emin repeats the lines, with Saffet acting as prompter: "Well . . . here I am . . . Earning my living as a farmer. What difference does it make? Nothing matters. But then, neither do I want to die. If God allows, I want to live at least for another twenty years." Emin's efforts to sound convincing become comical; at one point Muzaffer points out that each false take will cost the filmmaker another ten million Turkish lira. Theoretically, movies preserve the past for all time; through grainy black-and-white images we can learn something about our ancestors' ways of life. In practice this seldom happens: the media can only offer a superficial representation of experience. Young Ali (Muhammad Zimbaoğlu) visits his aunt's house and discovers a yellowing photograph of his relatives in a broken frame. He walks up the road and stuffs it into a crevasse in a dry-stone wall. The image is nothing more than a plaything, to be picked up and forgotten about immediately afterward.

The implication is obvious; the elements can only be appreciated through direct experience. *Mayıs Sıkıntısı* suggests that such sensations are under threat: a large slice of Emin's land is about to be seized by the government, even though it has been in the family's possession for generations. Saffet has been forced to work in a factory in an ambiance where no one cares for anything except money. He leans against a pile of used tires, a painful reminder of the apparently inexorable march of progress, with trucks bringing building supplies on newly created roads. Muzaffer actively embraces the urban way of life—at the end of the film he returns to İstanbul but refuses to take his brother with him. It is better for Saffet to remain "safe" in his hometown. In a single phrase, Muzaffer sums up the ideological opposition that continues to dominate mainstream Turkish cultures over the past quarter century: whereas urban development might destroy the landscape, it is perceived as vital to the country's future health. Anyone contemplating a successful career should participate in this new world. To remain wedded to the landscape is considered reactionary, an implicit denial of the republic's ability to compete economically with its partners in the East as well as the West.

As with all Ceylan's films, however, things are seldom that clear-cut. He told James Wood in a 2005 interview that he was "interested in the inner life of the people" in contemporary Anatolia (27–28), which changed after industrialization. Aziz Nesin's short story "Corruption Unlimited" tells of a *nouveau riche* man claiming that all his wealth has been distributed "in a most fair manner, keeping all canons of justice in view," even though he keeps his "own share of the 'booty' to the last penny," giving him the chance to have "a highly enjoyable life" (142–43, 145). This satiric tale emphasizes the destructive effect of wealth on personal morality. Ceylan expresses a similar view as he shows Ali leaving school and gazing in a shop window at a digital watch. The boy's covetous desires soon change, as Muzaffer's friend Sadık (Sadık İncesu) shows the little boy a musical cigarette lighter. The fact that it serves no useful purpose doesn't matter; it's the thrill of possession that matters to him. Ali admits he does not want the lighter any more, but the watch instead. We might dismiss his shifting views as childish whims but nonetheless understand how materialism blinds individuals to the beauties of the world they inhabit and the people within it. Ali could be much happier if he exercised his imagination, unburdened by the desire for trinkets.

In another sequence the entire family visits Çanakkale to view the Gallipoli monument: we might recall Tolga Örnek's treatment of the subject, in which ordinary soldiers were embroiled in a conflict they knew nothing about but, nonetheless, were brought together by the experience of adversity. In *Mayıs Sıkıntısı* no one appears particularly concerned with the area's historical significance. Sadık stops by a convenient bush to relieve himself, while Muzaffer keeps his movie camera rolling in the hope of securing some more material. After spending a requisite length of time at the site, the family takes a selfie next to the Straits, the sun setting behind them in a russet glow. Ceylan cuts to a quick close-up of the sea followed by another scene showing Emin performing once more in Muzaffer's film.

Mayıs Sıkıntısı has an upbeat ending, despite the impending destruction of Emin's property. Ali is told to keep a hen's egg in his pocket for thirty-five days; if he accomplishes this task successfully, he will have his watch. Time passes without incident until he carried a basket of tomatoes to a fellow villager; as he bends down to pick the basket up after taking a breather, the egg breaks. Looking furtively to the right of the camera to see if anyone is watching, he chases two hens into a farmyard, grabs their eggs, and flees. The promise has been kept in his family's view. The folkloric aspect of this ritual might be apocryphal, but Ali's determination to keep the egg intact recalls Semih Kaplanoğlu's film of the same name (*Yumurta*), released eight years after *Mayıs Sıkıntısı*, wherein everyday objects remind us of the timelessness of the universe. It's not the egg that matters, but its associations with new life and the birth of creation, a fundamental aspect of Mother Anatolia.[10] The little boy's dedication adumbrates the end of Ceylan's film, as Emin remains on the family homestead while Muzaffer and Sadık return to İstanbul, their film unfinished. Emin fetches water and begins his time-honored rituals—putting out the fire that burned all night beneath the trees, and picking up the detritus everyone has left behind. Ceylan cuts to a close-up of him picking up Ali's unbroken egg and savoring the morning air, with the mist lifting and the birds announcing the dawn. He eats a pear and dozes in the shadow of an oak tree—as he does so, the camera tilts upward to show the sun rising and setting. He appears to be communing with nature in a ritual that transcends time and space, a visual equivalent of the state of being described by Yahya Kemal:

> They that have fallen asleep with the beloved,
> And in that paradise pure pleasure have enjoyed,

Forgetting the world as they do for a time,

. . . .

O Communion! Shelter under thy spell the lover,
O sweet and heavenly night! Go on forever.

("Vuslat," 69)

As in *Kasaba*, Ceylan acknowledges inspiration from Chekhov in *Mayıs Sıkıntısı*. Nonetheless the melancholic aspect of Chekhovian writing has been set aside at the film's end as Emin understands the power of living in and for the moment.

The plot of *Uzak* (2002) emphasizes how difficult it can be to achieve this elevated mental state. The film completes Ceylan's provincial trilogy and deals with the kind of issues of acclimatization (or lack thereof) that have repeatedly cropped up throughout this book. Yusuf (Mehmet Emin Toprak) quits provincial life in Yenice for the bright lights of İstanbul: he is seen searching for Mahmut's apartment in the back streets of Beyoğlu. He turns right and knocks on a door; no one answers. In a neighboring block Kamil (Feridun Koç), a *kapıcı* (janitor), emerges on the way to the local grocery to run errands for a resident. Too busy to talk to anyone, he scuttles away from the camera. A woman comes out from another block, exchanges glances with Yusuf, and makes an awkward detour to avoid speaking to him. An elderly couple passes by, oblivious to his presence. As a stranger to a tight-knit community, no one wants to know him; he represents a threatening presence, especially when he touches a parked car and accidentally triggers the alarm. Another resident looks out of a first-floor window, scowls at Yusuf, and silences it with a gadget. The entire sequence has been shot in one take with no extraneous noise on the soundtrack save for the ringing of one resident's mobile phone. The silence speaks volumes as an expression of fear of the outsider: city life divides rather than unifies, as people confine themselves to their concrete fiefdoms without making any effort to embrace the stranger. Their indifference appears to fulfill the prophecy expressed by comic writer Ferhan Şensoy in 1992:

> Just play the dumb
> And have fun
> It's in full view before you.
> Save it nobody would dare
> Do you think the owners care?
> Let me tell you the moral of the story
> In the beginning of the play,

In case the audience is fickle as the city
Having sat a while, might not stay
. . . .
"Reach out to the skies, and find your concrete seat
You heavenscraper! What if the sky is a block of concrete?"

(81)

Once Yusuf discovers Mahmut's apartment and Mahmut decides—albeit reluctantly—to accommodate him, the two make every effort to avoid one another. Mahmut spends most nights slumped in an armchair watching television; he is mostly positioned at the center of the frame, forcing Yusuf to the periphery. Mahmut seldom pays attention to what he watches; the television functions as a means by which to avoid talking. In one sequence a power outage plunged the apartment into darkness as we hear a door creaking open. The lights come on again, revealing Mahmut and Yusuf facing one another to the left and right of the frame, the gulf between them emphasizing their reluctance to communicate. There follows a long and painful silence only interrupted by the creak of a window frame as Yusuf turns his back on Mahmut and quits the living room.

Diane Sippi comments on how Ceylan follows the example of the Russian director Andrey Tarkovsky by exposing "the character's interior" through spatial means as well as through clever management of the sets (37). In *Koza* and *Kasaba* the window frames denote imprisonment; in *Uzak* Ceylan extends that metaphor by showing how windows provide a convenient obstacle preventing Mahmut from talking to Yusuf. As Yusuf retires to the balcony to smoke and stare at the forbidding urban landscape, Mahmut remains indoors, slumped in the armchair. The film incorporates at least two direct references to Tarkovsky; in one of them Mahmut watches *Stalker* (1979) while Yusuf is in the living room but switches to a porn film once the young man leaves. Mahmut's friends taunt him about his quixotic dream to quit his profession as a photographer and pass the time like Tarkovsky in search of the perfect shot. While such references remind us of Ceylan's knowledge of European filmmakers, they also underline the barrenness of Mahmut's existence. While claiming to Yusuf that his move from the country to the city has been a success, his true aspirations dissipated long ago. Hoping to become a successful filmmaker in his own right, he now spends his days making commercials for tiles and other disposable commodities (Maheshwari). Mahmut's life reminds us of why Muzaffer returns to his hometown to make a film in *Mayıs Sıkıntısı*; with little or no prospect of advancement, both of them have reached dead ends career-wise.

Ceylan makes astute use of light as well as space. In one shot Yusuf talks on the phone to his mother; his face illuminated by a chink of light at the center of an otherwise darkened frame. The shot reappears, only this time Mahmut listens to Yusuf outside the door. Another sequence depicts Mahmut's ex-wife Nazan (Zuhal Gencer) in the bathroom, a light focusing on her face as she speaks. Meanwhile Mahmut can be seen in darkness lying on his bed. Ceylan cuts to Mahmut's darkened study, with Nazan exiting into the illuminated hallway, closing the door behind her. The camera tracks back to Mahmut shrouded in darkness as he buries his face in his hands. The fact that he is so often photographed like this not only suggests something about his isolated existence but also denotes his reluctance to form close relationships. He is much happier prying into others' lives to maintain dominance over them.

In exterior sequences Ceylan's use of light tells us something about life in contemporary İstanbul. As in Zaim's *Tabutta Rövaşata*, the Bosphorus is represented as a harsh, unforgiving expanse of gray: both protagonists sit alone on the shore, staring wanly out to sea. The weather proves equally unforgiving: Yusuf trudges the streets of Kadıköy looking for work, the slate-gray sidewalks obscured by snow. Alone in a park, with the evening fog descending rapidly, he thrusts his hands moodily into his pockets as he watches two children throwing snowballs at one another. Next day he shelters from the snow by entering a *kıraathane* frequented by sailors. Condensation prevents anyone from looking out of the filthy windows, while steam rises from the patrons' sodden overalls. The scene represents a microcosm of an unforgiving city where the elements turn against humankind, an ambiance vividly described in a stream of consciousness narration by Murat Gülsoy: "[This is a place] where it's easy to get lost or thought to be but you can't when you want, . . . rushing up and down up and down that road over and over again no time to stop. . . . no one cares about anyone no one knows anyone plus what is this place what kind of a city is this . . . welcome to the city" ("Welcome," 214–15). Ceylan's use of darkened lights and confined spaces denotes the confinement and repetitiousness of the protagonists' lives. We witness them cooped up in their apartment, unable (or perhaps unwilling) to acknowledge new experiences in a manner described by psychologist Jean Piaget in the late forties: "Repetition does not engender implication but that it appears only in the course of repetition, since implementation is the internal product of the assimilation that ensures the repetition of the external act" (97). Put more straightforwardly, we understand the implications of the repetitive act, and thereby assimilate it: adaptation occurs when we see the act repeated in different contexts and work out the implications of that act. The experience of watching *Uzak* reveals Mahmut's and Yusuf's reluctance to adapt to a harsh world, and, thereby, they simply go through the motions of existence.

Ceylan reinforces this sense of pointlessness through visual symbols, a technique first encountered in *Mayıs Sıkıntısı*. Mahmut torments Yusuf over the theft of a pocket watch that Yusuf never stole: we are reminded of that sequence when Ali coveted a watch in a local shop window. It is nothing more than a commodity designed to satisfy consumer desires, a product of the disposable world of capitalism. The fact that the two come to blows over it in *Uzak* reveals how far away they are from recognizing that true value emerges from reconciliation with the outside world. In another sequence in a photographic studio, Mahmut rolls two eggs across the floor, recalling Ali's adventures with the egg in his pocket in *Mayıs Sıkıntısı*. In *Uzak* the eggs serve as a painful reminder of a lost world of creation and tranquility, valueless in material terms but providing spiritual nourishment instead.

As the third film in the provincial trilogy, *Uzak* exposes the truth lurking behind the myth that moving from the country to the city automatically leads to prosperity. This is a familiar refrain in contemporary Turkish films; what distinguishes Ceylan's treatment is the way in which he uses light, space, and narrative to reinforce his points. Repetition in *Mayıs Sıkıntısı* or *Kasaba* assumes a positive construction—a rehearsal of rural traditions underpinning humanity's relationship to the elements. By contrast, repetition in *Uzak* denotes the opposite, a series of empty rituals passing the time. It is a confining film as well as a film about confinement, photographed in drab colors (by Ceylan himself) as opposed to the brightness of his two previous features. Its pessimistic aura is summed up in the final shot of the Bosphorus on another gray morning; the seagulls cry but Mahmut pays little heed to them. The camera moves tighter and tighter on his expressionless face as the wind begins to howl. He looks straight into the lens, his eyes blank, almost hollowed out; after one or two beats, the screen fades to black. Although the weather might change for the worse, he remains oblivious to it; in despair, he sees and hears nothing.

Rediscovering Mother Anatolia:
İklimler (2006) and *Kış Uykusu* (2014)

Previous critics have described the tripartite structure of *İklimler* and the way Ceylan constructs the narrative around three seasons—summer, autumn, and winter (Diken 84-100). This represents an extension of the director's concern with people's relationship to the environment, in this case Anatolia, the land of the Mother Goddess, the personification of nature, fertility, and destruction.

In both *İklimler* and *Kış Uykusu* he shows how the protagonists have become so wrapped up in their lives that they no longer appreciate where they came from or where they will end up.

The tone is set in the opening sequence of *İklimler* where İsa (Ceylan) takes photographs in the ancient city of Antiphellus near Kaş in the south of the republic.[11] His partner Bahar (Ebru Ceylan) watches him from the top of a hill; her expressions rapidly change from boredom to concern (as she sees İsa falling over) to indifference and despair.[12] The camera zooms in from her face to the tears trickling down her cheeks, while in the background birds chirrup and a bee buzzes. The sight of the columns set against a cloudless sky, coupled with the sounds of nature, emphasize timelessness: the site has remained the same since the early years of the previous millennium and will be untouched in the future. Neither İsa nor Bahar grasp the significance of their environment; like Mahmut in *Uzak*, İsa takes photos for professional reasons (to help him with his university classes), while Bahar cannot see beyond her self-pity. They could be anywhere: location does not matter. Ceylan emphasizes their emotional and physical imprisonment in the next sequence as they are photographed inside their car driving to the seafront. The windshield separates their faces from the camera lens as well as denotes a reluctance on their part to taste the sights, sounds, and smells of the coast road.

Later on we observe the ill-matched couple on a motorcycle returning to Kaş along a deserted track. The sequence commences with a shot of them in the far distance, their vehicle a speck on the horizon with the mountains dominating the foreground. Ceylan cuts to a tracking shot of the two driving apparently without a care in the world, followed by a stop-frame of Bahar putting her hands over İsa's eyes as they crash to the ground.[13] The sun sets inexorably behind the mountains as she walks out of shot, ignoring his entreaties to come back. İsa picks up the bike, watches her retreating into the distance, and glances out to sea as a boat chugs across the horizon. The sequence sums up the protagonists' detachment from the world: Bahar remains indifferent to it, while İsa looks out across a watery expanse, understanding as he does so his inability to reunite with the elements. He returns to Antephellus in the hope of rediscovering inspiration among the ruins. Life continues unruffled around him: birds fly hither and thither while a cock crows, signaling the break of a new day. İsa once again appears as a speck in the background, followed by a medium shot of him standing in the middle of the ruins, the shadows of the columns projected across his torso. Thunder rolls in the background as he takes another photograph, suggesting how nature takes revenge against those who dare to capture its glories within a camera lens.

The film's second movement takes place in and around İstanbul's İstiklâl Caddesi during autumn. The urban landscape is as bleak as that of *Uzak*: rain falls in torrents, forcing the locals to scurry for cover. For İsa life remains as meaningless, if not more so, as in Kaş: Bahar has walked out on him, leaving him to find whatever solace he can in the arms of Serap (Nazan Kırılmış). The sex scenes between the two of them are both violent and claustrophobic, unfolding in a sparsely furnished living room with Serap tearing İsa's sweatshirt and being pinned to the ground as a result, as İsa pulls her panties down prior to the sex act. Bülent Diken summarizes the violent motives for such behavior: İsa needs to "get rid of the violence within himself. . . . There is something he cannot handle in his soul; . . . with this violence another violence will go away" (90). Unable to mend his relationship with the world, he becomes bestial instead by exploiting someone weaker than himself.

Our focus of attention in this sequence centers not on the protagonists but on other aspects of the *mise-en-scène*. Thunder rolls once more outside, while raindrops trickle down the barred windows. A phone rings unanswered as the characters pursue their lovemaking, while Ceylan cuts to a close-up of a walnut on the floor beside Serap's head. The two are so self-centered that they neither talk to anyone else nor make any efforts to alleviate their voluntary imprisonment. The nut reminds us of the time of year this sequence takes place (they are customarily harvested in September and October).

The final act shows no improvement in İsa's condition as he ventures into the frozen wastes of Doğubeyazit in the east in a final attempt to win back Bahar's affections.[14] Ceylan once again emphasizes his insignificance in the universal scheme of things by photographing him at a distance, a small bleak figure in an otherwise whitened environment. Oblivious to anyone or anything else, he confronts Bahar in a series of confined spaces—a seedy café, the television production company van, a dirty hotel room. While protesting that he has transformed himself into "a different person," we understand how his sentiments are as insincere as those of Alper in *Issız Adam*. The weather—heavy snowfall followed by fog—sums up his inability to see either himself or others clearly; but as ever İsa pays little or no heed to his surroundings. He trudges off to Bahar's workplace to watch a film crew in the process of making a soap opera: a woman (Ceren Olcay) howls as she crouches next to a grave, while a man with a gun (Abdullah Demirkubuz) sidles up behind her. The sequence ends abruptly as the sound of a low-flying aircraft becomes too disturbing. Ceylan cuts to a medium close-up of Bahar watching the plane, followed by a long shot of Doğubeyazit under heavy snow with dogs barking off-screen. The fact that Bahar is so involved in a fictional representation of life renders her as myopic as her one-time partner. There is a brief hint at redemption in the hotel room, as Bahar briefly opens up and tells İsa of her beautiful dream of perfect sunshine and green meadows, where she could fly like a bird unencumbered by life's vicissitudes. This is followed by an imaginative recreation of a cemetery, with her mother (Fatma Ceylan) waving at her. She reveals a depth of insight hitherto unknown to us: death is not a final reckoning but an opportunity to reunite with Mother Anatolia. We should embrace freedom and move seamlessly from place to place in accordance with the movements of the seasons. Predictably İsa understands not one iota of what Bahar has said, as he asks her what time she will be on set the next morning. His mental myopia can be summed up by Yahya Kemal's poem "Longing," where the speaker, "lonesome and sad," yearns for those "summer days" when he and his beloved used "to chat over the hills at dawn" or watch the sun "vanishing over the horizon of sea" before returning to the village in a "dreamy" state. The fact that such visions are palpably fictional eludes the speaker ("Özleyen," 73).

Kış Uykusu can be viewed as a meditation on the third part of *İklimler*. Set in Cappadochia during the depths of winter, the action concentrates on Aydın, a retired stage actor (Bilginer) who runs the Hotel Othello while writing a column (under the pseudonym "Voice of the Steppes") for the local newspaper. Despite the remoteness of the location, the hotel attracts Japanese tourists (Masaki Murao, Junko Yokomizo) and provides a venue for local gatherings. Recent writing on Turkish cultures represents the region as a center of multiculturalism, especially during the final years of the Ottoman Empire. Hivren Demir-Atay discusses the fortunes of a translation of Edgar Allan Poe's short story "The Black Cat," which appeared in 1889 in Karamanlıdıka, using an orthography pioneered by the orthodox Christians of Cappadochia, thereby "illustrating both . . . Ottoman multiculturalism" as well as a prevailing tolerance for members of different religious faiths (131–32). Sadly, it seems that Aydın cannot recreate this spirit of tolerance in the present. His writings are full of diatribes against urban ugliness in rural Anatolia, as witnessed in his tenant Hamdi's (Serhat Kılıç's) shack, which has been ruined by the pile of rusting scrap metal left outside. Ceylan emphasizes the hotelier's distaste by means of a series of intercut close-ups between Aydın's Land Rover, a symbol of prosperity, the scrapheap, and shots of Aydın scowling at the sight in front of him.

Unable to pay the outstanding dues on his property, Hamdi comes to the hotel to plead his case. He peeps over the exterior wall into Aydın's wife Nihal's (Melisa Sözen's) well-appointed bedroom, prior to entering Aydın's study. Once inside, Aydın stares distastefully at Hamdi's muddy boots, prompting Hamdi to shift uncomfortably from foot to foot as if painfully aware of committing a social *faux pas* by not removing them. The action shifts forward to the evening;

as Aydın writes his next column, he describes the importance of religion being practiced by "neat, cultivated men of God who can uphold İslam as a religion of high culture and cleanliness." The *hodja* Hamdi clearly cannot meet such standards. Bearing in mind the significance attached to mud in Zaim's *Çamur*, it's clear that Aydın has no real grasp of Mother Anatolia and its people: religion has little spiritual significance, despite his desire for respectability. Mud might be natural, the product of the earth, but for him it denotes a lack of education. Aydın prefers to create an ersatz Turkish "culture" designed to appeal to foreigners, as represented by the earthenware clay pots put on display outside the hotel entrance. The interior décor is a mish-mash of objects: old playbills compete for our attention with Native Indian masks and ephemera from Aydın and Nihal's foreign travels, not to mention a photo of Omar Sharif, who evidently stayed there while filming *Monsieur İbrahim* (2003).[15]

Aydın assumes a Prospero-like omniscience over his kingdom — a world where men of God are expected to be clean and tidy and the landscape should be equally well kept. The irony of his situation is palpable: human beings cannot control Mother Anatolia but should rather accommodate themselves to her without expecting any reward, either material or otherwise. The acquisition of such self-knowledge has been vividly outlined in Bilge Karasu's novel *Gece* (*Night*) (written in the mid-seventies but not published in Turkish until a decade later, with the English translation remaining unpublished until 1994). One of the narrators views himself as "the power, the puppet master . . . responsible for making the decisions, setting the objectives, and coming up with the ideas" (126). He realizes that "we must give up yielding to the magic of words that are nothing more than clichés and sentimentalities." Once we accomplish that process and acknowledge the deity's perpetual presence, "our feelings, thoughts, and words finally become our own" (129). Aydın remains a slave to narcissism and thereby condemns himself to a life of perpetual role play; an actor performing on a self-created stage. In a climactic sequence, his sister Necla (Demet Akbağ) criticizes his naïve love for the romantic ideal of Anatolia and the Steppes that renders him impervious to anything happening around him.

Murat Nemet-Nejat, in an introduction to a collection of twentieth-century Turkish poetry, looks at the notion of *eda* as a register of the soul coming to terms with the world. It can be best defined as "the alien other, . . . the Asiatic mode of perception which contains an intense subjectivity at its center, . . . the distinction (any distinction) does not truly exist; 'it' (a bird, for example) is a link between the divine (he/she/it) and human (he/she) with the constant possibility of movement between them" (15-16). Gilles Deleuze offers a further definition of this state of being, "made up of qualities, substances, powers, and events. . . . The trajectory merges not only with the subjectivity of those who travel through a milieu, but also with the subjectivity of the milieu itself insofar as it is reflected in those who travel through it" (61). *Kış Uykusu* questions whether Aydın or his family have any awareness of *eda*'s significance, especially in terms of their relationship to the Anatolian landscape. Aydın embarks on a hunting expedition; he shoots a rabbit but derives no real pleasure from his kill. Ceylan photographs him driving home, his face scarcely visible behind the windshield. Once inside the hotel once more, he pleads with Nihal to stay (she had previously indicated her wish to leave him for good), then looks wistfully out the window at the snow-covered landscape outside. The action shifts to an interior shot of him facing his computer in an overstuffed study, looking once more out a barred window. Sitting in his self-created prison in almost total darkness, save for the glow of the screen, he begins his proposed *magnum opus* on the history of the Turkish theater. He can do little else other than reflect on what might have been, in terms of his complicated personal life as well as his ontological future. His decision to write about the theater underlines his devotion to acting, something he has pursued throughout his life. Unable to unify himself with his surroundings—a state of mind symbolized by the bars across his window—he resumes his "winter sleep," a half-life shared by many of Ceylan's male protagonists.

What about "Politics"?
Üç Maymun (2008) and Bir Zamanlar Anadolu'da (2011)

So far we have seen that while Ceylan reflects on the past, present, and future of humanity in general, he does not appear to be concerned with contemporary politics. In *Üç Maymun* (*Three Monkeys*) he redresses the balance somewhat; set just after the AKP (Justice and Development Party) election victory of 22 July 2009 (when they scooped 46 percent of the total vote), the film begins with a car accident on an isolated road.[16] Rain falls, thunder rolls, lightning flashes; it is difficult to see what happens. All we know is that the alleged suspect has driven off. Later it turns out that high-ranking AKP official Servet (Ercan Kesal) was at the wheel, but he has persuaded his driver Eyüp (Yavuz Bingöl) to take responsibility—and serve the jail sentence—in exchange for a lump sum of money. This scenario recalls Zaim's *Filler ve Çimen* in the way it shows politicians exploiting others for self-serving purposes. They are seldom interested in the people they allegedly represent.

Ceylan's interest in politics centers chiefly on the way it affects our daily lives. Eyüp's wife Hacer (Hatice Aslan) and son İsmail (Ahmet Rıfat Sungar) inhabit a rickety house in the suburbs of İstanbul adjoining a railway line: the regular sound of trains clattering past continually interrupts their lives. Their living room has a wide window opening out onto the landscape, with the Bosphorus in the background, while three doors separate the living room from the kitchen and the two bedrooms. The interior setting sums up the residents' lives; the windows and the doors denote their imprisonment, both emotional as well as physical, as they are unable to enjoy the sea view owing to pressure of work. Hacer works all hours in a local restaurant, including evenings; she barely earns enough money to survive, let alone prosper.

In such contexts it is hard not to accept financial help, even if it comes with strings attached. Hacer strikes up a friendship with Servet, which predictably culminates in the two of them going to bed together. The barrenness of this relationship is summed up in a shot of the two of them traveling in an official car, whose side windows prevent us from seeing their faces properly (also suggesting confinement). All we can hear is Servet talking monotonously about politics—especially his future within the AKP hierarchy. In the background the Bosphorus reminds us of how far removed the two of them are from the spiritual world. In such situations we feel very much like the poet Güven Turan in "Gizli Alanlar" (Secret Domain):

> Clouds gather and disperse
> no sun
> lurks in the corner of the window
>
> Nothing
> that comes into the world
> will be illumined
>
> Again it's hard
> to be content
> with words only.

(83)

The shortcomings of Hacer's life are set against the idealized world conjured up by seventies pop music (recreated on the soundtrack by Yıldız Tilbe) and Yeşilçam films and heard at moments of extreme despair—for example, when Hacer vows to repay Servet the money she has borrowed from him, although she has no means to do so. While the music plays in the background, Hacer watches Servet leaving her house after making love to him and subsequently takes a shower in a futile attempt to wash his sweat off her body. In a third sequence staged on an expanse of wasteground, Hacer declares undying love for Servet; he dismisses her abruptly and threatens to kill her if she comes near him anymore. This is a familiar situation from Yeşilçam; it should be followed by a retributive sequence in which the bad guy meets a violent end. Nothing similar happens in *Üç Maymun*: Hacer has to cope as best she can while Servet escapes scot free. The sequence concludes with a gust of wind that threatens to blow the politician's jacket into the Bosphorus—despite all his machinations, he remains at the elements' mercy.

The past casts a malign shadow over the present—perhaps more so than any other Ceylan film. İsmail sleeps in his bedroom, but wakes up with a start: the screen turns sepia as the door creaks open and the curtains blow in the wind. A little boy (Gürkan Aydın) enters soaking wet and calls out, *"Ağabey!"* (Brother). We discover that this is the ghost of İsmail's younger brother who drowned in tragic circumstances several years previously. Fate remains indifferent to human suffering, as Turan suggests:

> The resolve
> of a swell out to sea
>
> Naked sky
> Reflected
> in little tremors
> leeward
>
> Sunlight
>
> Weary of summer
> the shore
>
> is content to watch.
> ("Gizli Alanlar," 73)

One reaction might be to accept that the boy has reunited with nature; no one can possibly harm him. Yet the family cannot bear the loss so stoically; the memory of it prompts Eyüp into beating up his wife, especially when she rejects his amorous advances following his release from prison.

The family reenacts what happened to many Anatolians during and after the creation of the republic. They simply did not belong to the brave new world of capitalism (178). Nonetheless they could take comfort from the belief that

Anatolian cultures are transhistorical: Mother Anatolia represents "the essence of every form. You know all, but none can know you. . . . Only you are inexplicable and irreconcilable. . . . You have no beginning but you are the beginning of all" (Egemen 51). In *Üç Maymun* the family's connection to the Mother has been severed, thereby consigning them to a hand-to-mouth existence. Their plight is summed up in a lengthy shot toward the end, as Hacer stands aimlessly by the Sea of Marmara, accompanied by the sounds of a boat engine, dogs barking, and the gentle hiss of the waves. İsmail stands next to her but neither speaks nor looks toward her. Ceylan shifts the action further forward to show İsmail standing alone once more in the family kitchen while Eyüp lies silently on his bed. The ghost of the dead son is shown leaving the house, presumably to return.

The "Three Monkeys" of the film's title refer to the family whose lives are so emptied of meaning that they resemble performing animals carrying out their masters' bidding. Hacer works in the restaurant, Eyüp goes to prison for a crime he did not commit, while İsmail suffers a beating for involving himself in criminal activity. Eyüp seeks solace by entering a mosque; he watches everyone praying but finds himself incapable of participating. The deity cannot help him now. He stands outside his home once more, looking at the sea. Thunder rolls and rain starts to fall in torrents. The camera slowly tracks backward, so that, in the end, Eyüp resembles nothing more than a dot on a vast horizon as the screen fades to black. While the film makes some mild criticisms of the politicians' efforts to maintain their position at whatever cost, Ceylan is far more interested in how ordinary people's lives have been ruined. Eyüp and his family's lives resemble those vividly described in Bedri Rahmi Eyüboğlu's "İstanbul Destanı" (İstanbul Saga):

> Girls turn a trick all day long on their feet
> Sad and soaked in sweat
> Long faces long hands long days
> Windows up high close to the ceiling
> No daydreamers these fine girls with aching feet
> Outside are rows and rows of trees
> Walls walls high walls.
>
> (140–41)

Bir Zamanlar Anadolu'da shifts attention from national to local politics—specifically the investigation of the murder of Yaşar (Erol Eraslan) by the Ankara-based police force and the efforts of prosecutor Nusret (Taner Birsel) to determine precisely what happened, so that he can compile an accurate report.[17] He carries out the task with admirable thoroughness, accompanying the police from the scene of the crime to several local villages and subsequently attending the autopsy conducted by Cemal (Muhammet Uzuner). The basic scenario serves as a framework for another disquisition on humanity's relationship to the Anatolian landscape. The tone is set early on with a series of pans of the countryside at night, the mountains scarcely visible in the gloom; in the distance car headlamps burn like fireballs. The chief murder suspect Kenan (Fırat Tanış) is being taken to where Yaşar has been ostensibly buried: the only snag being that Kenan cannot remember the precise location, thereby forcing the group to travel nomadically from place to place. This analogy is not as far-fetched as it might seem: Ceylan invokes long-established traditions to indicate humanity's connection to the universe. Commissioner Naci (Yılmaz Erdoğan) expresses the point in a lengthy soliloquy: even if it rains, it makes no difference to Mother Anatolia, as she has been around for generations. By contrast everyone engaged in the fruitless search will have passed away in a century's time; not a trace of them will remain. Anatolia resembles "a fairytale" that draws attention to our mortality; either we accept it or we are doomed to perpetual unhappiness. Naci concludes his soliloquy by biting into an apple; it's time to fill the stomach on a dark and dingy night.

Nusret offers further insight into human insignificance in this region in a brief speech delivered within the confines of a police car. Although a lawyer by profession, he cannot make much sense of life: only Fate dictates what happens in the future. He recounts the possibly apocryphal tale of a woman with prior knowledge of her dying day. Fate might possess her, or she decides to commit suicide; it doesn't matter which. Nusret's sentiments cast doubt over his subsequent behavior; if life is as random as he claims, why does he spend so much time and energy poring over typed documents or attending the autopsy to ensure that due procedures are completed? The lawyer comprehends the futility of his task as he exclaims, "That's it!" and strides out of the morgue, never to return. It doesn't really matter how Yaşar passed away; what matters is that he has been restored to the bosom of Mother Anatolia.

It seems that *Bir Zamanlar Anadolu'da* emphasizes the absurdity of human life and the institutions underpinning it—the law, the medical profession. Far from it: Ceylan preoccupies himself with striking a balance between worldly and spiritual issues as a way of coping with existence. This concern is especially evident in a lengthy sequence taking place in the remote village of Ceceli in Central Anatolia, some seventy-five kilometers from Aksaray. Life here seems to have withstood the test of time: everyone kneels on the ground to eat while the *mukhtar*, or headman (Ercan Kesal), introduces the police officers, Nusret and Kenan, to the local elders. They partake of a communal meal, while discovering how the village youth has mostly migrated to İstanbul or to Germany, leaving most people back home condemned to a life of poverty. After the food has been distributed, the *mukhtar*'s daughter Cemile (Cansu Demirci) offers tea to the assembled company—as she takes it round on a brass tray, the shadows dance on the walls of the mud-brick building. Cemile begins to cry helplessly while Kenan has a ghostly vision of Yaşar sitting opposite him, peacefully sipping his tea.

The sequence is long and complex, transporting us back to a precapitalist world dependent on the seasons, where the villagers willingly endure long and cold winters so as to appreciate spring and summer even more. Mahmut Makal described this way of life as long ago as 1954: "Certainly these months [of spring and summer] more or less give one the strength to stand up to another winter. On such warm days, I find some green meadow in which to do lessons with the children. . . . One forgets the winter, its weariness, its hardships. There's no doubt about it; the sun is one of the greatest blessings. . . . The sound of our poet Yakup Kadri's noble words rings in my ears: 'O sorrowful land, a shame on those who know not how to love thee!'" (25). Being close to the land offers insight into its mysteries, a netherworld where distinctions between life and death assume scant significance. This accounts for Yaşar's unexpected reappearance. Ceylan's choice of names is especially significant, suggesting the fundamental links between human beings; likened to an angel in "a god-forsaken village" (Nusret's term), Cemile's name resembles that of Cemal. We are exposed to a much deeper awareness of ourselves, as described in Özdemir Asaf's "The Everlasting":

> I know well how to love, learnt how to think.
> Felt what dying is while still breathing.
> Now I can open and close every door.
> You understand what these mean.
>
> To you I am coming, only to you
> Without lies, undisguised.
> Shall tell all as it is,
> Know, let them know, let everyone know.
>
> You,
> Strike when strike, laugh when laugh.

> Your voice, your face, your hands, yours—all yours.
> You are the everlasting.
>
> ("Everlasting," 29)

Cemile understands such knowledge, as evidenced when she serves tea, her face illuminated by an antique gas lamp, giving her an otherworldly appearance contrasting with the exhausted masculine faces of the assembled guests. Not that this knowledge entitles her to special treatment; the next morning sees her taking in washing off the line, her hair blowing in the wind, before commencing her apparently endless round of chores.

Compared with this knowledge, most of the officers' activities seem futile. In a comic sequence involving Nusret, one officer produces a laptop and begins to tap something out but cannot decide whether the crime scene is in Sarıçullu or Kızılkullu, two districts divided by a line on a map. There is little or no concrete evidence to resolve the dispute; the only verifiable information they possess is that they are thirty-seven kilometers from Ankara. The comedy continues as the officers discover that they forgot to bring a body bag to take Yaşar's corpse back to the station. All they can do is tie him up, wrap him in a blanket and bundle him into a car trunk. Cemal becomes equally aware of the absurdity of human actions as he performs the autopsy on the corpse, while a group of schoolchildren happily play outside his dungeonlike room. He glances at them, sighs, and resumes his duties as the screen fades to black. There is basically no reason to continue the analysis, but Cemal feels unable to set his task aside. We might be reminded of a highly ironic poem "Yirmibirinci Yüzyılın İnsanlarına Şiirler" ("Songs for the Men of the Twenty-First Century") that first appeared in translation as long ago as 1945. Hasan Dinamo, a contemporary of Nâzım Hikmet, takes a look at life and scornfully asks:

> Aren't you all beautiful!
> Aren't you all at peace?
> Aren't you all happy?
>
> (26)

The answer to this question from Cemal's perspective is palpably no. Although in a socially superior position to Eyüp and Hacer in *Üç Maymun*, his life seems equally pointless as it prevents him from appreciating in any significant way the deeper truths of existence. In a world dependent on rational thought, where every occurrence needs to be thoroughly accounted for, spiritual reflection seems superfluous.

Questioning the Critics

Numerous criticisms have appeared about Ceylan's films, especially since he started gathering prizes at the Cannes Film Festival. In 2015 a book appeared containing several articles published in America, Great Britain, and elsewhere since 2003, with the final contribution dating from 2014. Five were interviews; the remainder consisted of critics' and academics' interpretations. Some of them have already been discussed; writing in 2006, Sippi likens Ceylan to the Iranian director Abbas Kiarostami in his use of the cinematic medium "as a non-didactic way of teaching" (53). Ceylan follows Tarkovsky by puncturing illusions while asserting the need to sustain them. Ali Rıza Taşkale (2008), writing about *İklimler*, draws on Deleuze's notion of the time image to draw a distinction between "old" and "new" strangers to İstanbul: the "new" stranger appears too traditional, too backward to fit into a cosmopolitan world (79). Julie Banks (2010) sees *Uzak* as an exposition of "the mundane nature of everyday life," wherein texture and richness assume more significance than narrative (162). Robert Cardullo believes that *Bir Zamanlar Anadolu'da* "uses the realistic film as an avenue to what lies onward, beyond, and beneath the realism" (237), while the anthology concludes with a piece by Jonathan Romney on *Kış Uykusu*, "as powerful and suggestive as any other Ceylan film. The script plays the long game, setting up early crises that play out much later, . . . a prime instance of the Kuleshov effect . . . [of] quietly but resolutely effective moments" (242). While these views possess their merits, it seems that Ceylan's films somehow remain elusive, especially from critics overzealously trying to categorize his work. When interviewed he has regularly acknowledged inspiration from Kiarostami and Tarkovsky; but this does not necessarily imply similarity in terms of style. Ceylan constructs his films slowly, forcing us to concentrate on the *mise-en-scène*, but that strategy does not suggest a focus on the everyday or whatever lies beneath it. And what exactly is meant by describing the director's fondness for "the long game" with "quietly . . . effective moments"? Do we conclude that he makes his films deliberately lengthy in the belief that other structural forms cannot accommodate "effective moments"? We have here what might be summed up as a conflict of expectations, with critics and reviewers trying to fit Ceylan's narratives into predetermined formal and/or cinematic categories, while the director himself offers experiences that resist such categorization. His narratives are not primarily based on other directors' work, concentrating far more on culture-specific issues such as the relationship between individuals and landscape. As a concept, "story" brings with it the expectation that the film must have a beginning, a middle, and an end, Ceylan deliberately subverts these divisions to show how past, present, and future are perpetually interconnected.[18] We should not approach his view of "history" as a chronicle of past deeds; the past has a profound effect on the ways in which his characters live now. His work is difficult to read (the verb implying that we can draw some kind of conclusions after watching the film), as we are not used to work that concerns itself with states of being and how people change—or do not change—as a result. This preoccupation does not exclude social criticism; many of Ceylan's films are quite vociferous in their comments on the consequences of rural migration to the metropolis, but the director wants to find out how such experiences affect his characters' ontological states. Sometimes we need to shun social and political issues and listen to ourselves. This is no easy task (as Naci and Nusret point out in *Bir Zamanlar Anadolu'da*), but we should aspire to that state of being to understand our position in the universe. Ceylan's characters are required to place themselves in the capacious arms of Mother Anatolia.

By stressing the culturally specific aspects of his oeuvre, I am not for one moment suggesting that Ceylan will prove inaccessible to the non-Turkish viewer. On the contrary, the sheer volume of critical commentary currently available proves the opposite. Yet I do aver that the kernel of the director's work can only be accessed if we set aside previously held assumptions about what constitutes an art house, "new Turkish," slow, or loosely plotted film (the meaning of all these terms depending on the degree to which they depart from or challenge the classical Hollywood structure) and treat Ceylan on his own terms as a native of Anatolia commenting on and rethinking the ways in which his fellow natives adapt (or fail to adapt) to changing times. We should embrace different ways of thinking, for it is only by doing so that we can discover more about ourselves.

Envoi

Discovery Learning

One interesting aspect of the films discussed is that most would probably not have been made if the Republic of Turkey had not opened itself up to the private sector from the last years of Turgut Özal's prime ministerial reign. New investments flourished as never before, while filmmakers could obtain funding from local sources such as TRT and commercial organizations as well as foreign companies and Council of Europe–sponsored initiatives such as Eurimages.[1] Kaplanoğlu's *Bal* was cofunded by Eurimages, ZDF (Germany), the Filmstiftung Nordrhein-Westfalen (also Germany), as well as the Media Program of the European Union, while *Yumurta* was supported by Efes Pilsen. *Kış Uykusu* acknowledged support from Bredok Filmproduction (Germany), while Örnek's *Senin Hikayen* received funding from Çağan Irmak's TAFF Pictures and obtained a foreign distribution deal from Warner Brothers.

The luxury of such funds enables filmmakers to make far-reaching criticisms of the destructive effects of industrial expansion. Although cynics might liken this approach to biting the hand that feeds them (capitalism funds the films, while the directors criticize capitalism), we learn about people equipped with the power to determine their own lives, who choose to pursue dreams of wealth and social status that frequently end unhappily. Temel in Zaim's *Çamur* is murdered by a gang of mobsters for failing to find sufficiently valuable relics, while Ayperi/Hatice in Irmak's *Unutursam Fısılda* has an equally turbulent life—in spite of enjoying the trappings of celebrity, she can only discover true happiness in obscurity with her sister. Alper in *Issız Adam* offers a classic example of someone whose narcissism renders him insensitive to others, especially his girlfriends, even though he enjoys being a well-known İstanbul restaurateur. Over time the pace of urban development has increased rapidly: the suburbs of the Republic's three major cities are ruined by unrestricted building of tower blocks, transforming them into latter-day equivalents of Russian cities under communist rule. Prospective residents are lured into buying properties through mortgages and the illusion of a better life. Many find themselves condemned to prisonlike existences, where they enjoy neither the sun's rays nor the benefits of an unpolluted atmosphere.

I am writing this piece on 19 May, one of the public holidays instituted at the beginning of the Kemalist period, officially titled the Commemoration of Atatürk, Youth and Sports Day (*Atatürk'ü Anma, Gençlik ve Spor Bayramı*). It celebrates Mustafa Kemal's landing at Samsun in the north of the country on 19 May 1919, regarded as the beginning of the Turkish War of Independence. Many of the rituals I can hear—taking place at the athletics track near my home—are designed to forge national unity: children recite poems, make parades, and sing the national anthem to acknowledge their common identity. Atatürk devised a maxim in 1933 that is frequently quoted on such occasions: "Ne Mutlu Türkum Diyene" (How happy is the one who says I am Turkish). Despite the significance of such tenets in daily life—as well as on public holidays—I would argue that the films surveyed in this book resist any attempts at national categorization. To treat Zaim, Kaplanoğlu, and Ceylan as specifically "Turkish" in their preoccupations overlooks their varied social, economic, and cultural backgrounds, encompassing Cyprus as well as different regions of the Turkish mainland. Their work depicts a multicultural world wherein life in the east is represented as very different from İstanbul or the Black Sea. More significantly we discover the importance of the distinction between country and city, not only geographically but psychologically. The shift from national cinemas to alternative constructions (supranational or transnational film) is nothing new: Tim Bergfelder's article on European cinema proposed a framework acknowledging interconnectedness at the levels of content and production (315–31). In the Turkish context Gökçen Karanfil and Serkan Şavk's piece on "Rethinking the Concept of 'Turkish Cinema' in Times of Mobility" argued that "the borders of containment for 'Turkish cinema' have never been so blurred and the vocabulary used to discuss it, is obsolete" (29).[2] Hence Asuman Suner's concept of the "New Turkish Cinema" (coined in 2010), used to describe the work of Ceylan, Zaim, Demibkubuz, and others, already seems outmoded.

I have tried to avoid such categories by invoking different traditions—for example mysticism (as embodied in the work of Rūmī) and the more culture-specific concept of the Mother Goddess Anatolia. To understand the significance of such traditions, and how they underpin many of the films analyzed here, is not quite as straightforward as it seems. If we focus on humanity's relationship to the universe using Rūmī's poetry as an example (as I suggested in my introduction), we should remind ourselves that his work has often been evaluated very differently by Westerners than their Turkish counterparts. İbrahim Garnard has argued that Rūmī was reconstructed as "one of the greatest sufi masters of the past," a representative of that "universal sufi tradition that was viewed as independent of İslam—in other words, he needed to be made into a non-İslamic sufi." This objective persuaded Western translators to render Rūmī "in a non-scholarly, poetic, and more 'alive' manner" (Garnard). Coleman Barks's best-selling versions (quoted in the introduction to this book) have been marketed as "translations," but are based on literal renditions of the Persian source text, some of which omit the term "God" altogether, and alter Rūmī's "prayers" into "spiritual insights." By transforming him from a Persian mystic into a "universal" prophet, the translators have invoked a rhetorical and political tradition described by Immanuel Wallerstein as "European [or American] universalism" (as opposed to "universal universalism") in an attempt to foreground First World—that is, Western—values (78).[3] Their task appears to have been wildly successful, as Franklin D. Lewis suggests:

> Along with self-help and personal improvement material, . . . spiritually driven commuters now unwind to audiobooks of Rumi's poetry as they sit in traffic jams on their way home from a hard day's work. . . . On Lafayette Street in New York City, a clientele of about four hundred people a day at the Jivamukti Yoga Center, including celebrities such as Mary Stuart Masterson and Sarah Jessica Parker, do spiritual aerobics to a background beat that sometimes mixes rock music and readings of Rumi. . . . Anthologies aimed at unchurched Westerners hungry for some form of non-institutional religion or non-traditional spirituality often include Rumi in the company of other visionaries, poets and seers. . . . It simply defies credibility to find Rumi in the realm of haute couture. But models draped in Donna Karan's new black . . . actually flounced down the runway to health guru Deepak Chopra's recent musical versions of Rumi. (7–9)

Enjoying the moment is not an exclusively Western metropolitan phenomenon: spiritual experiences are equally common in Native Indian traditions. Cheyenne Wooden Leg's sentiments (expressed in the nineteenth century) are remarkably close to those of Rūmī: "To 'make medicine' is to engage upon a special period of fasting, thanksgiving, prayer and self-denial, even of self-torture. The procedure is entirely a devotional exercise. The purpose is to subdue the passions of the flesh and to improve the spiritual self" (60).[4] What delineates the Turkish directors' interpretations of the same material is that they view it through the prism of the goddess Mother Anatolia, a tradition quite different from that of European universalism that also refutes alternative constructions such as the "third space," coined by Homi K. Bhabha to describe a means by which opposites (oppressed/oppressor, ruler/subaltern, West/East) can communicate with one another, free—if only temporarily—of hierarchies but embodied in their particularity [xvi]). Through a series of case studies, this book has shown that while the characters are equipped with freedom of choice, they need to be aware of Mother Anatolia's presence in and through the entire universe. Understanding this notion encourages moral and spiritual growth while at the same time fostering the belief that we are servants of nature. Our time on earth is limited; the only way we can discover eternity is to free ourselves from material concerns and unify ourselves with the world. We should give up greed or carnal desires and not be captivated by wealth but understand instead that we are servants of God (Yeniterzi 99-100). Such ideas apply to everyone, irrespective of religion or socioeconomic circumstances. At the end of Zaim's *Gölgeler ve Suretler* Ruhşar and Salih perform Karagöz in front of a refugee audience. Their moment of spiritual happiness might not last long, but it is worth savoring nonetheless. Both Yusuf at the end of Kaplanoğlu's *Bal* and Emin in *Mayıs Sıkıntısı* have similar experiences; the latter realizes that while the government has seized some of his land with no prospect of redress, no one can disrupt his experience of dozing underneath a tree on a sunny day.

This belief system parallels that of the Great Chain of Being, a worldview which, through the Middle Ages and down to the late eighteenth century, many philosophers, scientists, and most educated people embraced. The universe was believed to be divided into an immense number of worlds "ranging in hierarchical order from the meagerest kind of existents, which barely escape non-existence, through 'every possible' grade up to the *ens perfectissimum*, . . . the highest possible creature, between which and the Absolute Being the disparity was assumed to be infinite—every one of them differing from that immediately above and that immediately below it by the 'least possible' degree of difference" (Lovejoy 59). Alexander Pope's *Essay on Man* (1710) emphasizes the significance of this notion for the future of humankind:

> Vast chain of Being! which from God began,
> Natures aethereal, human, angel, man,
> Bear, bird, fish, insect, what no eye can see,
> No glass can reach; from Infinite to thee,
> From there to nothing—On superior pow'rs
> Were we to press, inferior might on ours;

Or in the full creation leave a void,
Where, one step broken, the great scale destroy'd;
From Nature's chain whatever link you strike,
Tenth, or ten thousandth, breaks the chain alike.

(Epistle 1, 237–45)

The great chain sustains the balance of the universe, which has been created by the Supreme Being: should we satisfy our individualistic desires, we are not only conniving against nature but consciously disregarding "the infinity of that power which gives forth from itself to all things" (Lovejoy 62). Those who assume that the world can be better fashioned only do so because they fail to recognize that the ideal state (offered by the Great Chain of Being) actively contains all possible evil. Working for the common good sustains "life stretched out to an immense span, in which each of the parts has its own place in the series, all of them different and yet the whole continuous, and that which precedes never wholly absorbed in that which comes after" (63). Humanity is just one race that provides a link in the chain, neither superior nor inferior to any other living creatures. It is therefore absurd for people to claim that they are more intelligent than other life forms as well as their fellow human beings (65).

Lovejoy ends his book with a discussion of how this belief system collapsed in the Romantic era, when writers considered it restrictive, promoting "uniformity of norms and universality of appeal," while curtailing the potential of the imagination. Ideally humankind should be given the potential to explore the limits of their psychology: "Nothing should be too strange or too remote, nothing too lofty or too low, to be included. . . . No *nuance* of character or emotion can be so delicate or elusive" (306). Romanticism demanded "a perpetual transcendence of the already-attained, for unceasing expansion. Romantic art must be progressive as well as universal" (306).

I don't want to push the parallels between Lovejoy's arguments and Anatolian traditions too far (they are underpinned by quite different worldviews, one deriving from Western rationalism, the other from more spiritual forms of identification). Yet it is nonetheless interesting that, for all its elaborate differentiation between historical periods, Lovejoy's history is structured around the idea of "seamless continuity" that rejects the fundamental contingency and discreteness normally implied by period distinctions (Bahti 33). It is this notion of "seamless continuity" that proves especially intriguing, suggesting a collapse between past, present, and future. While watching the end of *Mayis Sıkıntısı* or *Bal*, I am reminded of my high school days nearly forty years ago, when our educator introduced the concept of the Great Chain of Being through

Shakespeare's *Troilus and Cressida*: "Take but degree away, untune that string, / And hark! what discord follows" (I, iii, 109-10). We were studying *King Lear* at the time and interpreting the old king's decision to divide his kingdom among his three daughters as a break in the chain; the monarch no longer wanted to fulfill his divinely appointed role as ruler of the people, leading to societal destruction. The government's decision to seize some of Emin's land represents a challenge to the order of nature, especially if they cut down trees and shrubs and turn it into a building site. Zaim's *Balık* examines this issue in more detail as Kaya seeks quick riches (as well as satisfying the demands of the local market) by deliberately polluting the lake full of fish. This represents a crime against nature and its inhabitants (encompassing all creatures) as well as Mother Anatolia. The links between two such different experiences emphasize how the writing of this book provided me with a transcultural journey of discovery learning. I discovered for myself a framework analysis that disregards binaries in favor of acknowledging moments in my life as *different* yet *resembling* those in other cultures and/or historical periods.

Yet perhaps I should not be too complacent: several of the filmmakers covered in this book emphasize just how little of the contemporary world we understand; this helps to explain why so many of the male protagonists find it difficult, almost impossible, to communicate with one another. Partly this inability to communicate can be attributed to gender divisions: men like to fraternize with each other in the *kıraathane* while their partners simply exist as sex objects and/or domestic servants. Demirkubuz suggests that unknowability is a consequence of disrupting the balance of nature: if you expect people to live in urban rabbit hutches offering little or no access to the elements, then you cannot expect them to develop their powers of communication. They exist in a physical and emotional vacuum, unable to share thoughts either with their fellow residents or with the deity (through prayer). Unknowability also relates to the elements, as summed up through a familiar shot—used by Zaim, Irmak, and Ceylan—showing characters looking out over expanses of water, especially the Bosphorus, even if they cannot quite understand the significance of the experience. Likewise, when Yusuf sits by the tree during a rain shower at the end of *Bal*, listening to the splashing of water and the regular cheeping of birds, we understand that he is at one with nature, even though he would have no way of explaining it. Tolga Örnek's documentaries make similar points, especially *Mount Nemrud*, which suggests that its secrets remain perpetually undiscovered, despite regular archeological excavations and scholarly writing from all countries.

I recently watched a BBC documentary on the history of Jerusalem, looking at its turbulent story from the Judaist, Christian, and İslamic perspectives.

Through a familiar combination of computer graphics, interviews with academic experts, and historical artifacts, presenter Simon Sebag Montefiore claimed to offer "the most complete history" yet broadcast of the city. As Sebag Montefiore explained the Sunni İslam tradition,[5] I felt that there was a whole corpus of spiritual knowledge that could never be revealed to us. In 1923 George Santayana wrote that this belief was perfectly acceptable to any rational person: "Calling a substance unknowable, then, is like calling a drum inaudible, for the shrewd reason that what you hear is the sound of the drum. It is a play on words, and little better than a pun. . . . Mankind has always had ideas of matter, of God or the gods, and of a natural world, full of hidden processes and powers. . . . Everybody knew the quarter in which they lay and the circle of experiences in which each of them was manifested" (16–17). What distinguishes the protagonists in Ceylan or Kaplanoğlu's films is that they access the unknowable without being cognizant of "the circle of experiences" in which that communicative process occurs. It just *happens*. The only means by which we can share their state of ecstasy, however brief it might be, is to develop openness while accepting the unpredictable and the illogical. Only then can we understand Rūmī's experience of hearing "the ineffable silence of God, . . . an experience of speech-defying union of annihilation, . . . [in which] words [and logic] drop away" (Harmless 187–88).

Being exposed to the Anatolian tradition, its parallels in Rūmī's thought, and how both shape the work of contemporary Turkish filmmakers offers a fascinating commentary on the relationship between translation and language, both of which assume significance for non-Turkish viewers. I have written elsewhere of the shifting relationship between the two concepts and the ways in which both are culturally produced and reproduced (Raw, "Identifying Common Ground"). Since the days when the government appointed a Translation Bureau (*Tercüme Bürosü*) dedicated to rendering "Western classics" into Turkish, "translation" has been historically identified with fidelity: the target text should preserve the features of the source text, so that readers can understand the source text's claim to canonical status.[6] This approach still dominates university departments of Translation Studies, whose graduates are expected to become professional translators in a variety of fields. By contrast "adaptation" gives greater freedom to rewrite texts incorporating locally constructed stylistic conventions. Examples from the cinema include *Drakula İstanbul'da* (*Dracula in İstanbul*) (1953), a cult film of the period incorporating material derived from *Karagöz*; or *Şeytan* (1974), a version of *The Exorcist* based on the Koran rather than the Bible.[7] The experience of watching the films of Ceylan, Zaim, and Kaplanoğlu—in particular—casts doubt on the relevance of the terms "translation" or "adaptation" to our understanding of the material as we concentrate on every aspect of the *mise-en-scène*—sound, image, movement, as well as dialogue. Such complexities are nothing new: as long ago as 1960, Siegfried Kracauer proposed that film embodies our constructions of reality, combining realist with formalist tendencies, and permits us to view the unseen (i.e., imaginary) world. This experience sets in motion the intellectual—as well as the spiritual—process that will unify us with our environment and will reaffirm our participation in it (55–81). It doesn't really matter whether the dialogue is in Turkish (and hence requiring subtitles for non-Turkish viewers). We are asked to reflect on how our lives do not depend on linguistic or cross-cultural awareness but, rather, on the wordless understanding of elemental forces—the power of the sun, the wind, and the rain—and their significance for our ontology. Hence we can conclude that most of the films surveyed in this book are transcultural insofar as they acknowledge the interdependency between imagination and environment.

Since I began this project four years ago, the subject of Turkish cultures, their past, present, and future, has become widely popular among non-Turkish commentators. The liberal British newspaper the *Observer* reported on a recent statement from the Vote Leave campaign (i.e., those favoring a British exit from the European Union) claiming that free movement around Europe for Turks would "pose a threat to national security, as well as to [British] public services. . . . Since the birthrate in Turkey is so high, we can expect to see an additional million people added to the UK population from Turkey alone within eight years" (Boffey and Helm). Everyone, it seems, is ready and willing to offer his or her two-penn'orth on the country's bleak geopolitical future in Europe and the Middle East and its potentially "destructive" influence on other countries' foreign policies.[8] Even those non-Turks who have spent some considerable time living and working in the Republic participate in the chorus of criticism. The Canadian Don Randall, a member of the Department of English Literature at Bilkent University, Ankara from 1999 to 2016, published an article criticizing local colleagues for their shortcomings in spoken and written English, the products of "an under-performing educational system" (50). Their scholarly publications do not meet "international standards of quality" (53), a fault that has "quite important geopolitical implications" for the future of the country (65), condemning it to an inferior position *vis-à-vis* the "First World" of Europe and North America. The only solution is to engage more local academics who have spent time in the "First World," so as to help learners "discover the power to productively challenge and transform the purpose and meaning of English studies from a position outside the English-speaking world" (67). The Republic will always remain on the educational and geopolitical periphery unless it accepts further intellectual aid. These articles show how the colonialist mentality still dominates the Western psyche: while foreign intervention is necessary to improve the Republic's educational system (to bring it up to First World standards), those Turks who travel to improve themselves are perceived as potential "threats" to First World sociopolitical structures.[9] If I make such criticisms against my non-Turkish colleagues, I am sometimes accused of being a foreign appeaser, a latter-day Neville Chamberlain who has forgotten my true-blue British identity.

Not that such strictures really affect me: the experience of watching and writing about six Turkish filmmakers has proved personally revelatory. After more than a quarter of a century living in the Republic, I realized that I knew next to nothing about the culturally specific thought patterns that inspire much of their efforts. Hitherto my intellectual horizon was largely determined by First World binaries; a Westerner trying to make sense of living in non-Western cultures, looking at the work of (largely) independent filmmakers whose work positioned itself in opposition to "mainstream" Turkish cinema. I spent much time and effort concentrating on "Westernization" (a concept fundamental to the Republic's history from 1923 onward) and its attendant synonyms of modernity, forward thinking, and progress. I taught literature and film in my university so as to help learners engage in cross-cultural comparisons and thereby improve their second language abilities. Once they had graduated, they could hopefully exercise their improved critical thinking and/or linguistic capacities to communicate with other learners, especially in the First World. Although I did not like to admit it (to myself in particular), my pedagogic as well as my research agenda was not dissimilar to that embraced by colleagues such as Randall, even though I found most of his criticisms unfair. Writing and researching this book in the wake of my cancer operation altered my point of view entirely. I raised the issue in a recent blog post:

> It seemed much more useful to let the narrative[s] wash over me. . . . I allowed my imagination full rein rather than approaching the text objectively. . . . As someone acutely aware of humanity's connection to the elemental forces surrounding us, . . . [the authors] created a form . . . that was nothing less than primeval. . . . Understanding its meaning did not really matter; I gave myself to the language, and found myself transported into a magical world of sounds and emotions. ("The 'Inner Meaning'")

Not only did I became more aware of the importance of *sound* (both on and off the screen) but I also attempted to develop *deep listening*, "in which we are fully present with what is happening in the moment without trying to control it or judge it. We let go of our inner clamoring and our usual assumptions and listen with respect for precisely what is being said. . . . It is attentive rather than reactive listening" ("Deep Listening"). I no longer tried to reshape my pedagogic and/ or research experiences employing predetermined First World values. Rather I laid myself open to create new scholarly personal narratives—as explained in my introduction—based on complex and contradictory constructions of knowledge. When Derviş Zaim describes himself as an "alluvionic" filmmaker, he draws us into a world in which distinctions between past, present, and future no longer exist: history exerts a profound influence over our behavior as well as determining our future courses of action. Although Demirkubuz and Ceylan have acknowledged their debt to Russian literary giants such as Dostoyevsky and Chekhov, their representations of the Republic derive from a tradition that respects every aspect of the universe while drawing no distinction between inner and outer lives.[10]

Critics might accuse me of being slightly blinkered in my analysis; all of the filmmakers chosen for this book are men, with very fine women, such as Yeşim Ustaoğlu or Pelin Esmer, excluded. I would refer readers to my chapter on Esmer in *Exploring Turkish Cultures* for further discussion (Raw, *Exploring*, 299–333). I specifically selected these six personalities in the belief that their filmographies have proved consistently influential in determining the course of recent cinema history in the Republic as well as in helping me make sense of my state of mind as a professor living in Central Anatolia. Perhaps more so than any other book I have written, this has been simultaneously the most diffi- cult yet the most satisfying to write. I have occasionally felt like a cinephile, as I have shown how my daily experiences as a foreigner in the Republic have shaped—and continue to shape—my interpretations of the directors' work, and vice versa. But there have been other occasions when I have realized that I am not just writing a book on "film studies" (even though it is highly likely that the publishers will market it as such) but, rather, making sense of alternative metaphysical traditions. Hence the frequent use of noncinematic material, espe- cially literary texts in translation. I have specifically avoided the use of (ideo- logically loaded) geographical terms to describe it—for example, "Eastern" as opposed to "Western" thought—in the belief that anyone, irrespective of their subject position, can appreciate the significance of figures such as the Mother Goddess. We don't have to live in the Republic to understand how (and why) she assumes such importance for directors such as Kaplanoğlu. I would like to think that this book is both transcultural *and* transdisciplinary, with its intellectual content pitched not only at those involved in the production, distribution, and reception of films but also to anyone interested in reevaluating their ontological status in the contemporary world.

Notes

Introduction

1. Fazıl Hüsnü Dağlarca's "Af Gece" ("Night of the Amnesty") uses a similar analogy to dramatize the experience of a man released from jail after seventeen years, where he experienced perpetual

> Remorse for poplars and fields and cattle,
> Remorse for ships and weddings and rivers,
> Remorse from cradles and ox-carts in silence.
> Not by heaven and earth but in multitudes.
> . . . .
> A song of the native land renews the dark.
> Time is not light, yet it is. (96)

Human beings have their appointed place in the scheme of things, encompassing cities, territories, and the landscape. To imprison them upsets that scheme; hence Dağlarca's use of the word "remorse."

2. Much as I admire Talât Halman's work, I cannot agree with his demand for new methodologies that would analyze Turkish cultural products that eschew Western traditions and embrace local traditions instead. I'd prefer to approach texts on their own terms as potential sites for learning about oneself (Halman, "Difference," 327).

3. The Emek Cinema was constructed in 1884 and remodeled in 1924 in baroque and rococo styles. In 2010 plans were made to demolish the theater as part of a new shopping mall project. The idea was shelved, but the theater was demolished three years later.

Chapter 1. Derviş Zaim

1. The video is accessible through Facebook (Zaim, "Camii Cevresinde Rock").

2. The sight of the dog crossing the frame recalls the moment in Akira Kurosawa's *Yojimbo* (*The Bodyguard*) (1961), when Sanjuro Kuwabatake (Toshirô Mifune) walks down a deserted main street, only to find his attention diverted by a stray dog crossing the frame with a dead chicken in its mouth. The animal's obvious sense of well-being contrasts with the townspeople, who have all remained inside their houses watching Sanjuro, as if they are somehow loath to come out.

3. Also known as the Fatih Sultan Mehmet Bridge, the Second Bridge was opened in 1988. The Third Bridge (Yavuz Sultan Selim Köprüsü) opened in June 2016.

4. Cf. Abdüldadir Budak's "Babam ve Kalem" ("My Father and the Pen") (2000):

> Once my father was a pencil, now he is a fountain pen
> He's the Wall surrounding a garden by the name of Son
>
> My father penned the Wall and I, the roses he entwined about it
> Poetical aphorism: Oil lamps weep all day long.
>
> My father penned the oil lamp, which means he penned the night
> Does that explain why all the papers smell of soot?
>
> Some blood's seeped into the ink, the pen must now adjust to it
> Could the father be the ink and the sons of his the blood? (133)

5. Such material is not exclusive to Turkish films: Zhang Yimou's adventure epic *Ying Xiong* (*Hero*) (2002), set in China's past, suggests that to study the swordsperson's technique it is necessary to study calligraphy. This is a supreme art, one that permanently resists attack ("battle can never annihilate our written words") and invests special powers on those able to practice it ("merging the power of the wrist with the spirit in the heart"). I am indebted to Dennis Rothermel for this reference.

6. The power of music has been underlined in Güntekin's *Çalıkuşu*, when Feride is introduced to Yusuf Efendi, an aspiring composer. Flattered by her comments, he observes: "If there be a little virtue in a few of my pieces, it is no more than an attempt to express with a sincere voice that same divine melancholy that is to be found in the works of some of the great poets, such as [Abdülhak] Hamit [Tarhan] and [Tevfik] Fikret" (214).

7. Kurban Bayram commemorates the test that İbrahim (Abraham) was put to when asked to sacrifice his son. Before the sacrifice takes place, God sends a goat with his angel Gabriel and tells Abraham that he passed the test that God had placed before him. Prophet Abraham is then asked to sacrifice the goat instead of his son as the sign of his loyalty to God. Every year an animal is sacrificed. The meat is then divided into three portions—one is given to the poor, one to neighbors and relatives, and the third is kept for the household. The skin of the animal is donated, and the income obtained from the skins is shared with various social welfare organizations.

Chapter 2. Zeki Demirkubuz

1. Demirkubuz's latest film, *Kor* (*Ember*), was released in theaters in the Republic of Turkey on 22 April 2016, too late for analysis in this chapter.

2. The consumer desires that prompted many to opt for this form of existence have been explored in qualitative research by Güliz Ger and her fellow authors ("The Development of Consumer Desire," 102–7).

3. Despite this contrast, Demirkubuz has subsequently admitted that he disliked *C Blok* due to the film possessing too many characteristics of classical Turkish (Yeşilçam) cinema. Perhaps he had to make the film before he could go on to refine his style and work out his main concerns (Onaran 29).

4. While this style of filmmaking is used for parodic purposes in *Üçüncü Sayfa*, it has been employed highly successfully in other low-budget films, notably Robert Rodriguez's *El Mariachi* (1992), which uses intercut close-ups, rapid tracking shots, and brief two-shots in a breathless cinematic style suggesting urgency.

5. "While underlining the nature of fiction, *The Third Page* exposes the fiction within real life" (Çiftçi 42). Perhaps the film makes the point that in an absurd world the distinctions between "truth" and "fiction" hardly matter.

6. "These characters are not on a voyage of self-discovery but seek to escape from themselves—to give up, let go, and forget themselves in a fully imprisoned state of the other" (Aytaç 65).

7. Berke Gül suggests somewhat unfairly that "the somewhat dull atmosphere of Ankara" compared to that of İstanbul "finds its reflection in the gloomy, claustrophobic internal shots" (53).

8. Mükerrem's plight recalls that of Vittoria (Monica Vitti) in Michelangelo Antonioni's *L'Eclisse* (*The Eclipse*) (1962), who perpetually searches for stability in her relationships yet remains imprisoned by them. Antonioni's camera technique emphasizes her imprisonment by photographing her in confined spaces or by framing her in continual tight close-ups.

9. The name is incorrectly spelt "Seniye" on the Internet Movie Database.

Chapter 3. Semih Kaplanoğlu

1. I was not able to view a copy of *Herkes Kendi Evinde*.

2. A Turkish/German/French/Swedish coproduction, it was shot in Detroit, Germany, and the Republic of Turkey.

3. Yavuz Selim Söylemez takes a psychoanalytic view of Kaplanoğlu's work, arguing that the dream worlds created in the Yusuf trilogy not only relate to the director's personal experiences but also create new possibilities for "unrealized feelings" (143).

4. A useful summary of Kaplanoğlu's basic themes has been published (in Turkish) by Hasan Serdar Gergerlioğlu (128–34).

5. Kaplanoğlu has cited the Süleymaniye as an example of a "pure" work of architecture created by Sinan, inspiring the "minimalist/pure" approach to filmmaking in which the answers to life's basic questions might be provided ("Cinema Militans").

6. Fûzulî was the pen name of Muhammad bin Suleyman who wrote his collected poems (*dîvân*) in three different languages: Azeri, Persian, and Arabic.

7. Perhaps the educator is not necessarily to blame. One learner of Eastern Turkish origin (possibly Kurdish) opined, "Whenever I say something that discloses my identity,

I see that the atmosphere suddenly changes. A minority teacher who discloses his/her identity would never get a managerial position. To get such a position, s/he would have to prove that s/he is very nationalist. A Sunni-Turk would always be preferred" (Kaya 24).

8. Kaplanoğlu suggests that drinking milk is intrinsic to rural Anatolian cultures: "When workers sleep near the water, some snakes slither into their mouths and then into their stomachs. And people drink lots of milk so that the snake can go throughout their intestines with the milk and come out of their bodies at the other end. Or they hang upside down from a branch so that the snake falls out through their mouths" (qtd. in "Movies"). Or perhaps milk, as a natural product of the Anatolian landscape, has therapeutic qualities, having been produced from creatures nurtured by the Mother Goddess.

9. The 2012 film *Küf* (*Mold*) extends this metaphor of a train by having the central character Basri (Ercan Kesal) as an employee of the State Railway Company in a rural village. In one scene he walks through a tunnel to the end of a railway track, leading to nowhere—a suitable visual metaphor for his existence, much of which is spent trying and failing to find out about his son, who passed away eighteen years previously in anti-government protests. The bureaucracy, especially the police, makes every effort to frustrate Bedri's efforts by slowing down the process of investigation, rendering the old man's life even more meaningless.

10. The issue of slowness in cinematic narratives is a contentious one. Isolde Vanhee's piece on the legacy of Japanese director Yasujiro Ozu argues that slowness has become the hallmark of art cinema, demanding "great swathes of our precious time to achieve quite fleeting and slender aesthetic and political effects" (98). Such comments embody the kind of Westernized preoccupations that Kaplanoğlu's work tries to challenge—a preoccupation with "time" as a human construct; the desire for films to be both "aesthetic" as well as "political"; and a conscious distinction between "mainstream" (i.e., fast) and "art" (slow) cinema. I return to this issue in the chapter on Nuri Bilge Ceylan.

11. Kaplanoğlu's work has not always attracted critical plaudits. Writing in *Film Comment* on the Berlin Film Festival, Olaf Möller dismissed *Bal* as a "piece of arthouse fluff featuring a cute little boy, gorgeous rural landscapes, and a predictable coming-of-age story. . . . [The film] explains what makes this fucked-up poet tick. But so what?" (64). The fact that the film is categorized as an "arthouse" work denotes the Westerner's preoccupation with binaries.

12. I would therefore take issue with Ghislain Deslandes's and Jocelyn Maixent's claim that, like many contemporary Turkish directors, Kaplanoğlu is reliant on European funding for his films and therefore adopts "a deeply European way of making movies" (81). I do not believe that physical geography plays such an important part in the director's aesthetic. This is especially true of his most recent film, the coproduction funded by Germany, Sweden, France, and Turkey. On the other hand, his understanding of "Anatolia" as a state of mind is intrinsic to an understanding of his work.

Chapter 4. Çağan Irmak

1. This was not strictly true. Although the Ankara State Theater tended to favor this kind of acting style, many private companies were more naturalistic in terms of technique, especially Genco Erkal, whose company Dostlar Tiyatrosu specialized in Brecht. See my article "Genco Erkal: The Theatre of Commitment," in *Exploring Turkish Cultures*, 181–99. Some of my reviews can also be accessed on my blog at başkent .academia.edu/LaurenceRaw/theater-studies.

2. The Royal Shakespeare Company's style was formed on the basis of scholarly analysis of the text using methods pioneered by New Criticism. See Michael L. Greenwald, *Directions by Indirections*.

3. Irmak's decision to separate the two elements contrasts in particular Demirkubuz, whose representations of human isolation are often the result of an increasingly alienated metropolitan life, especially in İstanbul.

4. The Turkish spy Ahmet Esat Tomruk (1887–1966) was a celebrated spy during the War of Independence. Colloquially dubbed İngiliz Kemal (the English Kemal), he became the subject of a series of popular novels during the forties and fifties. The film *İngiliz Kemal Lavrens'e Karşı* (*English Kemal Against Lawrence*) (1952) pitted him against T. E. Lawrence (a.k.a. Lawrence of Arabia).

5. For a good introduction to Yeşilçam and its principal preoccupations, see Arslan, chapters 1–4.

6. We must remember that in the mind of Western writers, this is an oriental construction of melodrama, shaped by traditions like those practiced in Great Britain or Europe. See Elmas Şahin, "[The] Fall of Women in British Literature and Turkish Literature of [the] 19th Century: A Comparative Approach," *International Journal of Social Science* 31, no. 2 (2015): 83–97.

7. See Renee Hirschon, ed., *Crossing the Aegean: An Appraisal of the 1923 Compulsory Population Exchange between Greece and Turkey*.

8. Kahraman is a fictional name; Belgin Doruk (1936–95) was a popular female performer who made between five and six films a year in a career lasting from 1952 to 1970.

9. Redd appear as themselves in the film. Established in 1996, their last album was released in 2016.

10. Ayperi/Hatice is a fictional character.

11. "Nostalgia is shown to be both a driver of empathy and social connectedness, and a potent internal antidote for loneliness and alienation, . . . the 'perfect internal politician, connecting the past with the present, pointing optimistically to the future' and a mental state 'absolutely central to human experience'" (Adams).

12. This is not always the case: Şavkar Altınel's poem "Nostalji" ("Nostalgia") talks about nostalgia conjuring up memories of Auschwitz, "a terrible experience; but it was an experience all the same" (155).

13. *Çalıkuşu* is based on the novel by Reşat Nuri Güntekin. It was previously made into a film (by Osman F. Seden) in 1966 and subsequently televised by Turkish Radşo

and Television (TRT) in 1986. A further remake, as a multipart soap opera, appeared in 2013–14.

14. İnyemli is actually an able-bodied actor with considerable experience in television *diziler*.

15. This kind of worldview made the headlines only recently when members of a constitutional commission admitted that they did not know who Oscar Wilde was and confused him with the Oscar film awards. One member objected to the reference by saying: "Do you not have any examples from this [Turkish] culture, this civilization?" ("Oscar Wilde-Oscars References").

16. In the recently published *Dictionary of Turkish Cinema*, Gönül Dönmez-Colin devotes no more than a page (out of a total of 374) to Irmak's work. She calls him an "audience favourite," but concludes that he is a popular filmmaker oscillating between film and television (179).

17. Irmak released *Benim Adım Feridun* (*My Name Is Feridun*) in November 2016.

Chapter 5. Tolga Örnek

1. In light of Johnson's support for the Brexiteers (those favoring exit from the European Union) at the referendum held on 23 June 2016, which produced a vote of 51.89 percent to 48.11 percent in favor of leaving the Union, we might wonder whether the writer himself has not been guilty of participating in a "mesmerising disaster."

2. Such sentiments echo those made by the Ottoman officer Lieutenant İbrahim Nacï, whose diary begins by expressing the fear that he might die "without seeing the enemy, without striving for my country and for the nation" (111), and ends with a description of a conflict where "the bullets [were] resounding in the valleys, whistling through our skies, breaking the air with terrible noises [that] seemed like announcing to us the reality in this time of evening with its black shadows" (287).

3. Harvey Broadbent's essay "The Ottoman Army Response to the Gallipoli Campaign" offers a useful summary of English translations of Ottoman soldiers' diaries and other memories of the conflict. Broadbent concludes that not all the testimonies might be viewed as accurate representations of what happened, but they give an accurate picture of the atmosphere of desperation that pervaded many battalions forced to fight day after day (88–89).

4. Produced in New Zealand, the film *Chunuk Bair* (1992) retells this story from an Anzac perspective.

5. Pugsley is now senior research fellow in the Humanities Research Institute, University of Buckingham, UK.

6. For more on this subject, see my piece "Reconstructing Englishness" (1999), reprinted in *Exploring Turkish Cultures*, 21–34.

7. This policy continued after Atatürk's passing in 1938—as late as the seventies, younger academics and teachers were given full state scholarships to pursue their graduate research abroad. Now the funds are provided by the Higher Education Council (YÖK) or the Scientific and Technical Research Council (TÜBİTAK).

8. The whole story of Atatürk's personal life has been shrouded in secrecy. Even Latife was reluctant to tell anything, partly out of loyalty and partly out of fear. A twenty-five-year court order banning the publication of her letters and diaries expired in 2006. See "Wife of the Nation's Father: A New Book on an Old Taboo," *The Economist*, 22 June 2006.

9. For a full analysis of the shah's policies and personality, see Hassan Amini's recent television documentary *Decadence and Downfall* (2016).

10. I am writing this piece on 18 March, the 101st anniversary of the beginning of the Ottoman defense. A ceremony marks the occasion, attended by all heads of state as well as the ambassadors of the United Kingdom, Australia, and New Zealand. At my university the senior faculty watches a series of events including a lecture, some songs, and poetry readings.

11. This subject also forms the basis for Ahmet Ümit's detective novel *Patasana* (2011).

12. Narrated by Jeremy Irons (English) and Zafer Alagöz (Turkish).

13. Recalling Çağan Irmak's use of old Turkish popular songs for similar dramatic effect.

14. The music radio station exists (www.kentfm.com.tr).

15. Dündar has seldom been frightened of court controversy. As I write, he has been sentenced to prison following an accusation of aiding terrorism when his newspaper *Cumhuriyet* (*The Republic*) published footage of the State Intelligence Service (MİT) sending weapons to anti-Assad fighters in Syria.

16. This is certainly true of his latest work, *Sen Benim Herşeyimsin* (*Instructions not Included*) (2016), a remake of the Mexican comedy (2013).

Chapter 6. Nuri Bilge Ceylan

1. Following the tradition established by several critics, Ira Jaffe sees this kind of "slow" filmmaking style as symptomatic of a particularly Western style of melodramatic filmmaking pioneered by Jim Jarmusch and Gus Van Sant. Other "influences" include Michelangelo Antonioni (83, 85). This chapter argues that Ceylan is much more interested in local cultures.

2. In different cultures, including Turkish cultures past and present, the tortoise has been represented as the ancient wisdom seeker, content and peaceful in his journeys.

3. The distinction is an important one. In Western cultures, eco-filmmakers are constructed as "radical," committed to social action through films that often include disturbing content. Ceylan's films might evince a similar reaction, but they are more concerned with the inner life. See Laura Sevler, "How a New Generation of Eco-filmmakers Are Challenging Broadcasting Convention," *Ecologist*, 28 Oct. 2010.

4. The spiritual meaning of the duck speaks the message: "Be in the moment, for this is where all your power exists and is available to you, . . . a strong sense of knowing, which leads to a graceful self confidence, having a connectedness to ancient ancestor wisdom" ("Duck Symbolism").

5. Following the tradition of several non-Turkish commentators, Diane Sippi sees the film as being inspired by the work of Ozu and Tarkovsky: "The image, embodying life in all its uniqueness, stretches out into infinity. . . . It is the form that comes closest to expressing the filmmaker's world, to making incarnate his longing for the ideal" (52). I would argue that this "ideal" is represented by the elements.

6. Ceylan's photographic exhibition "Panorama Bakış" (Panoramic Views), which opened at Cer Modern, Ankara, in mid-2014, continues this theme.

7. Such experiences would seem to substantiate the claim made in an Organization of Economic Co-operation and Development (OECD) report dated October 2013 that education at the tertiary level often fails to meet learner expectations or meet the standards of its regional competitors" ("Education Policy Outlook," 4–5).

8. *Kasaba* deliberately foregrounds the progress of the seasons to emphasize this relationship. The film opens in winter with children playing in the snow. The second and third sections unfold in spring when the leaves reappear on the trees and the inhabitants gather for the carnival (Suner 136).

9. Ceylan would have sympathized with the sentiments of the Dogme95 documentary film movement that explicitly repudiated the efforts of the "decadent filmmaker," who is dedicated simply to illusions, and the true documentarist, who is preoccupied with "a more casual, observational style" committed to verisimilitude. See Charles Lee, "Dogme95," *Encyclopedia of the Documentary Film*, 1:314–16.

10. "Egg Symbolism."

11. A Lycian settlement now listed by the Catholic Church as a titular see, or site of a former church that no longer functions.

12. Kristi McKim, perhaps inspired by the film's title, likens this moment to those seen in Woody Allen's and Ingmar Bergman's films: "Bahar's mournful expression betrays her isolation from İsa as the close-up reveals her vulnerability to the audience. That the long take (which lasts approximately two minutes and even includes a fly that lands in her hair) insists upon our sustained look at her sun-soaked teary face visually connects the sun with her sadness" (175).

13. Compare a similar sequence in Çağan Irmak's *Karanlık Takiler*.

14. McKim believes that this sequence has attracted most critical attention: "The high-definition snow at once enhances the distance between them [İsa and Bahar] . . . and collapses the space, enabling a seeming intimacy as they share . . . a view of this photogenic atmospheric phenomenon" (178).

15. Another meeting of fact and fiction: Sharif made the film, but the Hotel Othello does not actually exist.

16. The party have been in power since 2002. For a look at the implications of their election victories, see Ali Çarkoğlu and Kerem Yıldırım, "Election Storm in Turkey: What Do the Results of the June and November 2015 Elections Tell Us?"

17. J. Hoberman, perhaps a little confused by the apparently meandering structure of the film, describes it as "a shaggy-dog story or a fairy-tale or you could call it an epistemological murder mystery" (277). Three definitions are better than one.

18. Again we have a problem of terminology here. Geoff Andrew sees this technique of collapsing past, present, and future as evidence of Ceylan's universality: "His characters eloquently evoke the disappointments of all those who had no small talent but who for one reason or another never lived up to their initial promise or fulfilled their dreams" (59). Ceylan makes very particular points about characters in culture-specific locations; the fact that non-Turkish audiences can empathize with them emphasizes his skill in creating transcultural cinema. For an analysis of the Western-influenced origins of the term "universal," see the Envoi that concludes this volume.

Envoi

1. See Ziya Ünis, "The Evolution of Privatization in Turkey."

2. The proceedings from the conference were published by Cambridge Scholars Publishing two years later. Karanfil and Şavk summarized their ideas in the introduction (1–6), while Serhan Mersin and Pınar Yıldız also looked at transcultural models for Turkish cinema (23–37).

3. This strategy even affects those writing in defense of Turkish identities. As explained in the first chapter, Chris Rumford uses binaries to make distinctions between universalism and particularity in recent Turkish history (145). This is a characteristic rhetorical strategy employed by Western scholars in their treatment of Turkish affairs.

4. The importance of spirituality rather than succumbing to the pleasures of the flesh is also evident in Christianity. Janina Ramirez's documentary on the East Window of York Minster in the north of England (2011) purports to explain everything about its significance but only succeeds in proving the existence of the unknowable (*Britain's Most Fragile Treasure*).

5. Al-Aqsa Mosque in Jerusalem is the third holiest site after the mosques of al-Haram in Mecca and al-Nabawi in Medina.

6. See Şehnaz Tahir Gürçağlar, *The Politics and Poetics of Translation in Turkey*.

7. See my discussion of both films in *Turkey: Directory of World Cinema*, 70–71, 88–89.

8. See Mark Townsend, "Why Are They Making Us Out to Be Such a Threat?"

9. Himmet Umunç and I published a reply to Randall's claims ("Reassessing").

10. The thriller writer Ahmet Ümit summarizes this relationship succinctly: "Do you know why the ancient people of Anatolia chose her [the goddess] as their mother god? Because men were not aware of their roles as impregnators. They thought that it was the wind, the rain, the rivers, in short, nature, that impregnated women. And it was not at all a strange idea at the time. People viewed themselves as a part of nature" (356).

Works Cited

Bibliography

Adams, Tim. "Look Back in Joy: The Power of Nostalgia." *Guardian*, 9 November 2014.

Akçalı, Emel. "The Ambivalent Role of National Landmarks in the Age of Globalization: The Case of Atatürk's Mausoleum in Turkey." *Borderlands* 9, no. 2 (2010): 1–23.

Akın, Gülten. "Aşağı Canbolat Musa Akbaba Sağ Kolu İçin ağıt" ["Elegy for the Right Arm of Musa Akbaba from Lower Canbolat"]. 1983. Translated by Saliha Paker and Mel Kenne. In *What Have You Carried Over? Poems of 42 Days and Other Works*, 22. Jersey City, NJ: Talisman House, 2014.

———. "Şiir, Ideoloji ve Vicdan" ["Poetry, Ideology and Conscience"]. 2006. Translated by Saliha Paker. In *Aeolian Visions/Versions: Modern Classics and New Writing from Turkey*, edited by Mel Kenne, Saliha Paker, and Amy Spangler, 23–27. Horsham, UK: Milet, 2013.

Akyol, Miustafa. "Was Atatürk Not a Dictator?" *Hürriyet Daily News*, 21 April 2012.

Altınay, Ayşe Gül. "Ebru: Reflections on Water." In *Ebru: Reflections of Cultural Diversity in Turkey*, edited by Attila Durak, 19–25. 2nd ed. İstanbul: Metis Yayınları, 2009.

Altınel, Şavkar. "Nostalji" ["Nostalgia"]. Translated by Alan Levi Stark. *Agenda: Modern Turkish Poetry* 38, no. 3–4 (2002): 155.

Amani, Aslan. "Football in Turkey: A Force for Liberalism and Modernity?" *Open Democracy*, 19 July 2013.

And, Metin. *Turkish Miniature Painting: The Ottoman Period*. New ed. İstanbul: Dost, 1982.

Anderson, Benedict. *Imagined Communities: Reflections on the Origin and Spread of Nationalism*. Rev. ed. London: Verso, 1991.

Andrew, Geoff. "Beyond the Clouds: The Films of Nuri Bilge Ceylan." In *Exile Cinema: Filmmakers at Work beyond Hollywood*, edited by Michael Atkinson, 57–63. Albany: State University of New York Press, 2008.

Arslan, Savaş. *Cinema in Turkey: A New Cultural History*. Oxford: Oxford University Press, 2010.

Asaf, Özdemir. "The Departed." Translated by Yıldız Moran. In *To Go To: Poems*, 26–27. İstanbul: Sanat Basimevi, nd.

———. "The Everlasting." Translated by Yıldız Moran. In *To Go To: Poems*, 29. İstanbul: Sanat Basimevi, nd.

"Atatürk Film Draws Turkish Crowds, Controversy." *NBCNews.com*, 13 November 2008.

Atay, Oğuz. "Unutulan" ["The Forgotten"]. Translated by İdil Aydoğan. In *Aeolian Visions/Versions: Modern Classics and New Writing from Turkey*, edited by Mel Kenne, Saliha Paker, and Amy Spengler, 121–26. Horsham, UK: Milet, 2013.

Aydın, Kamil. *Images of Turkey in Western Literature*. Huntingdon, UK: Eothen, 1999.

Aytaç, Senem. "Destiny." In *Mental Minefields: The Dark Tales of Zeki Demirkubuz*, edited by Zeynep Dadak and Enis Köstepen, 64–66. New York: Lincoln Center, 2007.

Ayvazoğlu, Beşir. "Keder Aniden Vurur" ["Grief Strikes Suddenly"]. In *101 Poems by 101 Poets: An Anthology of Turkish Poetry*, edited by Mevlut Ceylan, 116. İstanbul: Metropolitan Municipality, 1996.

"Babam ve Oğlum." *The Remains of the Day*, 15 January 2014.

Bahti, Timothy. "Literary Criticism and the History of Ideas." In *The Cambridge History of Literary Criticism*. Volume 9, *Twentieth Century Historical, Philosophical and Psychological Perspectives*, edited by Christa Knellwolf and Christopher Norris, 31–43. Cambridge: Cambridge University Press, 2001.

Banks, Julie. "The Texture of Distance: Approaching Nuri Bilge Ceylan's *Distant*." 2010. In *Nuri Bilge Ceylan: Essays and Interviews*, edited by Robert Cardullo, 153–64. Berlin: Logos Verlag GmbH, 2015.

Barks, Coleman, ed. *Rumi: The Book of Love: Poems of Ecstasy and Longing*. New York: HarperCollins, 2013.

Barnes, Elizabeth. *Love's Whipping Boy: Violence and Sentimentality in the American Imagination*. Chapel Hill: University of North Carolina Press, 2011.

Barnes, Julian. *Keeping an Eye Open*. London: Vintage, 2015.

Baumbach, Nico. "All That Heaven Allows: What Is, or Was, Cinephilia?" *Film Comment* 38, no. 2 (March–April 2012): 47–53.

Baybars, Taner. "Gerçek" ["Reality"]. Translated by Mehmet Yaşin. In *Selected Poems/ Seçme Şiirler*, 64–65. İstanbul: Yapı Kredi Yayınları, 1997.

———."Memlekete Mektup" ["Letter to Homeland"]. Translated by Mehmet Yaşin. In *Selected Poems/Seçme Şiirler*, 32–36. İstanbul: Yapı Kredi Yayınları, 1997.

Beckett, Samuel. *Worstward Ho!* 1983. samuel-beckett.net.

Behramoğlu, Ataol. "Akıp Giden Zaman Türküsü" ["The Song of Time Passing"]. Translated by Walter G. Andrews. In *I've Learned Some Things: Selected Poems*, 70–71. Austin: Center for Middle Eastern Studies, University of Texas, 2008.

———. "Yaşadıklarımdan Öğrendiğim Bir Şey Var" ["There's Something I Have Learned from What I've Lived." 1995. Translated by Suat Karantay. In *Contemporary Turkish Poetry: A Selection*, edited by Suat Karantay, 92–93. İstanbul: Boğaziçi University Press, 2006.

Bell, Jamie. "An Interview with Zeki Demirkubuz." *Sight and Sound* (February 2006). 6th Atlanta Turkish Film Festival, October 2007.

Bennett, Lucy, and Tom Phillips. "An Introduction: The Fan Studies Network. New Convictions, New Research." *Participations* 10, no. 1 (May 2013): 52–55.

Bergfelder, Tim. "National, Transnational or Supranational Cinema? Rethinking European Film Studies." *Media, Culture, and Society* 27, no. 3 (2005): 315–31.

Bezel, Nail. *Word Seed on the Wind.* Bloomington, IN: AuthorHouse, 2007.

Bhabha, Homi K. *The Location of Culture.* 1994. New York: Routledge, 2004.

"Birth Traditions." *Turkish Culture Portal,* January 2016.

Boffey, Daniel, and Toby Helm. "Vote Leave Embroiled in Race Row over Turkey Security Threat Claims." *TheGuardian.com,* 22 May 2016.

Bora, Tanıl, and Nuri Bilge Ceylan. *Taşraya Bakmak [Looking at the Countryside].* İstanbul: İletişim Yayıncılık, 2005.

Broadbent, Harvey. "The Ottoman Army Response to the Gallipoli Campaign: From English Translations of Documents in Turkish Military Archives and Other Sources by the Gallipoli Centenary Research Project." In *Gelibolu: Tarih, Efsane ve Anı [Gallipoli: Legend and Memory],* edited by İbrahim Güren Yumurşak and M. Mehdi İlhan, 79–95. İstanbul: İstanbul Medeniyet Üniversitesi, 2013.

Bruner, Jerome. *Making Stories: Law, Literature, Life.* Cambridge, MA: Harvard University Press, 2002.

Brunwasser, Matthew. "Dengbej: Kurdish Storytellers Revive Their Tradition in Turkey." *Public Radio International,* 24 May 2013.

Budak, Abdülkadir. "Bamam ve Kalem" ["My Father and the Pen"]. 2000. Translated by Deniz Tufan and Jean Carpenter Efe. In *Contemporary Turkish Poetry: A Selection,* edited by Suat Karantay, 133. İstanbul: Boğaziçi University Press, 2006.

Büker, Seçil, and Hasan Akbulut. "Journey to the Soul of the Provinces: Semih Kaplanoğlu's Film *The Egg.*" *Kocaeli Journal of the Faculty of Communication* (2012): 19–39.

Calloway-Thomas, Carolyn. *Empathy in the Global World: An Intercultural Perspective.* Thousand Oaks, CA: Sage, 2010.

Campbell, Verity. *Turkey.* London: Lonely Planet, 2010.

Camus, Albert. *The Outsider.* 1942. Translated by Sandra Smith. Harmondsworth, UK: Penguin Classics, 2013.

Cardullo, Robert. "Nuri Bilge Ceylan's *Once Upon a Time in Anatolia.*" 2011. In *Nuri Bilge Ceylan: Essays and Interviews,* edited by Robert Cardullo, 219–28. Berlin: Logos Verlag GmbH, 2015.

Carlyon, L. A. *Gallipoli.* London: Doubleday, 2002.

"Celebrity and Development." *The Twenty Ten Theme,* 2010.

Ceylan, Nuri Bilge. "Introduction." In *Emine Ceylan: Photographs,* 4–5. İstanbul: privately printed, 1987.

Cizre-Sakallıoğlu, Ümit, and Erinç Yeldan. "Politics, Society and Financial Liberalization: Turkey in the 1990s." *Development and Change* 31, no. 2 (March 2000): 491–508.

Clabbatari, Jane. "Why Is Rumi the Best-Selling Poet in the US?" *BBC Culture,* 21 October 2014.

Clark, Peter. *Marmaduke Pickthall: British Muslim.* London: Quartet, 1986.

Cook, Pam. "Rethinking Nostalgia: *In the Mood for Love* and *Far from Heaven*." In *Screening the Past: Memory and Nostalgia in Cinema*, 1-23. Abingdon, UK: Routledge, 2005.

Cumming, Charles. *A Colder War*. London: HarperCollins, 2014.

Çamlıbel, Faruk Nafiz. "İlkbahar/Yaz/Sonbahar/Kış Günesi" ["Spring/Summer/Autumn/Winter Sun"]. Translated by S. Behlül Toygar. In *Fifteen Turkish Poets: 75 Poems*, 46-48. İstanbul: İskender Matbaası, 1969.

Çarkoğlu, Ali, and Kerem Yıldırım. "Election Storm in Turkey: What Do the Results of the June and November 2015 Elections Tell Us?" *Insight Turkey* 17, no. 4 (Fall 2015): 57-81.

Çiçekoğlu, Feride. "Kimini Şahin Tırmalar" ["Some Get Clawed by Falcons"]. 1990. Translated by Suat Karantay. In *Contemporary Turkish Short Fiction: A Selection*, vol. 2, edited by Suat Karantay, 47-50. İstanbul: Çitlembik, 2010.

Çiftçi, Ayça. "The Third Page." In *Mental Minefields: The Dark Tales of Zeki Demirkubuz*, edited by Zeynep Dadak and Enis Köstepen, 40-42. New York: Lincoln Center, 2007.

Çolakoğlu, Ayşe. *Beyond Gallipoli*. İstanbul: Doğan Egmont Yayıncılık, 2008.

Dadak, Zeynep, and Senem Aytaç. "The Scraps of Time: Zeki Demirkubuz's Canon." *zekidemirkubuz.com*, 2007.

Dadak, Zeynep, and Enis Köstepen, eds. *Mental Minefields: The Dark Tales of Zeki Demirkubuz*. New York: Lincoln Center, 2007.

Dağlarca, Fazıl Hüsnü. "Af Gece" ["Night of the Amnesty"]. Translated by Talât Saït Halman. *Third World Resurgence* 96 (1999): 40.

Daloğlu, Tülin. "Turkey Misunderstands Its 'Magnificent Century.'" *Al-Monitor*, 17 February 2011.

Dazkır, Sibel Seda, and Marilyn A. Read. "Interviews with Turkish Women: Rise of Consumerism and Its Influence on Home Interiors." *Researchgate*, 2014.

De Beauvoir, Simone. *The Prime of Life*. 1960. Translated by Peter Green. New York: Lancer, 1966.

"Deep Listening." *The Center for Contemplative Mind in Society*, 2015.

Deleuze, Gilles. "What Children Say." In *Essays Critical and Clinical*, translated by Daniel W. Smith and Michael A. Greco, 61-68. London: Verso, 1998.

Demir-Atay, Hivren. "Edgar Allan Poe in Turkish Translations in Three Alphabets." In *Translated Poe*, edited by Emron Esplin and Margarida Vale de Gato, 131-41. Bethlehem, PA: Lehigh University Press, 2014.

Deslandes, Ghislain, and Jocelyn Maixent. "Turkish Auteur Cinema and European Identity: Economic Influences on Aesthetic Issues." *Journal of European Popular Culture* 2, no. 1 (2012): 81-98.

Dickens, Charles. *Hard Times*. 1854. Harmondsworth, UK: Penguin, 1976.

Diken, Bülent. "Climates of Nihilism." 2008. In *Nuri Bilge Ceylan: Essays and Interviews*, edited by Robert Cardullo, 84-104. Berlin: Logos Verlag GmbH, 2015.

Dilmen, Güngör. *Ben Anatolia* [*I, Anatolia*]. 1984. Translated by Talât Sait Halman. In *I, Anatolia and Other Plays*, edited by Halman and Jayne L. Warner, 203–45. Syracuse, NY: Syracuse University Press, 2008.

Dinamo, Hasan. "Yirmibirinci Yüzyılın İnsanlarına Şiirler" ["Songs for the Men of the Twenty-First Century"]. In *The Star and the Crescent: An Anthology of Modern Turkish Poetry*, edited by Derek Patmore, 25–26. London: Constable, 1945.

Doane, Mary Ann. *The Desire to Desire: The Woman's Films of the 1940s*. Basingstoke: Macmillan, 1988.

Dostoyevsky, Fyodor İlyich. *Notes from the Underground*. 1864. Translated by Richard Pevear and Larissa Volokhonsky. New York: Vintage, 1994.

Dönmez-Colin, Gönül. *The Routledge Dictionary of Turkish Cinema*. London: Routledge, 2014.

"Duck Symbolism and Duck Meaning." *Universe of Symbolism*, 2016.

"Ebru: The Art of Paper Marbling." *MuslimHeritage.com*, 2005.

"Education Policy Outlook: Turkey." *OECD*, October 2013.

Egemen, Reşit. *Anatolia: Land of Mother Goddess*. Translated by Mary Işın. Ankara: Hitit, 1988.

"Egg Symbolism." *Egglovers.blogspot.com*, 5 October 2010.

"Egyptian Account of the Battle of Kadesh." In *Ancient Records of Egypt*, edited and translated by James Henry Breasted III, 136–47. Chicago: University of Chicago Press, 1906.

Elsaesser, Thomas. "Cinephilia or the Uses of Disenchantment." In *Cinephilia: Movies, Love and Memory*, edited by Martin de Koning, Marijke de Valck, and Malte Hagener, 27–45. Amsterdam: Amsterdam University Press, 2005.

Erdem, Gizem Öztürk. "New Turkish Cinema: Interview with Professor Deniz Bayrakdar." *Nouvelle-Europe*, 10 June 2013.

Ergülen, Haydar. "Kayip Kardeş" ["Lost Brother"]. Translated by Arzu Eker Roditakis and Elizabeth Pullitto. In *Aeolian Visions/Versions: Modern Classics and New Writing from Turkey*, edited by Mel Kenne, Saliha Paker, and Amy Spangler, 177. Horsham, UK: Milet, 2013.

Ersöz, Cezmi. *Derinliğine Kimse Sevgili Olamadı* [*Confessions of a Love Gone Wrong*]. 2011. Translated by Leyla Tonguç. İstanbul: Çitlembik, 2012.

Eyüboğlu, Bedri Radmi. "İstanbul Destanı" ["İstanbul Saga"]. Translated by Clifford Endres and Selhan Savcıgıl Endres. In *Turkish Poetry 2014*, edited by George Messo, 122–45. New York: Red Hand, 2014.

Faik, Saït. "Arkadaş" ["The Friend"]. Translated by Talât S. Halman. In *Sleeping in the Forest: Stories and Poems*, edited by Talât S. Halman, 183. Syracuse, NY: Syracuse University Press, 2004.

———. "Geri Zaman" ["Back When"]. Translated by Talât S. Halman. In *Sleeping in the Forest: Stories and Poems*, edited by Talât S. Halman, 190. Syracuse, NY: Syracuse University Press, 2004.

Farzanefar, Amin. "Interview with Semih Kaplanoğlu: On the Enigmatic Beauty of Reality." Translated by John Bergeron. *Quantaa.de*, 23 September 2010.

Fasih, Mehmed. *Gallipoli 1915: Bloody Ridge (Lone Pine) Diary.* Translated by Hasan Basri Danışman. İstanbul: Denizler Kitabevi, 1997.

Fitzgerald, F. Scott. *The Great Gatsby.* 1925. Harmondsworth, UK: Penguin, 1977.

"Free Circumcision Makes Good Politics in Turkey." *Jerusalem Post*, 14 July 2011.

Freud, Sigmund. *The Psychopathology of Everyday Life.* 1901. Edited and translated by Angela Richards. Harmondsworth, UK: Penguin, 1988.

"Gallipoli 2015: Hundreds of Thousands Attend Anzac Centenary Service across Australia and Turkey." *ABC News*, 26 April 2015.

Garnard, İbrahim. "Western Views of Mawlana Rumi's Muslim Identity." *Dar-Al Masnevi*, August 2006.

Gasimova, Aida. "If All the Trees on Earth Were Poets: A Survey of the Qu'ranic Symbolism of the Pen in Medieval Azeri Turkic Sufi Poetry." *Journal of Turkish Literature* 11 (2014): 7–33.

Ger, Güliz, Russell W. Bek, and Dana-Nicoleta Lascu. "The Development of Consumer Desire in Marketing Economies: The Case of Romania and Turkey." In *Advances in Consumer Research*, vol. 20, edited by Leigh McAlister and Michael L. Rothschild, 102–7. Provo, UT: Association for Consumer Research, 1993.

Gergerlioğlu, Hasan Serdar. "Semih Kaplanoğlu Sineması Üzerine Sosyolojik bir Deneme" [The Sociological Aspects of Semih Kaplanoğlu's Cinema]. *Selçuk Üniversitesi Soysal Bilimler Enstitüsü Dergisi* (2013): 128–34.

Germen, Murat. *Ankara: Öncü Modernizmden Öykünmeci Mimesis ve Sahte Fütürizme* [*Ankara: From Pioneering Modernism to Revivalist Mimicry and Fake Futurism*]. Ankara: Erimtan Müzesi, 2015.

Gibbons, Fiachra. "Jail Made Me a Film Director." *Guardian*, 30 January 2006. *zekidemirkubuz.com*.

"Girl with a Pearl Earring." *Artble.com*, 2012.

Greenwald, Michael L. *Directions by Indirections: John Barton of the Royal Shakespeare Company.* Newark, NJ: University of Delaware Press, 1985.

"Grueling Work No Fairy Tale on Turkey's Famed Soap Operas." *Hürriyet Daily News*, 26 March 2015.

Gül, Berke. "Confession." In *Mental Minefields: The Dark Tales of Zeki Demirkubuz*, edited by Zeynep Dadak and Enis Köstepen, 52–54. New York: Lincoln Center, 2007.

Gülsoy, Murat. "My Life's a Lie" ["Hayatım Yalan"]. Translated by Emine Deliorman and Jonathan Ross. In *Contemporary Turkish Short Fiction: A Selection*, vol. 2, edited by Suat Karantay, 253–65. İstanbul: Çitlembik, 2009.

———. "Welcome to the City [Deniz]" ["Burası Bir Şehir (Deniz)"]. Translated by İdil Aydoğan. In *Aeolian Visions/Versions: Modern Classics and New Writing from Turkey*, edited by Mel Kenne, Saliha Paker, and Amy Spengler, 214–16. Horsham, UK: Milet, 2013.

Günersel, Tarık. *Muhafizgücü 1, Hayalgücü 0*. İstanbul: Gölge Yayınları, 1989.

Güntekin, Reşat Nuri. "Bir Yudum Su" ["One Drink of Water"]. Translated by John Taylor. In *An Anthology of Modern Turkish Short Stories*, edited by Fahir İz. Minneapolis: Bibliotheca İslamica, 1977.

———. *Calıkuşu* [*Autobiography of a Turkish Girl*]. 1922. Translated by Sir Wyndham Deedes. London: George Allen and Unwin, 1949.

Gürçağlar, Şehnaz Tahir. *The Politics and Poetics of Translation in Turkey, 1923–1960*. Amsterdam: Rodopi, 2008.

Halman, Talât Saït. "Difference and the Future of Turkish Literary Studies." In *The Turkish Muse: Views and Reviews*, edited by Talât Saït Halman and Jayne L. Warner, 327–28. Syracuse, NY: Syracuse University Press, 2006.

———. "Introduction." In *The Art of the Turkish Tale*, edited and translated by Barbara Walker, vol. 1, iii–xvi. Lubbock: Texas Tech University Press, 1990.

———. *Love Is All: Rumi's Life and Poems of Ecstasy*. Amkara: Bilkent Kültür Girişiml, 2012.

———. "Near Eastern Literatures: A Generation of Renewal." In *Rapture and Revolution: Essays on Turkish Literature*, edited by Jayne L. Warner, 59–71. Syracuse, NY: Syracuse University Press, 2007.

Hamzic, Amina, Maja Nedelovska, Donjeta Demolli, and Nemanja Cabric. "Turks Bewitch the Balkans with Their Addictive Soaps." *Balkan Insight*, 1 May 2013.

———. "Rumi: Soaring to Ecstasy." *Live Journal*, 22 November 2006.

Harmless, William, SJ. *Mystics*. Oxford: Oxford University Press, 2008.

Hepçilingirler, Feyza. *Kırmızı Karanfil Ne Renk Solar* [*As the Red Carnation Fades*]. Translated by Mark David Wyers. Horsham, UK: Milet, 2015.

Hikmet, Nâzım. "Benim Şiir Hakkında" ["About My Poetry"]. 1994. Translated by Randy Blasing and Mutlu Konuk. In *The Poems of Nâzım Hikmet*, 3. New York: Persea, 2002.

———. "Denize Hakkında" ["About the Sea"]. 1994. Translated by Randy Blasing and Mutlu Konuk. In *The Poems of Nâzım Hikmet*, 164–65. New York: Persea, 2002.

———. "Eğer Alan Vardır" ["You Are the Field"]. Translated by Larry Clark. In *An Anthology of Turkish Literature*, edited by Kemal Silay, 328–29. Bloomington: Indiana University Press, 1996.

———. "Senin Yüzünden" ["Because of You"]. 1994. Translated by Randy Blasing and Mutlu Konuk. In *The Poems of Nâzım Hikmet*, 239. New York: Persea, 2002.

———. "Şeyler Ben Sevdim Bilmiyordum" ["Things I Didn't Know I Loved"]. 1994. Translated by Randy Blasing and Mutlu Konuk. In *The Poems of Nâzım Hikmet*, 261–64. New York: Persea, 2002.

———. "Üzücü Özgürlük" ["Sad Freedom"]. Translated by Talât S. Halman. In *The Penguin Book of Turkish Verse*, edited by Nermin Menemencioğlu, 215–16. Harmondsworth, UK: Penguin, 1978.

Hirsch, Alan R. "Nostalgia: A Neuropsychiatric Understanding." *Advances in Consumer Research* 19 (1982): 390–95.

Hirschon, Renée, ed. *Crossing the Aegean: An Appraisal of the 1923 Compulsory Population Exchange between Greece and Turkey.* Oxford: Berghahn, 2003.

Hoberman, J. "*Once Upon a Time in Anatolia* (Nuri Bilge Ceylan, 2011, Turkey)." In *Film after Film: Or, What Became of 21st Century Cinema?*, 277–81. London: Verso, 2012.

Huntington, Samuel. "Democracy's Third Wave." *Journal of Democracy* 2, no. 2 (Spring 1991): 12–34.

Ibn'Arabi, Muhyiddin. "Listen, O Dearly Beloved." 1958. Translated by Henry Corbin. In *The Poetry of Ibn'Arabi.* London: The Muhyiddin Ibn'Arabi Society, 2014.

———. "Wild Is She, None Can Make Her His Friend." 1911. Translated by R. A. Nicholson. In *Tarjuman al-Ashwaq.* London: The Muhyiddin Ibn'Arabi Society, 2014.

İleri, Selim. *Yarım Yapayalnız* [*Boundless Solitude*]. Translated by Mark David Wyers. Horsham, UK: Milet, 2014.

Jaffe, Ira. *Slow Movies: Countering the Cinema of Action.* New York: Wallflower, 2014.

Johnson, Boris. *The Churchill Factor: How One Man Made History.* London: Hodder and Stoughton, 2014.

Kaelan, James. "The Director's POV: From Concerned Observer to Storyteller by Michael Rabiger and Mick Hurbis-Cherrier." *Moviemaker,* 16 February 2013.

Kanık, Orhan Veli. *I Am Listening to İstanbul: Selected Poems.* Translated by Talât Saït Halman. New York: Corinth, 1971.

———. "Separation." Translated by Murat Nemet-Nejat. In *I, Orhan Veli,* 96. New York: Hanging Loose Press, 1999.

Kansu, Ceyhun Atuf. "Anadolu Ristoranlar" ["Anatolian Restaurants"]. Translated by Nermin Menemencioğlu. In *The Penguin Book of Turkish Verse,* edited by Nermin Menemencioğlu, 315–17. Harmondsworth, UK: Penguin, 1978.

Kaplan, Sam. *The Pedagogical State: Education and the Politics of National Culture in Post-1980 Turkey.* Stanford, CA: Stanford University Press, 2006.

Kaplanoğlu, Semih. "The Cinema Militans Lecture 2012." Translated by Semih Kaplanoğlu and Zeynep Büyükcoşkun. Utrecht, 29 September 2012. *Bfi.org.uk.*

———. "Tractatus." Translated by Mary Işın. In *Ayşe Erkmen: Selected Works,* 1–15. İstanbul: Ofset Yayınevi, 1990.

Karanfil, Gökçen, and Serkan Şavk. "An Introduction from the Editors." In *Imaginaries Out of Place: Cinema, Transnationalism and Turkey,* 1–6. Newcastle-upon-Tyne: Cambridge Scholars, 2013.

———. "Rethinking the Concept of 'Turkish Cinema' in Times of Mobility." In *Topographies of 'Turkish Cinema': Hybrids, Hyphens and Borders: Book of Abstracts.* İzmir: İzmir University of Economics, 2011.

Karasu, Bilge. *Gece* [*Night*]. 1985. Translated by Bilge Karasu and Güneli Gün. Baton Rouge: Louisiana State University Press, 1994.

Karpat, Kemal H. *Turkey's Politics: The Transition to a Multi-Party System.* Princeton, NJ: Princeton University Press, 1959.

Katapish, Dawn. "A Conversation with Tarık Günersel." *World Literature Today* (January/February 2011): 24-27.

Kaya, Nurcan. *Forgotten or Assimilated? Minorities in the Education System of Turkey.* New York: Minority Rights Group International, 2009.

Kemal, Yahya. "Açık Deniz" ["Open Sea"]. Translated by S. Behlül Toygar. In *Selected Poems of Yahya Kemal Bayatlı*, 30-31. İstanbul: İskender Matbaası, 1962.

———. "Özleyen" ["Longing"]. Translated by S. Behlül Toygar. In *Selected Poems of Yahya Kemal Bayatlı*, 72-73. İstanbul: İskender Matbaası, 1962.

———. "Vuslat" ["Communion"]. Translated by S. Behlül Toygar. In *Selected Poems of Yahya Kemal Bayatlı*, 67-69. İstanbul: İskender Matbaası, 1962.

Kemal, Yaşar. "Teneke" ["The Drumming-Out"]. Translated by Thilda Kemal. In *Anatolian Tales*, 46-103. London: Collins and Harvill, 1968.

Kılıçbay, Barış, and Mutlu Binark. "Media Monkeys: Intertextuality, Fandom, and *Big Brother Turkey*." In *Big Brother International: Formats, Critics, and Publics*, edited by Ernest Matthijs and Janet Jones, 140-49. London: Wallflower, 2009.

Kinzer, Hans-Lukas. *A Quest for Belonging: Anatolia beyond Empire and Nation (19th-21st Centuries).* İstanbul: Isis, 2007.

Kissinger, Henry. *World Order.* London: Allen Lane, 2014.

Kotaman, Aslı. "*Yazgı* or *Kadar*: Not of Great Importance, or Taking a Stand against Kader." In *Cinema and Politics: Turkish Cinema and the New Europe*, edited by Deniz Bayrakdar, 232-40. Newcastle-upon-Tyne: Cambridge Scholars, 2009.

Kracauer, Siegfried. *Theory of Film: The Representation of Physical Reality.* 1960. Princeton, NJ: Princeton University Press, 1997.

Lago, Colin. *Race, Culture, and Counselling.* Buckingham, UK: Open University Press, 1996.

Lee, Charles. "Dogme95." In *Encyclopedia of the Documentary Film*, vol. 1, edited by Ian Aitken, 314-16. London: Routledge, 2008.

Lepeska, David. "İstanbul's Gentrification by Force Leaves Locals Feeling Overwhelmed and Angry." *Guardian*, 2 July 2014.

Lewis, Franklin D. *Rumi—Past and Present, East and West.* London: Oneworld, 2000.

Lovejoy, Arthur O. *The Great Chain of Being: The Study of the History of an Idea.* 1936. New York: Harper, 1960.

Lury, Karen. "Children in an Open World: Mobility as Ontology in New Iranian and Turkish Cinema." *Feminist Theory* 11, no. 3 (2010): 283-94.

Machiorlatti, Jennifer A. "Ecocinema, Ecojustice, and Indigenous Worldviews: Nature and First Nations Media as Cultural Recovery." In *Framing the World: Explorations in Ecocriticism and Film*, edited by Paula Willoquet-Maricondi, chap. 4. Charlottesville: University of Virginia Press, 2010.

Mackenzie, Compton. *Gallipoli Memories.* 1929. London: Panther, 1965.

Maheshwari, Laya. "Nuri Bilge Ceylan's Time." *Fandor.com*, 24 May 2014.

Makal, Mahmut. *A Village in Anatolia.* Translated by Sir Wyndham Deedes. London: Valentine, Mitchell, 1954.

McKim, Kirsty. *Cinema as Weather: Stylistic Screens and Atmospheric Change*. New York: Routledge, 2013.

Menken, Robin. "A Conversation with Turkish Film Director Derviş Zaim." *Cinema without Borders*, 5 July 2012.

Mersin, Serhan, and Pınar Yıldız. "Forming New Transcultural Fields in Turkish Cinema." In *Imaginaries Out of Place: Cinema, Transnationalism and Turkey*, 23–37. Newcastle-upon-Tyne: Cambridge Scholars, 2013.

Miller, Olaf. "Prison as Metaphor Is the Guiding Light of the Turkish Director's Literary Vision." In *Mental Minefields: The Dark Tales of Zeki Demirkubuz*, edited by Zeynep Dadak and Enis Köstepen, 70–74. New York: Lincoln Center, 2007.

Morrow, Lisa. *Waiting for the Tulips to Bloom: Adrift in İstanbul*. İstanbul: Lisa Morrow, 2015.

Morsünbül, Ümit. "Analyzing *Honey (Bal)*, *Milk (Süt)*, and *Egg (Yumurta)* Movies in Terms of Erikson's Theory of Psychosocial Development." *Elementary Education Online* 14, no. 1 (2015): 181–87.

"Movies That Make You Think 135: *Süt*." *Moviessansfrontieres*, 26 November 2012.

Möller, Olaf. "Double Trouble Ethical Lapses in Potsdamer Platz." *Film Comment* 46, no. 3 (May/June 2010): 64–66.

Mulvey, Laura. "Visual Pleasure and Narrative Cinema." 1975. In *Visual and Other Pleasures*, 14–27. Basingstoke, UK: Macmillan, 2009.

Mungan, Murathan. "Doğu Dağı" ["Eastern Mountain"]. 2007. Translated by Mel Kenne and Ruth Christie. In *Aeolian Visions/Versions: Modern Classics and New Writing from Turkey*, edited by Mel Kenne, Saliha Paker, and Amy Spangler, 127. Horsham, UK: Milet, 2013.

Naci, İbrahim. *Farewell: A Turkish Officer's Diary of the Gallipoli Campaign*. Translated by Nilüfer Epçeli, edited by Z. Alp Çeviri. Çanakkale: General Directorate of Nature Conservation and National Parks, 3rd Regional Directorate, 2013.

Nash, Robert J. *Liberating Scholarly Writing: The Power of Personal Narrative*. New York: Teachers' College Press, 2004.

Nash, Robert J., and Jennifer J. J. Jang. *Preparing Students for Life Beyond College: A Meaning-Centered Vision for Holistic Teaching and Learning*. New York: Routledge, 2015.

Nemet-Nejat, Murat. "Introduction." In *Eda: A Contemporary Anthology of Twentieth Century Turkish Poetry*, 2–27. Jersey City, NJ: Talisman House, 2004.

Nesin, Aziz. "Sınırsız Yolsuzluk" ["Corruption Unlimited"]. In *Laugh or Lament: Selected Short Stories*, translated by Masud Akhtar Sheikh, 141–50. İstanbul: Nesin Books, 2011.

Oden, Ike. "Journeyman Filmmakers on Hollywood's A-List." *Styleblazer*, 15 March 2013.

Onaran, Gözde. "Blok C." In *Mental Minefields: The Dark Tales of Zeki Demirkubuz*, edited by Zeynep Dadak and Enis Köstepen, 28–30. New York: Lincoln Center, 2007.

"Oscar Wilde-Oscars References Confuse Turkey's Polarized Parliament Commission." *Hürriyet Daily News*, 3 May 2016.

Önal, Hülya. "From Clichés to Mysticism: Evolution of Religious Motives in Turkish Cinema." *Religions* 5 (2014): 199–218.

Örik, Nahid Sırrı. *Kıskanmak*. 1946. İstanbul: Oğlak Yayıncılık, 1994.

Özkan, Derya. "From the Black Atlantic to Cool İstanbul: Why Does Coolness Matter?" In *Cool İstanbul: Urban Enclosures and Resistances*, edited by Derya Özkan, 13–35. Bielefeld, Germany: Transcript, 2015.

Pala, İskender. *Babil'de Ölüm İstanbul'da Aşk* [*Death in Babylon, Love in İstanbul*]. Translated by Fulya Vatansever. İstanbul: Kapı, 2015.

Partington, Angela. "Melodrama's Gendered Audience." In *Off-Centre: Feminism and Cultural Studies*, edited by Sarah Franklin, Celia Lury, and Jackie Stacey, 49–69. London: HarperCollins, 1991.

Pembecioğlu, Nilüfer. *Narratives through [the] Turkish Perspective: Transmedia Storytelling and Intertextuality in the Post-Network Era*. Cluj-Napoca, Romania: Argonaut, 2014.

Piaget, Jean. *The Psychology of Intelligence*. 1947. Translated by Malcolm Piercy and D. E. Brethyne. Totowa, NJ: Littlefield, Adams, 1960.

Pickthall, Muhammad Marmaduke. *The Cultural Side of Islam (Islamic Culture)*. 1927. New Delhi: Kitab Bhavan, 1981.

Poirier, Agnes. "'*Winter Sleep*': A Wake-Up Call for Turkey's Erdoğan?" *Al-Jazeera*, 26 May 2014.

Pope, Alexander. *Essay on Man*. 1710. Edited by Henry Morley. *Project Gutenberg*, 20 August 2007.

Randall, Don. "English Studies in Turkey: An Assessment." *Ariel: A Review of International English Literature* 46, no. 1–2 (2015): 45–68.

Raw, Laurence. "Ayhan Işık: Long Live the King." In *Exploring Turkish Cultures: Essays, Interviews and Reviews*, 250–60. Newcastle-upon-Tyne: Cambridge Scholars, 2011.

———. "Ayhan Işık's Film Career: A Survey." *Academia.edu*, 2010.

———."A Criticism of Indifference in Nuri Bilge Ceylan Style." *IMDb.com*, 21 March 2016.

———. "Cyprus Past, Present, and Future: The Derviş Zaim Trilogy." In *Cypriot Cinemas: Memory, Conflict, and Identity in the Margins of Europe*, edited by Costas Constandinides and Yiannis Papadakis, 98–117. New York: Bloomsbury, 2015.

———. "Derviş Zaim: To Return to the Past." In *Exploring Turkish Cultures*, 281–99. Newcastle-upon-Tyne: Cambridge Scholars, 2011.

———. "*Drakula İstanbul'da*." In *Turkey: Directory of World Cinema*, edited by Eylem Atakav, 70–71. Bristol: Intellect, 2013.

———. *Exploring Turkish Cultures: Essays, Interviews, and Reviews*. Newcastle-upon-Tyne: Cambridge Scholars, 2011.

———. "Genco Erkal: The Theatre of Commitment." In *Exploring Turkish Cultures*, 181–98. Newcastle-upon-Tyne: Cambridge Scholars, 2011.

———. "Identifying Common Ground." In *Translation, Adaptation and Transformation*, 1–29. London: Continuum, 2012.

———. "The 'Inner Meaning' of a Poem." *Academia.edu*, 1 December 2015.

———. "Reconstructing Englishness." 1999. In *Exploring Turkish Cultures*, 21–34. Newcastle-upon-Tyne: Cambridge Scholars, 2011.

———. "Şeytan." In *Turkey: Directory of World Cinema*, edited by Eylem Atakav, 88–89. Bristol: Intellect, 2013.

———. "Telling It Like It Is." In *Exploring Turkish Cultures*, 299–333. Newcastle-upon-Tyne: Cambridge Scholars, 2011.

———. "Tolga Örnek: A Fresh Look at Old Stories." In *Exploring Turkish Cultures*, 333–53. Newcastle-upon-Tyne: Cambridge Scholars, 2011.

———. *Türk Sahnelerimden İzenimler* [*Impressions of the Turkish Stage*]. İstanbul: Mitos Boyut, 2009.

Rıfat, Oktay. "Sandalda" ["In the Rowing Boat"]. Translated by Richard McKane. In *The Penguin Book of Turkish Verse*, edited by Nermin Menemencioğlu, 269–70. Harmondsworth, UK: Penguin, 1978.

Rimbaud, Arthur. Letter to Paul Deminy, 15 May 1871. *Abelard.fr*.

Rogerson, Barney. "Long before Islamic State." *TLS*, 28 November 2014, 32.

Romney, Jonathan. "Nuri Bilge Ceylan: Four Reviews: From *Distant* to *Winter Sleep*." 2014. In *Nuri Bilge Ceylan: Essays and Interviews*, edited by Robert Cardullo, 228–44. Berlin: Logos Verlag GmbH, 2015.

Rumford, Chris. "Turkish Identities: Between the Universal and the Particular." In *Dialogue and Difference*, edited by Laurence Raw and Ayşe Lahur Kırtunç, 139–49. Ankara: British Council, 2000.

Sacks, Oliver. *The Mind's Eye*. London: Picador, 2010.

Salih-al-Bukhari. Translated by M. Muhsin Khan. *Center for Muslim-Jewish Engagement*. Los Angeles: University of Southern California, 2009.

Santayana, George. "The Unknowable: The Herbert Spencer Lecture Delivered at Oxford, 24 October 1923." *Archive.org*, 2014.

Sartre, Jean-Paul. *Nausea*. 1938. Translated by Robert Baldick. Harmondsworth, UK: Penguin Modern Classics, 2000.

Scheff, Thomas. "Emotion and Depression." *Psychology Today*, 15 July 2011.

Sevler, Laura. "How a New Generation of Filmmakers Are Challenging Broadcasting Convention." *Ecologist*, 26 October 2010.

Shakespeare, William. *A Midsummer Night's Dream*. In *The Complete Works*. Edited by John Jowitt, William Montgomery, Gary Taylor, and Stanley Wells, 403–25. Oxford: Clarendon Press, 2005.

Shelley, Mary. *Frankenstein*. 1818. *Archive.org*, 2009.

Silas, Ellis. *Crusading at Anzac: Anno Domini 1915*. London: The British-Australasian, 1916.

Sippi, Diane. "Ceylan and Company: Autobiographical Trajectories of Cinema." 2005. In *Nuri Bilge Ceylan: Essays and Interviews*, edited by Robert Cardullo, 34–58. Berlin: Logos Verlag GmbH, 2015.

Sönmez, Nedim. *The Turkish Art of Marbling*. Translated by Margaret O. Johnson-Kubinski and Klaus Kubinski. Hickelhoven, Germany: Verlag Anadolu, 1996.

Söylemez, Yavuz Selim. "Türk Sinemasında Rüya Gerçeği: Semih Kaplanoğlu ve Yusuf Üçlemesi" ["Dream Reality in Turkish Cinema: Semih Kaplanoğlu and the Yusuf Trilogy"]. *Mustafa Kemal Üniversitesi Sosyal Bilimler Enstitüsü Dergisi* 11, no. 25 (2014): 143-57.

Spinelli, Ernesto. "The Existential-Phenomenological Paradigm." In *Handbook of Counselling Psychology*, edited by Ray Woolfe, Wendy Dryden, and Sheelagh Strawbridge, 180-96. London: Sage, 2003.

Staiger, Janet. *Modern Reception Studies*. New York: New York University Press, 2005.

Suner, Asuman. "Home, Belonging, and Other Aspects of Nuri Bilge Ceylan's Early Films." 2010. In *Nuri Bilge Ceylan: Essays and Interviews*, edited by Robert Cardullo, 123-53. Berlin: Logos Verlag GmbH, 2015.

———. "Horror of a Different Kind: Dissonant Voices of the New Turkish Cinema." *Screen* 45, no. 4 (Winter 2004). nbcfilm.com, 2013.

———. "The New Aesthetics of Muslim Spirituality in Turkey: *Yusuf's Trilogy* by Semih Kaplanoğlu." In *Religion in Contemporary European Cinema: The Postsecular Constellation*, edited by Costica Bradatan and Camil Ungureanu, 44-60. New York: Routledge, 2014.

———. *New Turkish Cinema: Belonging, Identity and Memory*. London: I. B. Tauris, 2010.

Sutton, Jan. *Healing the Hurt Within: Understand Self-Injury and Self-Harm and Heal the Emotional Wounds*, 3rd ed. Oxford: How to Books, 2007.

Sweet, Corinne. *The Mindfulness Journal: Exercises to Help You Find Peace and Calm Wherever You Are*. London: Boxtree, 2014.

Şafak, Elif. "Goodbye to All That." BBC Radio 3, 7 July 2015.

Şahin, Elmas. "[The] Fall of Women in British Literature and Turkish Literature of [the] 19th Century: A Comparative Approach." *International Journal of Social Science* 31, no. 2 (2015): 83-97.

Şensoy, Ferhan. *İstanbul'u Satıyorum [I am Selling İstanbul]*. 1988. Translated by Tomris Uyar. *The Turkish Pen Reader* (Summer 1992): 78-81.

Taft, Michael W. "Five Ways Our Need to Fit In Controls Us." *Science 2.0*, 14 March 2012.

Tamborini, Ron, Kristen Salomonson, and Changmo Bahk. "The Relationship of Empathy to Comforting Behavior following a Film Exposure." *Communication Research* 20, no. 5 (October 1993): 723-38.

Tanpınar, Ahmet Hamdi. *Saatleri Ayarlama Enstitüsü [The Time Regulation Institute]*. 1954. Translated by Ender Gürol. Madison, WI: Turko-Tatar Press, 2001.

———. *The Time Regulation Institute*. 1954. Translated by Maureen Freely and Alexander Dawe. London: Penguin Classics, 2014.

Tasker, Yvonne. "Having It All: Feminism and the Pleasures of the Popular." In *Off-Centre: Feminism and Cultural Studies*, edited by Sarah Franklin, Celia Lury, and Jackie Stacey, 85-97. London: HarperCollins, 1991.

Taşkale, Ali Rıza. "On Nuri Bilge Ceylan's *Distant*." 2008. In *Nuri Bilge Ceylan: Essays and Interviews*, edited by Robert Cardullo, 66-84. Berlin: Logos Verlag GmbH, 2015.

"10 Turkish Contemporary Artists to Know Now." *Art Reader*, 30 May 2014.

Tibbetts, John C., ed. *Peter Weir: Interviews*. Jackson: University Press of Mississippi, 2014.

Torres, Sasha. "Melodrama, Masculinity, and the Family: *Thirtysomething* as Therapy." In *Male Trouble*, edited by Constance Penley and Sharon Willis, 283–302. Minneapolis: University of Minnesota Press, 1993.

Townsend, Mark. "Why Are They Making Us Out to Be Such a Threat? Turks React to Vote Leave." *TheGuardian.com*, 21 May 2016.

Turan, Güven. "Gizli Alanlar" ["Secret Domain"]. Translated by Ruth Christie. In *Turkish Poetry 2014*, edited by George Messo, 31–119. New York: Red Hand, 2014.

"The Turkish Art of Marbling." *Turkish Culture Portal*, 2015.

Ulusay, Nejat. "A Transformational Experience within the Contexts of 'National' and 'Transnational': The Case of Turkish Cinema." In *Imagination out of Place: Cinema, Transnationalism, and Turkey*, edited by Gökçen Karanfil and Serkan Şavk, 6–23. Newcastle: Cambridge Scholars, 2013.

Usher, Bethany. "Twitter and the Celebrity Interview." *Celebrity Studies* 6, no. 3 (2015): 306–21.

Uslu, Ayşe Didem. "Grotesque and Gothic Comedy in Turkish Shadow Plays." In *Asian Gothic: Essays on Literature, Film and Anime*, edited by Andrew Hock Soon Ng, 224–37. Jefferson: McFarland, 2008.

Uzuner, Buket. *Balık İzlerinin Sesi* [*The Sound of Fishsteps*]. 1993. Translated by Pelin Arıner and Elızabeth Maslen. İstanbul: Remzi, 2002.

———. *İki Yeşil Su Samuru* [*Two Green Otters*]. 1991. Translated by Alexander Dawe, edited by Alexander Christie-Miller. İstanbul: Everest, 2013.

———. *Uyumsuz Defne Kaman'ın Maceraları* [*The Adventures of the Misfit Defne Kaman*]. Translated by Clare Frost and Alexander Dawe. İstanbul: Everest, 2012.

Ülgener, Sabri F. "Value Patterns of Traditional Societies: Turkish." In *The Turkish Administrator: A Critical Survey*, edited by Jerry R. Hopper and Richard I. Levin, 119–29. Ankara: USAID, Public Administration Division, nd.

Ümit, Ahmet. *Patasana*. Translated by Amy Spangler. İstanbul: Everest, 2011.

Ümunç, Himmet, and Laurence Raw. "Reassessing English Studies in Turkey." *Ariel* 48, no. 1 (2017): 137–45.

Ünis, Ziya. "The Evolution of Privatization in Turkey: The Institutional Context of Public-Enterprise Reform." *International Journal of Middle East Studies* 23, no. 2 (May 1991): 163–76.

Vanhee, Isolde. "Too Slow to Handle? Ozu, Malick, and the Art-House Family Drama." In *Ozu International: Essays on the Global Influences of a Japanese Auteur*, edited by Wayne Stein and Marc DiPaolo, 93–116. New York: Bloosmbury Academic, 2015.

Wadsworth, Darryl Cameron. "Popular Sentiments: Victorian Melodrama, Class, and Sentimentality." Doctoral dissertation, University of Pennsylvania, 1996.

Wallerstein, Immanuel. *European Universalism: The Rhetoric of Power*. New York: New Press, 2006.

Webster, Donald Everett. *The Turkey of Atatürk: Social Processes in the Turkish Reforma-tion*. Philadelphia: American Academy of Political and Social Science, 1939.

"Wife of the Nation's Father: A New Book on an Old Taboo." *The Economist*, 22 June 2006.

Willemen, Paul. "Notes on Subjectivity." In *Looks and Frictions: Essays in Cultural Studies and Film Theory*, 56-87. Bloomington: Indiana University Press, 1994.

Williams, Chris. *Overcoming Anxiety, Stress and Panic: A Five Areas Approach*. London: CRC Press, 2012.

Wood, James. "A Quick Chat with Nuri Bilge Ceylan." 2005. In *Nuri Bilge Ceylan: Essays and Interviews*, edited by Robert Cardullo, 26-34. Berlin: Logos Verlag GmbH, 2015.

Wood, Robin. "*Climates* and Other Disasters: The Films of Nuri Bilge Ceylan." 2006. In *Nuri Bilge Ceylan: Essays and Interviews*, edited by Robert Cardullo, 58-66. Berlin: Logos Verlag GmbH, 2015.

Wooden Leg. "Cheyenne." In *Native American Wisdom*, 60-61. Philadelphia: Running Press, 1994.

Wordsworth, William. "Ode: Intimations of Immortality from Recollections of Early Childhood." 1807. In *The Oxford Book of English Verse, 1250-1900*, edited by Arthur Quiller-Couch. 1919. *Bartleby.com*.

Yeniterzi, Emine. *Jalâl Al-Din Al-Rumi: A Muslim Saint, Mystic and Poet*. Translated by A. Bülent Baloğlu. Ankara: Türkiye Diyanet Vakfı, 2000.

Yıldırım, Leylâ. *Orada Herkes Ölüyor* [*Unfulfilled Promises*]. Translated by John Winston Baker. Gita Yayınları, 2015.

Yıldız, Bekir. "Resho Agha." 1968. Translated by Thomas F. Brosnahan. In *An Anthology of Modern Turkish Short Stories*, edited by Fahir İz, 266-72. Minneapolis: Bibliotheca İslamica, 1977.

Zaim, Derviş. "Camii Cevresinde Rock/Rock around the Mosque." *Facebook*, 18 January 2010.

Zarzosa, Augustin. *Refiguring Melodrama: Captive Affects, Elastic Sufferings, Vicarious Objects*. Lanham, MD: Lexington, 2013.

"Zeki Demirkubuz Adapts 'Notes from [the] Underground' for New Film." *Today's Zaman*, 5 February 2011.

Filmography

All the King's Men. Directed by Julian Jarrold. Performance by David Jason, Maggie Smith, William Ash. BBC/WGBH, 1999. Television.

The Art of Gothic: Britain's Midnight Hour. Directed by Ian Leese. Performance by Andrew Graham-Dixon. BBC Four, 23 October-7 November 2014. Television.

Atatürk. Directed by Tolga Örnek. Performance by Donald Sinden, Stanford Shaw, Donald Everett Webster. Ekip Film, 1998.

Babam ve Oğlum. Directed by Çağan Irmak. Performance by Fikret Kuşkan, Çetin Tekindor, Hümeyra. Avşar Film, 2005.

Bal. Directed by Semih Kaplanoğlu. Performance by Bora Altaş, Erdal Beşikcioğlu, Tülin Özen. Kaplan Film, 2010.

Balık. Directed by Derviş Zaim. Performance by Bülent İnal, Sanem Çelik. Maraton Film, 2014.

Bana Şans Dile. Directed by Çağan Irmak. Performance by Rıza Kocaoğlu, Melisa Sözen, Berke Üzrek. Muhteşem, 2001.

Bekleme Odası. Directed by Zeki Demirkubuz. Performance by Zeki Demirkubuz, Nurhayat Kavrak, Nilüfer Açıkalın. Mavi Film, 2003.

Benim Adim Feridun. Directed by Çağan Irmak. Performance by Suzan Aksoy, Güngör Bayrak, Özge Borak. TAFF Pictures, 2016.

Bir Zamanlar Anadolu'da. Directed by Nuri Bilge Ceylan. Performance by Muhammet Uzuner, Yılmaz Erdoğan, Taner Birsel. Zeynofilm, 2011.

Body of Lies. Directed by Ridley Scott. Performance by Russell Crowe, Leonardo DiCaprio, Mark Strong. Warner Bros./Scott Free, 2008.

Britain's Most Fragile Treasure. Directed by Paul Tilzey. Performance by Janina Ramirez. BBC/Victoria and Albert Museum, 2011. Television.

Bulantı. Directed by Zeki Demirkubuz. Performance by Zeki Demirkubuz, Şebnem Hassanisoughi, Öykü Karayel. Mavi Film, 2015.

C Blok. Directed by Zeki Demirbubuz. Performance by Serap Aksoy, Ajlan Aktuğ, Ülkü Duru. Mavi Film, 1994.

Cenneti Beklerken. Directed by Derviş Zaim. Performance by Serhat Tutumler, Melisa Sözen, Nihat İleri. Sarmaşık Sanatlar, 2006.

Chunuk Bair. Directed by Dale G. Bradley. Performance by Robert Powell, Kevin J. Wilson, Jed Brophy. Avalon, 1992.

Çalıkuşu. Directed by Osman F. Seden. Performance by Türkân Şoray, Kartal Tibet, Kadir Savun. Kemal Film, 1966.

Çalıkuşu. Performance by Aydan Sener, Kenan Kalav, Sadri Alışık. TRT, 1986. Television.

Çalıkuşu. Directed by Çağan Irmak. Performance by Bengü Ergin, Ebru Helvacıoğlu, Fehmi Karaarslan. Kanal D, 2013–14. Television.

Çamur. Directed by Derviş Zaim. Performance by Engin Alkan, Taner Birsel, Yelda Reynaud. Downtown Pictures, 2003.

Çanakkale Aslanları. Directed by Turgut Demirağ, Nesret Eraslan. Performance by Cüneyt Gökçer, Muzaffer Tema, Ajda Pekkan. And Film, 1964.

Çanakkale 1915. Directed by Yeşim Sezgin. Performance by Baran Akbulut, Özgür Akdemir, Rıza Akın. Fida Film, 2012.

Çemberimde Gül Oya. Directed by Çağan Irmak. Performance by Mehmet Ali Nuroğlu, Özge Özbek, Kenan Bal. Kanal D, 2004–5. Television.

Decadence and Downfall: The Shah of Iran's Ultimate Party. Directed by Hassan Amini. Amber Entertainment, 2016. Television.

Dedemin İnsanları. Directed by Çağan Irmak. Performance by Çetin Tekindor, Yiğit Özsener, Gökçe Bahadır. Most Production, 2011.

The Defiant Ones. Directed by Stanley Kramer. Performance by Tony Curtis, Sidney Poitier, Theodore Bikel. Stanley Kramer Productions, 1958.

Devir. Directed by Derviş Zaim. Performance by Ramazan Bayar, Ali Özel, Mustafa Salman. Maraton Film, 2013.

Devrim Arabaları. Directed by Tolga Örnek. Performance by Haluk Bilginer, Taner Birsel, Charles Carroll. Ekip Film, 2008.

Djeca. Directed by Aida Begic. Performance by Marija Pikic, İsmir Gagula, Bojan Navojec. Film House Sarajevo/Kaplan Film. 2012.

Drakula İstanbul'da. Directed by Mehmet Muhtar. Performance by Arif Kaptan, Annie Ball, Bülent Oran. And Film, 1953.

Educating Rita. Directed by Lewis Gilbert. Performance by Julie Walters, Michael Caine, Michael Williams. Acorn Pictures, 1983.

El Mariachi. Directed by Robert Rodriguez. Performance by Carlos Gallardo, Consuelo Gómez, Jaime De Hoyos. Columbia, 1992.

The Exorcist. Directed by William Friedkin. Performance by Linda Blair, Max von Sydow, Ellen Burstyn. Warner Bros., 1973.

Fetih 1453. Directed by Faruk Aksoy. Performance by Devrim Evin, İbrahim Çelikkol, Dilek Serbest. Aksoy Film, 2012.

Filler ve Çimen. Directed by Derviş Zaim. Performance by Ali Sürmeli, Sanem Çelik, Bülent Kayabaş. Maraton Film, 2000.

Gallipoli. Directed by Peter Weir. Performance by Mel Gibson, Mark Lee, Bill Kerr. Australian Film Commission, 1981.

Gelibolu. Directed by Tolga Örnek. Performance by Sam Neill, Zafer Ergin. Ekip Film, 2005.

Gölgeler ve Suretler. Directed by Derviş Zaim. Performance by Osman Alkaş, Popi Avraam, Mustafa Bölükbaşı. Maraton Film, 2010.

Günaydın İstanbul Kardeş. Directed by Çağan Irmak, İrfan Tözüm. Performance by Esin Akkaya, Volkan Severcan, Güler Ökten. ATV, 1998–2001. Television.

Hayal-i-Cihan. Directed by Çağan Irmak. Performance by Okan Yalabık, Çetin Tekindor, Bilge Şen. Avşar Film, 2006. Television.

Herkes Kendi Evinde. Directed by Semih Kaplanoğlu. Performance by Tolga Çevik, Şükran Güngör, Devrim Parscan. Haylazz Prodüksiyon, 2001.

Hititler. Directed by Tolga Örnek. Performance by Haluk Bilginer. Ekip Film, 2003.

Instructions not Included. Directed by Eugenio Derbez. Performance by Eugenio Derbez, Hugo Stiglitz, Leia Freitas. Alebrije Cine y Video, 2013.

Issiz Adam. Directed by Çağan Irmak. Performance by Melis Birkan, Cemal Hünal, Şerif Bozkurt. Most Production, 2008.

İki Dil Bir Bavul. Directed by Özgür Doğan, Orhan Eskiköy. Bulut Film, 2008.

İklimler. Directed by Nuri Bilge Ceylan. Performance by Nuri Bilge Ceylan, Ebru Ceylan, Nazan Kesal. Pyramide Films, 2006.

İngiliz Kemal Lavrens'e Karşı. Directed by Osman F. Seden. Performance by Ayhan Işık, Muzaffer Tema, Pola Morelli. Kemal Film, 1952.

İtiraf. Directed by Zeki Demirkubuz. Performance by Taner Birsel, Başak Köklükaya, İskender Altın. Mavi Film, 2002.

Jerusalem: The Making of a Holy City. Directed by Tom Sheahan. Performance by Simon Sebag Montefiore. BBC, 2011. Television.

Kabuşlar Evi. Directed by Çağan Irmak et al. Performance by Çetin Tekindor. Avşar Film, 2006. Television.

Kaçan Fırsatlar Limited. Directed by Ufuk Bayraktar. Performance by Levent Üzümcü, Ali Duşenkalkar, Bennu Yıldırımlar. Avşar Film, 2006. Television.

Kader. Directed by Zeki Demirkubuz. Performance by Vildan Atasever, Ufuk Bayraktar, Engin Akyürek. Greek Film Center/Highway, 2006.

Karanlıktakiler. Directed by Çağan Irmak. Performance by Erdem Akakçe, Rıza Akın, Derya Alabora. Most Productions, 2009.

Kasaba. Directed by Nuri Bilge Ceylan. Performance by M. Emin Ceylan, Havva Sağlam, Cihat Bütün. NBC Ajans, 1997.

Kaybedenler Külübü. Directed by Tolga Örnek. Performance by Nejat İşler, Yiğit Özsener. Ekip Film, 2011.

Kıskanmak. Directed by Zeki Demirkubuz. Performance by Serhat Tutumluer, Barrak Tütünataç, Nergis Öztürk. Yerli Film, 2009.

Kış Uykusu. Directed by Nuri Bilge Ceylan. Performance by Haluk Bilginer, Melisa Sözen, Demet Akbağ. Zeynofilm, 2014.

King Kong. Directed by Merian C. Cooper, Ernest B. Schoedsack. Performance by Fay Wray, Robert Armstrong, Bruce Cabot. RKO Radio, 1933.

Kor. Directed by Zeki Demirkubuz. Performance by Aslıhan Gürbüz, Caner Cindoruk, Taner Birsel. Mavi Film, 2016.

Koza. Directed by Nuri Bilge Ceylan. Performance by Mehmet Emin Ceylan, Fatma Ceylan, Turgut Toprak. TRT, 1995.

Kuruluştan Kurtuluşa Fenerbahçe. Directed by Tolga Örnek. Ekip Film, 1999.

Küf. Directed by Ali Aydın. Performance by Ercan Kesal, Muhammet Uzuner, Tansu Bicer. Motiva Film, 2012.

Labirent. Directed by Tolga Örnek. Performance by Timücin Esen, Meltem Cumbul, Sarp Akkaya. Ekip Film, 2011.

L'Eclisse. Directed by Michelangelo Antonioni. Performance by Alain Delon, Monica Vitti, Francisco Rabal. Cineriz, 1962.

Masumiyet. Directed by Zeki Demirkubuz. Performance by Güven Kıraç, Haluk Bilginer, Derya Alabora. Mavi Film, 1997.

Mayıs Sıkıntısı. Directed by Nuri Bilge Ceylan. Performance by Emin Ceylan, Muzaffer Özdemir, Fatma Ceylan. NBC Ajans, 1999.

Mâsuk'un Nefesi. Directed by Murat Pay. Performance by Abdurrahman Düzcan, Mustafa Başkan, Hadi Duran. Kaplan Film, 2014.

Meleğin Düşüsü. Directed by Semih Kaplanoğlu. Performance by Tülin Özen, Budak Akalın, Musa Karagöz. Greek Film Center, 2005.

Monsieur İbrahim. Directed by François Dupeyron. Performance by Omar Sharif, Pierre Boulanger, Gilbert Melki. ARP Sélection, 2003.

Mount Nemrud: Throne of the Gods. Directed by Tolga Örnek. Ekip Film, 2001.

Muhteşem Yüzyıl. Directed by Durul Taylan, Yağmur Taylan, et al. Performance by Selen Öztürk, Ezgi Eyüboğlu, Tuncel Kurtiz. Tim's Productions, 2011-14. Television.

Mustafa. Directed by Can Dündar. Performance by Can Dündar, Yetkin Dikinçiler, Beyhan Saran. NTV, 2008.

Mustafa Herşey Hakkında. Directed by Çağan Irmak. Performance by Fikret Kuşkan, Nejat İşler, Başak Köklükaya. ANS Production, 2004.

Nadide Hayat. Directed by Çağan Irmak. Performance by Demet Akbağ, Sevil Aki, Batuhan Begimgil. TAFF Pictures, 2015.

New York'ta Beş Minare. Directed by Mahsun Kırmızıgil. Performance by Haluk Bilginer, Danny Glover, Gina Gershon. Boyut Film, 2010.

Nokta. Directed by Derviş Zaim. Performance by Serhat Kılıç, Mehmet Ali Nuroğlu, Numan Acar. Maraton Film, 2008.

Paralel Yolculuklar. Directed by Derviş Zaim, Panikos Chrysanthou. Maraton Film, 2004.

Prensesin Uykusu. Directed by Çağan Irmak. Performance by Çağlar Çorumlu, Genco Erkal, Şevval Başpınar. Most Production, 2010.

Richard III [III. Richard]. Directed by Semih Sergen. Performance by Burak Sergen. Ankara Devlet Tiyatrosu, 2001. Theater performance.

Rüya. Directed by Derviş Zaim. Performance by Gizem Akman, Zafer Altun, Dilşad Bozyiğit. Maraton Filmcilik, 2016.

Sen Benim Herşeyimsin. Directed by Tolga Örnek. Performance by Tolga Çevik, Cengiz Bozkurt, Tuna Çevik. Globalgate Entertainment, 2016.

Senin Hikayen. Directed by Tolga Örnek. Performance by Timuçin Esen, Selma Ergeç, Nevra Serezli. Taff Pictures, 2013.

Sense and Sensibility. Directed by Ang Lee. Performance by Emma Thompson, Alan Rickman, Kate Winslet. Columbia, 1995.

Stalker. Directed by Andrey Tarkovsky. Performance by Alisa Freyndilkh, Aleksandr Kaydanovsköy, Anatoliy Solonitsyn. Kinostudiya "Mosfilm," 1979.

A Star Is Born. Directed by George Cukor. Performance by Judy Garland, James Mason, Jack Carson. Warner Bros., 1954.

Süt. Directed by Semih Kaplanoğlu. Performance by Melih Selçuk, Başak Köklükaya, Rıza Akın. Kaplan Film, 2008.

Şeytan. Directed by Metin Erksan. Performance by Canan Perver, Cihan Ünal, Meral Taygun. Saner Film, 1974.

Tabutta Rövaşata. Directed by Derviş Zaim. Performance by Ahmet Uğurlu, Tuncel Kurtiz, Ayşen Aydemir. İstisnai Filmler ve Reklamlar, 1996.

Tahıl. Directed by Semih Kaplanoğlu. Performance by Jean-Marc Barr, Ermin Bravo, Grigoriy Dobrygin. Kaplan Film, 2017.

Tamam Mıyız? Directed by Çağan Irmak. Performance by Deniz Çeliloğlu, Aras Bulut İnyemli, Uğur Güneş. Taff Pictures, 2013.

Taxi Driver. Directed by Martin Scorsese. Performance by Robert de Niro, Jodie Foster, Cybill Shepherd. Columbia, 1976.

Titanic. Directed by James Cameron. Performance by Leonardo DiCaprio, Kate Winslet, Billy Zane. Twentieth Century-Fox/Paramount, 1997.

Ulak. Directed by Çağan Irmak. Performance by Çetin Tekindor, Melis Birkan, Şerif Sezer. Avşar Film, 2008.

Unutursam Fısılda. Directed by Çağan Irmak. Performance by Hümeyra, Isıl Yücesoy, Farah Zeynep Abdullah. Taff Pictures, 2014.

Uzak. Directed by Nuri Bilge Ceylan. Performance by Muzaffer Özdemir, Emin Toprak, Zuhal Gencer. NBC Ajans, 2002.

Üç Maymun. Directed by Nuri Bilge Ceylan. Performance by Yavuz Bingöl, Hatice Aslan, Ahmet Rıfat Şungar. NBC Film, 2008.

Üçüncü Sayfa. Directed by Zeki Demirkubuz. Performance by Başak Köklükaya, Ruhi Sarı, Erol Babaoğlu. Mavi Film, 1999.

The Water Diviner. Directed by Russell Crowe. Performance by Russell Crowe, Yılmaz Erdoğan, Cem Yılmaz. Fear of God Films, 2014.

When Pop Ruled My Life: The Fans' Story. Directed by Sam Bridger. Performance by Kate Mossman, Rick Wakeman, Dave Hill. BBC Four, 29 May 2015. Television.

Written on the Wind. Directed by Douglas Sirk. Performance by Rock Hudson, Lauren Bacall, Dorothy Malone. Universal International, 1956.

Yazgı. Directed by Zeki Demirkubuz. Performance by Serdar Orçin, Zeynep Tokuş, Engin Günaydın. Mavi Film, 2001.

Yeraltı. Directed by Zeki Demirkubuz. Performance by Engin Günaydın, Serhat Tutumler, Nihal Yalçın. Mavi Film, 2012.

Ying Xiong. Directed by Zhang Yimou. Performance by Jet Li, Tony Chiu Wai Leung, Maggie Cheung. Beijing New Picture Film Co., 2002.

Yojimbo. Directed by Akira Kurosawa. Performance by Toshirô Mifune, Tatsuya Nakadai, Yôko Tsukasa. Kurosawa Production Co., 1961.

Yol. Directed by Yılmaz Güney. Performance by Tarık Akan, Şerif Sezer, Halil Ergün. Güney Film, 1982.

Yumurta. Directed by Semih Kaplanoğlu. Performance by Nejat İşler, Saadet Aksoy, Ufuk Bayraktar. Kaplan Film, 2007.

Index